ROUTLEDGE LIBRARY EDITIONS:
EDUCATION MANAGEMENT

Volume 23

THE STRUGGLE FOR CHANGE

THE STRUGGLE FOR CHANGE

The story of one school

M.F. WIDEEN

Routledge
Taylor & Francis Group
LONDON AND NEW YORK

First published in 1994 by Falmer

This edition first published in 2018
by Routledge
2 Park Square, Milton Park, Abingdon, Oxon OX14 4RN

and by Routledge
711 Third Avenue, New York, NY 10017

Routledge is an imprint of the Taylor & Francis Group, an informa business

British Library Cataloguing in Publication Data
A catalogue record for this book is available from the British Library

ISBN: 978-1-138-48720-8 (Set)
ISBN: 978-1-351-04158-4 (Set) (ebk)
ISBN: 978-1-138-48801-4 (Volume 23) (hbk)
ISBN: 978-1-138-54549-6 (Volume 23) (pbk)
ISBN: 978-1-351-04062-4 (Volume 23) (ebk)

The Struggle for Change: The story of one school

M.F. Wideen
with
Ivy Pye

The Falmer Press
(A member of the Taylor & Francis Group)
London • Washington, DC

USA The Falmer Press, 4 John St, London WC1N 2ET
UK The Falmer Press, Taylor & Francis Inc., 1900 Frost Road, Suite 101, Bristol, PA 19007

First published 1994

A catalogue record of this publication is available from the British Library

ISBN 0 7507 0168 4 cased
ISBN 0 7507 0169 2 paper

Library of Congress Cataloging-in-Publication Data are available on request

Jacket design by Caroline Archer

Typeset in 10/12 pt Caledonia by
Graphicraft Typesetters Ltd., Hong Kong

Printed in Great Britain by Burgess Science Press, Basingstoke on paper which has a specified pH value on final paper manufacture of not less than 7.5 and is therefore 'acid free'.

Contents

Preface

This book is about the struggle of the teachers and principal in one school to bring about a change in the teaching of language arts. That struggle occurred within the constraints and support of systems outside the school; it occurred within the limitations of what they knew about the things they attempted to change; and it also occurred within the limitations of what they knew about the change process. The introduction in Chapter 1 briefly describes the flavor of that change. This first chapter also provides some indication as to why I found the change to be important and the role I played as a researcher over the five year period of this study.

Social and educational change also occurs within the context of an understanding about school change that has grown up over time through similar experiences in other schools. This understanding can be seen in the growing body of literature which deals with various aspects of educational change. The second chapter, 'The background context: Promises and problems' sets this context drawing on five areas, curriculum reform, school improvement, school effectiveness, teacher research, and teacher development. Here I take a critical perspective of this research and attempt to ferret out where and how it can be useful to teachers and where it appears to break down. In the second chapter I also attempt to trace some of the threads from those areas that have brought us to where we are now in our thinking about teaching and how to change it. In this chapter I discuss how these five areas show a promise for the future that is also burdened by many problems when it comes to informing teachers about changing their work.

Chapter 3, 'The story of one school' and Chapter 4, 'The substance of the change' build on the first chapter to describe the change occurring in the school in more detail. Old habits had to be broken and new ground forged before the change could become institutionalized in the school. I attempt to trace that struggle in Chapter 3. One of the factors that became very evident to me was that subject matter, namely language arts, became an important factor in the change itself. I devote Chapter 4 to a discussion of this idea.

The final four chapters of the book deal with what has been learned from this case study about the roles of different people, the unit of change, and the factors at work in the change at Lakeview. A final chapter provides some overall reflection.

As I read the literature for these and other sections of the book, I found myself becoming increasingly critical of that research and what it had to say in terms of assisting teachers to bring about change and in terms of improving our understanding of the change process. I make no apologies for this critical stance. I believe that it is only from a perspective that takes the literature about school change as being problematic that we can ultimately improve both our practice and our understanding of the process that leads to improvement in that practice.

The book is written for an audience of practitioners, policy makers and academics, although often those categories become blurred. I wrote the book primarily for those in schools — teachers and principals — who ultimately will bring about those changes that we outsiders so glibly talk about. I make the assumption, based on my experience working with teachers and principals, that they are not only the doers of change, but also the consumers and contributors to the literature that contains our understanding of change. But the book is also written for students, for those who attempt to understand school improvement and for those who seek to contribute toward our understanding of change through research.

In attempting to identify the people who helped me put this book together I was taken back to my first years of teaching. A group of us, all teachers, struggled with implementing a new science program that we had helped develop based on the curriculum reforms of the 1950s and 1960s. To us it reflected a new and exciting kind of science teaching. As a curriculum committee, we set out to explain this new and wonderful program to our fellow teachers thinking that they too would be eager to put it into practice. But it was not to be so. While some successes occurred, we encountered all those problems of change in schools that have been talked about in the literature since that time. I am grateful to those with whom I worked at that time and from whom I gained first-hand some glimpses of what the stuggle for change was all about.

My formal introduction to the change theory and its application came through IMTEC, an institute in Norway directed by Per Dalin. The year I spent there and the contacts I made as a result could not have been a better learning experience. The Canadian study of change in faculties of education that emerged from that experience brought me in contact with Michael Fullan, David Hopkins, Ken Eastabrook, and Nancy Watson. From that experience I learned that studying the process of change was just as difficult as attempting to undertake it.

But it is my most recent experience at Lakeview that led to this work. I am particularly indebted to the staff at Lakeview Elementary who did everything possible to ensure that I saw all aspects of life in that school, the good, the bad, and the ugly. Not only did they invite me into their school, they shared with me their hopes and aspirations, their uncertainties and fears, and, most importantly, their ideas. Their candour provided the material for what you are about to read.

The research would not have been possible without the financial support I received from the Social Sciences and Humanities Council, Simon Fraser

University, and one British Columbia School District who must go unnamed for purposes of anonymity.

I would also like to thank Ivy Pye for her efforts in editing and helping to keep the ship on course. Much gratitude also goes to Pat Holborn, David Hopkins, Wendy Strachan, David Reynolds, Carolyn Manchur, Judith McPhie, Bev Craig, Ron Brooke, Barbara Moon, Peter Stretton and Gary Doige for their invaluable suggestions and critiques of the manuscript at different stages. I would also like to acknowledge the students of Lakeview whose work appears throughout this volume.

Finally, I want to thank my partner, Loretta, for her contributions to the book but also for her patience and understanding during periods of turbulent weather. That I owe a lot to all these people, I gratefully acknowledge. Much of what is commendable in the following pages is due to them. The errors and interpretation of events are mine alone.

M.F.W.

Acknowledgment

The author and publisher wishes acknowledge the kind permission to reproduce selected material from Good Apple, 1204 Buchanan St., Box 229, Carthage, IL.

to
Loretta

Hansel and Gretel

To Be Read By
The Town Crier:

Town Crier Role

Hear Ye, Hear Ye, Hear Ye, NEW EVIDENCE! A NEW ACCOUNT AT THE SCENE OF THE CRIME WHICH JUST CAME TO PUBLIC ATTENTION!

The police arrived on the scene and discovered the old lady, Mrs Salem, burned to a crisp in her own large hearth oven.

When the police had decently removed her remains, they questioned the children, Hansel and Gretel, who were smiling and were not visibly upset. They seemed to show no regret or sorrow.

Hansel said the old lady threatened him with a kettle of boiling water just because he threw her cat into the well. Little Gretel said the old lady fussed just because they broke her broom in two. And she said she would lock up Hansel in a cage for damaging her house.

Both children said they heard she was a witch and they were just trying to tease her a little But Mrs Salem didn't seem to have a sense of humor.

So the court, considering their age, ruled that there was some evidence that the two children had been frightened and acted to defend themselves and they were released to their parents on probation.

Chapter 1

Introduction

An open, inviting school greeted me the morning I first visited Lakeview. Friendly faces and student art work brightened the halls and I felt comfortable and at ease as I made my way to visit Barbara, a fourth grade teacher. When I entered her classroom she was discussing the story of Hansel and Gretel, the two children who had been abandoned in the woods by their parents only to have come into the clutches of, what for me had always been, 'the wicked witch'.

'Most of you have read the story. Most versions pretty well end up the same,' Barb told the students. Both Barb and the students recalled different versions of the story and how the endings changed. She then asked how many students would like to have Hansel and Gretel as their friends. Several hands were raised and a chorus of answers replied, 'yes!'

'But are you sure? After all, they pushed an old lady into a hot oven, killed her, and stole her property.'

'But the witch was an evil person,' said one of the boys. Several others agreed.

'How do you know that?' asked Barb.

'She was getting the oven ready to bake Hansel and Gretel.'

'But that is what Hansel and Gretel said. How do we know for certain that the witch was not just checking her bread or baking cookies for the children?'

A lively, noisy discussion followed. Most of the children held fast to their view that Hansel and Gretel were the heroes in the story and that the wicked witch was the bad one. But some students began to question this accepted view of Hansel and Gretel.

As the pros and cons around this argument were taking place, the class was interrupted by a student carrying a placard and shouting 'HEAR YEA! HEAR YEA!' His costume and rotund shape suggested some indiscriminate European town crier of several centuries ago. The placard he carried read:

HANSEL AND GRETEL TO BE TRIED FOR ROBBERY AND MURDER ! ! !

Hansel & Gretel-Guilty or Innocent

→ Hansel & Gretel are innocent because they would have died if they didn't Kill Mrs. Salem.
They should be set free and they should stay with their dad.
Mrs. Salem was a nosty, old, fat person and deserved to be killed because she hated childern and she threatend the Kids.
The stepmother is responsible because she kicked them out of the house.
Hansel & Gretel are responsible for taking the jewells and they shoald be returned.

Hansel and Gretel v.s. Mrs. Salem

1. I think that Hansel and Gretel are guilty.
2. I think they are guilty because the witch has alot of friends and they have known her for a long time and she wouldn't do anything like that.
3. I would put Hansel and Gretel in jail because they cooked Mrs Salem.
4. I think that Mrs. Salem is a nice old women that minds her own bissness. I think that Hansel and Gretel are two little nosey kids.

by: Tracy

The class appeared startled at first, but soon joined into the spirit when it was announced that they would be holding a trial of Hansel and Gretel and that some of them would be serving as lawyers and jurors, with others taking the important role of audience participants. The transition from talk about a nursery story to setting up court in the classroom involved explanation on Barb's part, plenty of discussion and interruption on the students' part, and generally a lot of noise. But by recess-break the 'courtroom' was ready, the players identified, and their roles more or less understood.

Time was made available for the prosecution and defense to hold internal discussions while the rest of the class engaged in speculation and argument about the possible outcome. The prosecuting attorney presented arguments based on discussions with a small group of advisors who had taken on the role of identifying the case against Hansel and Gretel. The defense attorney's case was built on the input of a similar support group.

The court case unfolded amid some time-outs to review and explain procedure — and occasionally decorum. After hearing the evidence the jury brought down a guilty verdict against Hansel and Gretel. It caused an uproar in the classroom. Those students who had taken the side of Hansel and Gretel from the beginning expressed their dismay and disappointment by reviewing what for them was a clear-cut case supporting a 'not guilty' verdict. The arguments continued until the noon hour bell rang. Students left the room still arguing the case. It was clear this discussion would go on for some time.

This little vignette involving two characters from most of our early childhoods may strike the reader as an odd choice for a book on school improvement. My first reason for having begun this way arises out of the literature on educational reform. Having argued at one time that schools had remained stubbornly the same over the years despite enormous changes in society, (Wideen and Andrews, 1987), I was intrigued to find something unusual happening on my first visit to Lakeview. My own years in school had followed a pattern: students all read the same passage in the basal readers silently and the teacher then asked questions about it. We seldom held discussions, either about the stories, or how the authors had developed them. Later, as a university supervisor of student teaching, I had seen the same pattern of language arts teaching over the years which confirmed for me the commonly-held notion that the act of teaching had stubbornly resisted change over a long course of time. This language arts lesson in the fall of 1986, however, which saw a familiar fairy tale turned upside down struck me as a significant shift in the teaching of language arts. These children were involved, they were excited and at times even angry over the interpretation of a story — something I had rarely seen in a school where the mode of language arts teaching rested on the use of basal readers. They were also being encouraged by example to challenge certain fixed beliefs. Yet a comfortable and safe feeling existed in the classroom. I enjoyed the morning, was sorry that it was over, and wished only that I, too, could have participated. After having seen so many lessons that held all the excitement of time spent watching paint dry, this was an event that left me feeling stimulated and excited about further possibilities.

As I left the class and glanced once more around the halls of the school I realized that this was not an isolated happening; other interesting things appeared to be taking place here. The walls were decorated with a variety of students' work that reflected their writing; in several corners of the building students of different ages were reading to other students; the doors of classrooms were open revealing a mixture of instructional activity. My subsequent visits would reveal that the school was now in the process of becoming what they called 'a writing school' which would eventually lead to whole language, subject integration, and several other innovations that would constitute a major change in this school. (A sample of one student's story — completely unedited — is included in Appendix A.) The school would come to be seen as a 'light house' school for the district to which the superintendent would send visitors. Many of the staff would become leaders in their district. The school was much more than Barb's morning classroom.

That first visit to the school and subsequent interviews with the principal and staff convinced me to return to find out more about the changes that had occurred during the previous two years. I became intrigued with the dynamic situation in the school which seemed to change with every visit. Even the concept of what had changed, changed. With some seed money from the local school district, and later from a national funding agency, I returned again on several occasions to watch the teachers teach and to interview the teachers, principal, and district people. From this case study of one school I learned a great deal. This book is my opportunity to share what I learned with you.

What you read here represents my story, my observations, of a school that managed to change itself from within. In one sense it is the story of a researcher who examined a school over a period of several years, observing, reflecting and trying to come to some understanding of what was happening there. But in another sense it is also an attempt to relate, in retrospect, what has been learned from this case that might help other schools undertake change.

Meanwhile, over the same period the literature on school improvement has become ever more refined and insightful. First I had to wrestle with the question, 'With all this growing literature, why write yet another book on school improvement?' But, as I will show in the next chapter, which attempts to summarize selected parts of this literature, many gaps still remain in our understanding of how schools change in ways that make them better places for children to learn and for teachers to teach. Most of these gaps lie in the phenomenology of change and what it means to individuals and groups working to improve their practice. In the opening section to *New meaning of educational change*, Fullan (1991) puts it this way:

> The problem of meaning is central to making sense of educational change. In order to achieve greater meaning, we must come to understand both the small and the big pictures. The small picture concerns the subjective meaning or lack of meaning for individuals at all levels on the educational system. Neglect of the phenomenology of change — that is how

> people actually experience as distinct from how it might be intended — is at the heart of the spectacular lack of success of most social reforms (p. 4).

This book is about the small picture; about what change means to those who undertake it, and how that experience relates to the larger social, political picture.

But I included this story of an interpretation of a fairy tale for another reason: the conviction — firmly held and deeply felt — that school improvement should be understood by how it changes or improves teaching. Little else matters. Talking about school change, and indeed even effecting it, becomes merely an empty exercise unless it means an improvement in the education of children. However, while I feel that student learning remains our principle and most important focus, I also feel that another aspect of change within a school deserves attention and that is the link between the change in the teaching of a subject and the change process itself. I return to this theme later. For now I simply comment that this teaching episode illustrated a significant shift in the way teachers at Lakeview had come to view instruction. And in many ways the change in instruction paralleled, or mirrored, the change occurring in the school itself. To the cynic who might ask, 'What else would one expect school improvement to mean?' I respond by pointing out the number of textbooks on school improvement that never mention teaching or instruction. For example, in Fullan's landmark book on educational change, to which I just referred, no time is devoted to the content of the change process, namely the subjects that teachers deal with on a day-to-day basis. Similarly, in Huberman and Miles' (1984) careful study of twelve innovative sites virtually no attention is given to analyze the effects that the substance of the change in those twelve schools may have had on the change itself. Change is treated as something generic that applies across innovations whether one is implementing a new means to discipline children or changing science instruction. As Stodolsky (1988) points out, the subject does matter. Even where the literature on school effectiveness places an emphasis on curriculum and instruction, that emphasis tends to take a generic approach.

In this book I contend that the teacher remains central to the process of reform in the schools, and thus, I set out to examine closely the role teachers play in school reform. As this study evolved, it became clear to me that much of what is written about educational reform often fails to address issues that matter to teachers and principals, to those who ultimately are responsible for implementing change. Although researchers and policymakers typically pay lip-service to the importance of teachers in school reform, they act as though they have not completely internalized the concept. Once acknowledgment has been made to the role of teachers, researchers and policymakers proceed to satisfy their own interests which often have little to do with either the work or the understanding of teachers as they go about the task of school reform.

This contention is not to argue that research on educational reform and policymaking cannot occur at different levels and encompass many perspectives and concerns. Rather, it is to contend that the centrality of the teacher's role has thus far been under-emphasized and poorly understood.

This teaching episode and many others I observed in this school in 1986 reflected an approach to teaching that would eventually become a major reform in the province of British Columbia. In short, the little picture that is described in this book represented a wedge of progressive practice, initiated by the staff at Lakeview and other schools throughout the province, that was later to be mandated by the Ministry of Education.[1]

The fact that other schools in the province were undertaking similar changes at about the same time does not take away from the perception of teachers at Lakeview that they were operating in apparent isolation. The sense of isolation was underscored by the observation that the changes made in the practice of these teachers created anxiety and a certain amount of anomie as they sensed that they were now out-of-step with the rest of the educational community. This anxiety sprang from not knowing where the changes would take them, and in feeling inadequate and at risk in trying something new. Essentially, they were concerned about trying and failing, and ultimately being held accountable.

On the other hand, changes such as those happening in Lakeview do not occur in a vacuum. They arose partly from local conditions, and partly from developments within the big picture of sociopolitical processes which were taking place at some distance. As I watched and talked to these teachers, I was constantly aware of the contextually-bound nature of their work and by the way in which that context influenced what they did in their classrooms. To place some of these contextual forces in a perspective, I next describe some selected aspects of the big picture.

Note

1 Ministry of Education (1990) *Year 2000: A framework for learning*, Victoria: Province of British Columbia.

I
Remember...

Chapter 2

The background context: Promises and problems

During the last several decades, researchers, program developers, policymakers and a host of other players in most nations in the Western world have turned their attention to the schools. A growth industry has been created around attempts at school reform. Although reformers have been around since schools began, the current pressures for reform that began shortly after the Second World War and were driven by political, economic and educational forces, have now taken on more serious overtones as nations struggle to compete in the global marketplace. Schools have once again become the focal point of social, political, and economic concerns.

The response to these pressures has generally taken two forms. One finds reform attempts being imposed on teachers by policymakers, with researchers at their side attempting to find ways of assisting schools to implement this particular style of reform. We also find reform that teachers initiate and undertake with outside support. Throughout the history of school reform these two approaches have created a tension. More recently, however, this tension has been heightened as we see a shift toward teacher development and school-based reform in which change comes from within the schools. We see this tension at work when we examine the broad areas shown in Figure 1 which include educational change, curriculum development, school improvement, school effectiveness, teacher research and teacher development. The thinking in these areas provides the broad context for the case study that follows in the next chapter and for my analysis in the concluding chapters.

Interest in educational change has been a continuing interest to educators throughout the period shown in Figure 1. It serves as a backdrop to other areas. The curriculum reform movement was a series of developments that took place after the Second World War. School improvement and school effectiveness developed as areas of study somewhat later, with each attracting its own advocates. Teacher research, begun in the 1940s and established as a persistent niche in curriculum thinking since, has, in the last few years, come to occupy a key place in educational thinking. The field now being called 'teacher development' has emerged recently and presents something of an alternative to the others. By placing an emphasis on problems faced in the classroom and supporting the teacher in developing the ways and means of solving those problems, the emphasis for school change now shifts from the policymakers to the classroom teacher. To understand the pressures on schools to bring about change and the ways they might attempt to achieve it, is to understand at least something about the developments in these five areas.

Each of these areas provides a rich source of knowledge about education in general and school improvement in particular. In each we also see opportunities for making our schools better places in which children can learn and teachers can teach. However, in each we find problems and limitations as we try to apply the knowledge that has been gained. Perhaps it seems obvious to point out that these areas did not occur independently of each other and that they do not have clearly defined boundaries, but this point must be kept in mind as we consider the impact they have had, and continue to have, on the education of our young people. Figure 1 shows the five areas from a temporal perspective.

These areas, as well as the developments within them, created a tension between those who would direct change from outside and those who would argue for change from within. In a very general sense, curriculum reform, school improvement and school effectiveness represent a paradigm within which the impetus for change lies with those on the outside who either direct or support school change. The school improvement advocates would perhaps not agree with that statement because they see themselves in sharp contrast to the curriculum reformers and the school effectiveness advocates, as we will see later in this section.

The fields of teacher research and teacher development stand in some contrast to the other three since they represent a paradigm in which the teacher stands at the centre of school change. They present a different paradigm for conceptualizing how change comes about, and how one interprets what I saw at Lakeview. So what we see in Figure 1 may well be more than a temporal shift; it may illustrate the passing of real control in education from the policymakers and external agents to schools and teachers.

Staff development, yet another concept used in the literature, has played a role throughout these attempts at reform in the schools. But typically, the form staff development has taken has been driven by the perspectives of those proposing the reform. In general, it has been a means of 'fixing' teachers so that they can implement projects according to the designs of policymakers. Some notable exceptions to this practice do exist as we will see in this chapter.[1]

Curriculum reform

The roots of the curriculum reform movement in the United States lie deep in the political substructure. In the summer of 1952 newspaper headlines announced that the USSR had achieved supremacy in space; the communists had circled the earth with a satellite. The gauntlet had been thrown down; the space race was on.

Figure 1: The background context[1]

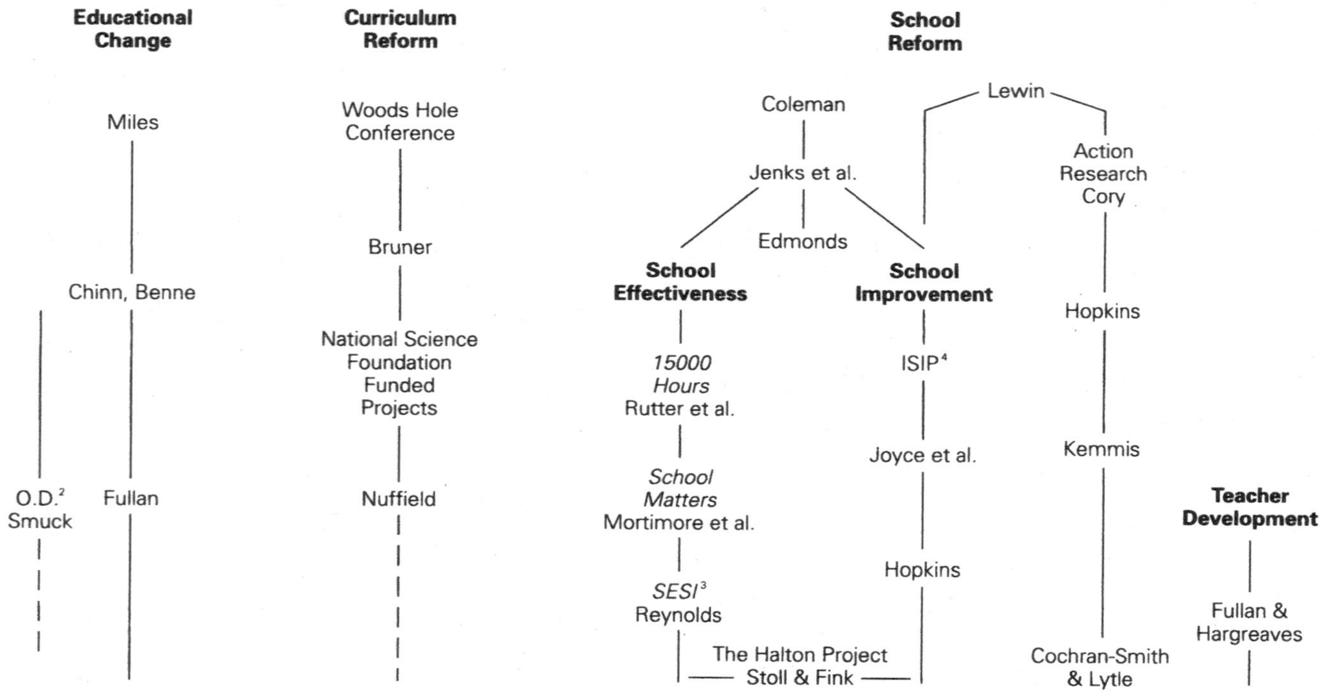

[1] The Figure provides examples only to illustrate these fields of research and development
[2] Organizational Development
[3] School Effectiveness and School Improvement Journal
[4] International School Improvement Project

To win it the Americans would need more and better scientists. These political concerns led to Congress suddenly opening the coffers and making unprecedented amounts of money available for curriculum development. Other Western countries soon followed suit. Since the field of curriculum development had been virtually moribund[2] up to the period following the Second World War, these developments were enthusiastically welcomed by educators. With curriculum development receiving a huge boost, a new excitement filled the air. Those who had long laboured in a rather barren patch now found that political pressure for reform produced resources which would support various educational prerogatives and designs to improve the schools. Throngs of educators, psychologists and academics from other disciplines also saw an opportunity for developing their particular ideas to provide a better education for the young.

Suddenly the educational establishment was filled with the thinking of scholars such as Bruner and Gagné whose seminal work in curriculum projects was to affect thinking in the field of education for the next several decades. Bruner's work in the 1960s set out several themes that would revolutionize thinking in education generally and science and mathematics in particular (Bruner, 1960). He focused attention on the structure of the subject matter and argued that any subject contained an essential structure such that its foundations could be taught to anyone at any time in some form. He also emphasized the notions of discovery learning, intellectual risk and the processes of scientific thought. Gagné's (1963; 1965) assertion that the learning of processes and skills, such as observation, inferring and classification should be the purpose for classroom instruction and enquiry, would become the central core of many curriculum projects. He began with the question, 'What do you want the learner to be able to do?' This capability became a type of terminal behaviour placed at the top of a pyramid made up of skills or processes to be learned in sequence. Once these learning hierarchies had been identified, the specified parts would then be taught and evaluated. Gagné saw objectives as capabilities or behavioural products specifiable in operational terms. The work of these and other theorists found their way into projects aimed at producing curriculum materials. By 1967, some sixty curriculum projects had been funded in mathematics and science alone in the United States. The seeds for major change had been sown. Educational thinking would never be the same.

Others who were to become the educational leaders of the 1970s and 1980s soon became involved at levels more closely related to the classroom. In *Models of teaching*, Joyce and Weil (1986) capture the variety of teaching approaches that typified the developments during the curriculum reform movement. This landmark book legitimized the notion of plurality and argued that good teaching essentially involved learning to use a variety of approaches to instruction.

The curriculum reform movement held great promise for education. Scholars, teachers and educators had come together to develop curriculum packages that were not only novel and interesting but which reflected the best possible thinking in subject area disciplines and in educational theory. But it also presented many problems to schools and teachers. The development of new ideas and new approaches to teaching produced an unprecedented amount of material on how the work of classroom teachers could be improved. Now teachers had many more ways in which to be ignorant. The gulf between the theory of how teaching ought to be done and the practice of putting it into place had become even wider.

However, the problem that became most central in terms of school change — and one that persists today — rested on the top-down, managerial approach taken to curriculum implementation and school change by those who developed curriculum materials. While developers may have taken quite different perspectives toward the curriculum, all seemed to base their work on the assumption that if enough front-end loading could be put into the curriculum and implementation packages then teachers would not alter the curriculum materials in ways that the developers had not intended. This came to be known as 'teacher proofing'. Plenty of development work, carefully planned in-service training, the provision of adequate resources, and time for the teacher to learn how to use the materials would hopefully ensure a high degree of fidelity between the intention of the developers and what teachers did with the materials (Havelock, 1969). But much to the chagrin of the developers and policymakers, 'curriculum proof teachers' proved to be far more robust than a 'teacher proof curriculum'. So, while the curriculum reform movement had produced a powerful new generation of ideas about how teaching could be improved, it remained largely a theoretical exercise and had little effect upon what was being taught in schools.

The evidence for this observation comes from many sources. As early as 1969, Hoetker and Ahlbrand reviewed attempts to improve classroom instruction that went back to the early days of educational reform and concluded:

> . . . studies that have been reviewed show a remarkable stability of classroom verbal behaviour patterns over the last half century, despite the fact that each successive generation of educators . . . has condemned the . . . pattern of instruction (p. 48).

In the early 1970s, Goodlad and his co-workers took a critical look at the extent to which the new developments resulting from a decade of curriculum reform were being used in the classrooms in the United States. Their work followed on the heels of the curriculum reform movement, which included organizational and technological changes as well as new curriculum packages and methods of instruction. In *Looking behind the classroom door* (1974) they reported finding little evidence of the reforms that were to have changed the schools of that country. They argued:

> The highly recommended and publicized innovations of the past decade were dimly conceived and at best partially implemented in schools claiming them. The novel features seem to be blunted in the effort to twist the innovation into familiar conceptual frames or established patterns of schooling (p. 72).

Goodlad characterized the curriculum reform movement as a solution in search of a problem.

With so many resources and so much brainpower behind these developments in curriculum reform it behoves us to pause and consider what went wrong with the implementation of the multitude of projects that sprang up as a result. Those who have analyzed the events with the advantage of hindsight point up an important issue which has to be kept in mind as we look to the future for improving schools. The curriculum reform movement took what House (1981) called the technical perspective toward implementation. It emphasized systematic planning and a rational approach to implementation. Factors such as goal ambiguity (so typical of schools), low quality of innovation, and lack of time to discuss innovation were seen as barriers to implementation. Proponents of this perspective argued that better technical assistance and planning could overcome these problems. Havelock's work (1969) in developing the Research, Development, and Diffusion model aimed at providing this assistance. It sought to make curriculum implementation a rational process through research and development.

Staff development within this context became a process of 'fixing' teachers so that they implement the curriculum packages that had been so carefully put together. They came to workshops and listened to charismatic presenters and worked through the materials that they would use in their classroom. Seldom were they asked if these programs would solve their own classroom problems. Seldom were they asked if the culture of their school would support the changes that were proposed by these new curriculum materials. The emphasis was on the fidelity of putting into practice the materials as they had been developed. However, as Corbett and Rossman (1989) pointed out after their study of several schools, 'innovation cannot succeed on technical considerations alone' (p. 186). The cultural and political considerations also have to be thought about in school change. During the heyday of curriculum reform, the culture of schools and the political dimensions of schools received little attention.

The problem with the efforts of these reformers and the policymakers who followed them went beyond a system of implementation that did not work. Many in the educational field now contend that teachers who have had mandates imposed on them show low morale, dissatisfaction, and reduced commitment to their jobs. Sikes (1992) points out that mandated change can cause teachers to feel that their initial grounding and the ideas that underpin their educational ideologies are no longer viewed favourably; they feel that they may have been wrong and may have disadvantaged their pupils. Stoll (1992) uses the term 'inadequate' and Hargreaves[3] uses the concept of 'guilt' to explain this phenomenon. If teachers were, in fact, teaching poorly, then perhaps they should have been made to feel guilty, but the question of good and bad teaching seemed less important to the developers than putting their particular template for teaching into place. This period produced a myriad of approaches that were often in conflict with each other. Times changed and fads changed. We saw 'discovery learning' one decade and 'back to the basics' another. This seesawing led one teacher to comment that if he never changed his teaching, he would be out in front at least once every ten years.

The efforts during this time — and many that have followed since — did not seem to consider teachers in any way other than as objects to be moved about in an education chess game by grandmasters blessed with superior knowledge. Not only has that manipulation of teachers been proved to be faulty, but the approach to curriculum development on which it was based has failed utterly. As many have pointed out, teachers do have the option of simply ignoring mandates and retreating to the isolation of their classrooms.[4] Given some of the excesses proposed by many developers and policymakers far removed from classroom practice, the schools may be better places because many of them did.[5]

This period of curriculum reform which had its origins with the launching of sputnik flourished through the 1960s and early 1970s. In Figure 1 its demise is shown by a dotted line, since while developmental activity came to an end with the withdrawal of much of the funding, many of the ideas were to remain and continue to influence educational thinking right up to the present.[6] The period has been characterized in many different ways by many different people. MacDonald (1991) in his critical introduction to Rudduck's, *Innovation and change,* divided the last three decades of curriculum and planning into three main stages: from package development to teacher development to school development (p. 4). While one might wish to argue that teacher development is a more recent happening than MacDonald suggests, no one would question that package development was the first main thrust for improving schools. Fullan (1991) labelled this stage as implementing failure. He wrote:

> Up to this point, then, one could say that in the 1960s educators had been busy developing and introducing innovations, while in the first half or so of the 1970s they were busy failing to put them into practice (p. 6).

Those who criticized this period of curriculum reform because it did not create the revolution in schooling that people expected had a legitimate argument. In fact, as Goodlad (1987) pointed out, the heralded period of curriculum reform hardly created a ripple. Many have since used that weakness to justify their own, alternate approach to school reform. The advocates of school improvement are among them. However, after a couple of decades of applying their solutions to improving the schools they have had little more success. Meanwhile, what has been lost, at least to many of the current-day reformers, is the rich source of ideas that came out of the period of curriculum reform. It accomplished several things that were to be of lasting importance, for instance, the strong emphasis taken toward subject matter, beginning with mathematics and science and later spreading to other subjects. Other more generic ideas were also tried. For example, this period saw the emergence of cooperative learning, inquiry teaching and the application of systems theory to instruction. While we may not react warmly to all these ideas, we can at least appreciate a period that set them out to be tried.

School improvement

The notion of school improvement probably began with the work of Edmonds in the late 1960s (cited in Carlsen and Ducharme, 1987). It came about because, in their words, 'one of the implications of the various studies . . . is that some schools clearly do make a difference' (p. xvii). Edmond's concern involved the equitable distribution of goods and services to all people; schools were the means for achieving this goal. He saw inequity arising from our failure to educate the children of the poor (Edmonds, 1987). Since his early work, the use of the term 'school improvement' has grown substantially; one routinely finds it in titles of books, in journals and reports, and discussed at conferences and by organizations. The school improvement advocates have taken a quite different approach to reform from those who proposed to change the schools through the implementation of better curriculum packages (which occurred during the curriculum reform movement) or through the manipulation of variables from a distance (which typified the school effectiveness research which I discuss later). Much more attention is given to the school as a unit, to the problems within that school, and to addressing how schools can be improved. In fact, in many ways the beginning of the school improvement movement was given impetus by the failure of curriculum reform. Writing in 1984, Hopkins put it this way:

> The curriculum reform movement, despite the blaze of publicity, the glossy, colourful and imaginative products, dramatically failed to alter life in the schools (Hopkins and Wideen, 1984, p. 8).

But in that same chapter, in which he sets the frame for a series of essays on school improvement, Hopkins presents a further argument which illustrates another perception of many who were to drive the school improvement movement. He sees school improvement as a reaction to the pervading norms of Western thought which are based on instrumental reason, scientism and technology. Because that empirical/analytic paradigm had not served to support the reforms they felt were needed in the schools, advocates of school improvement began to stress the value of allowing the teachers to 'own' the process of reform. They argued that the focus should be on the school, and adopted a more phenomenological approach to change. The outcomes of schooling were issues to be debated in ways that were to make the values of those in schools explicit. Although general similarities appeared in their different approaches, the advocates of school improvement did not speak with a single voice. The International School Improvement Project reported in Van Velzen (1985) captured one approach to school improvement as:

> . . . a systematic, sustained effort at change in learning conditions and other related internal conditions in one or more schools with the ultimate aim of accomplishing educational goals more effectively (p. 48).

This definition places the emphasis on the school as a unit. It also recognizes the need for a systematic approach to involve such things as goal setting, planning, implementation and monitoring.

The work of Hargreaves and Hopkins (1991), who use the notion of 'the empowered school's, provides an illustration of this position. Drawing on their work with the School Development Plans project in Great Britain, they designed a practical guide for school leaders and practitioners. Such planning aims 'to improve the quality of teaching and learning in a school through the successful management of innovation and change' (p. 3). Schools examine where they are now, what changes they will need to make, how they will manage these over time, and how they will know whether such changes have been successful. In their view, developmental planning provides a staff with the means of managing rapid and substantive changes and encourages a focus on teaching and learning within a school while keeping an eye on external policy requirements.

Hargreaves and Hopkins' work rests on a longitudinal three-year study of schools that have been engaged in developmental planning.[7] Other projects such as the League of Professional Schools operated out of the Program of School Improvement at the University of Georgia (Glichman, Allen and Lunsford, 1992) follow a similar path. The approach taken by these people and others fits quite nicely into the definition of school improvement offered by the International School Improvement Program in Britain. Hargreaves and Hopkins characteristically exclude such things as the professional development undertaken by individual teachers, or large mandated change efforts undertaken by governments. However, they do acknowledge the reality of those external pressures and contend that a strong planning process provides the means to manage such mandates.

Goodlad (1987) and a group of contributors to the *Eighty-sixth yearbook of the national society for the study of education* take what they term an 'ecological' approach to school improvement. In this edited volume, Goodlad presents an alternative to the present 'top-down, authoritarian, linear approach' to school renewal which, he argues, has failed to produce sustained and ongoing reform in our schools. In this new paradigm the school is viewed from an ecological stance where multiple interactions replace one-way directions, leadership by knowledge replaces leadership by authority, inquiring behaviour replaces mandated behaviour, and high expectations replace accountability. These changes are predicated on a shift in power from those at the top of the educational pyramid to the principals and teachers at its base. Others in that volume such as Henshaw, Wilson and Morefield (1987) develop this ecological metaphor, making the case for the school as the unit of reform. They argue that the school should become an open community seeking change through critical inquiry. Williams, Moffett and Newlin (1987) suggest that policymakers outside the school, such as superintendents and school board officials, take on different roles from those they have played in the past. To suit modern realities, policymakers must build school and school district capabilities and disperse the leadership function. Frazier (1987) traces the role of the state in school reform and concludes with an argument for collaboration among all players. All these authors have attributed primary importance to the school as the unit for renewal and view everything beyond it as secondary.

These authors share a conviction that the aim of school renewal should be to achieve better functioning of the school as a healthy unit rather than the emphasizing of outcomes such as test scores. Such health comes from better connections to society's expectations and to the growing knowledge base regarding sound educational practices. They use the metaphor of an ecological system to explain school reform. Since ecosystems are complex and interrelated, they require certain types of external energy sources for survival but can be damaged by others. If we think of the school as an ecosystem, then it is not difficult to understand why schools have not changed as they might have been expected to. Ecosystems do not change as a result of simple interventions; neither do schools. It alerts us to the fact that schools are delicate cultures that can be damaged, and indeed that have been damaged, by quick-fix remedies. This metaphor also alerts us to the complexities of the entire process of schooling, its interconnectedness, and to the difficulties that change implies. But any metaphor carried to its limit breaks down. Schools, unlike biological systems, are made up of intelligent, thoughtful individuals who are capable of producing their own action plans for change in keeping with their understanding of the expectations of the external environment.

The central argument in the school improvement literature sees the onus for reform placed on the shoulders of teachers and schools and suggests that if we leave schools alone, they will rise from the ashes. That proposal becomes naive and even dangerous when it is not accompanied by more specific suggestions about how such change should come about and in which milieu. In making this assertion I do not wish to be classed among those who think that schools can be managed in the process of reform (or indeed that they should be — assuming that were possible). In fact, this book itself is about a school managing its own change process. However, it would be naive to place the task of reform on schools which lack the resources and capabilities, and indeed the energy, to carry out the job. The danger lies in the extremes to which such an approach to reform can lead; for example, apart from asking whether it is reasonable to expect schools to undertake any reform without some type of external pressure, we have to consider to what extent expecting schools to go it alone serves to relieve policymakers of their responsibility. The role of outside groups in reform remains critical in terms of providing support and setting the ethos under which such reform will take place. What needs to be explored more carefully than many in the school improvement area seem to recognize is how policymakers can set the stage and create a climate for change in schools and districts. They need to ask: What forms of support are most productive? And, most importantly, what does change mean to the teacher?

The strength of the school improvement movement lies in its focus on the school and its recognition of the cultural aspects of change. The value placed by its proponents on equity in schooling and strong support of the teacher's role in school change provide a firm base from which to begin. The problems, on the other hand, lie in the movement's incompleteness and the fact that while it identifies with the teacher, it typically deals with issues far removed from classroom practice. Moreover, although the proponents generally support the school as the basis for change, their orientation remains somewhat technical and top-down. As external agents of change, the proponents still appear to be searching for the correct formulae for changing schools.

One finds little in the literature on school improvement that a teacher can do much about. Once one has said that the school is the basis for change, what does one do next? One also wonders how the ecological metaphor that Goodlad refers to can be brought about; surely it requires intense interplay between the staff and principal in a school? In the meantime, what does an individual teacher do? School improvement advocates appear to ignore or underestimate the complexity of the process.

The school improvement movement has also failed to connect to other work in education such as the developments in curriculum reform, discussed in the previous section, the work in school effectiveness, and many of the more fundamental ideas about what it means to be educated. An example of the disconnectedness of these movements can be seen in the way in which both school effectiveness and school improvement elected to ignore the developments coming out of the period of curriculum reform. That movement saw numerous projects which attempted to move schools away from recitation teaching, or what Schwab (1964) had termed, the 'rhetoric of conclusions' — a style of teaching typical during the post-war years. The implementation of these curricula saw efforts to bring teaching strategies, such as inquiry teaching and cooperative learning, to the classrooms. The research on school improvement appeared to move ahead as if none of this reform had occurred. Few links were made to the previous decades of curriculum thinking.

School effectiveness

The question of whether differences between schools do make a difference in student learning gave rise to another approach to the study of schools. The group who pioneered this approach in the 1960s began to examine the characteristics of the 'effective' school. This paradigm had an outcome focus, a quantitative methodology, a focus on easily-measured behaviours and an aim of generating truthful knowledge about the schools, whether those in the schools liked it or not. Effectiveness was defined in terms of student achievement (Reynolds, 1992). Different characteristics which varied from school to school, such as the emphasis on curriculum and instruction, were then correlated to achievement. Research over time produced a cluster of characteristics typical of some schools which were found to be strongly related to high achievement. Such schools were described as being 'effective' schools. Mortimore (1991), who has been central to this movement, describes the effective school in a slightly different way, as one in which students show greater academic progress than might be expected given its particular intake of students.

The notion that differences from one school to the next made a difference in student outcomes was not always accepted by educators. The studies of the American sociologists, Coleman (1966) and Jencks (1972), as well as the Plowden report (1967) in Great Britain showed quite conclusively that schools made no difference to student achievement. The authors of these reports argued that factors such as cost per student, internal school policy and provision, and school facilities had no effect upon student test scores (Reynolds, 1991). The legacy of doubt created by these large-scale studies about the links between school differences and student learning provided much of the impetus for both the school effectiveness and school improvement movements as shown in Figure 1.

The Coleman report drew on a large-scale survey of over 60,000 students in 4,000 schools and concluded that educational achievement was largely independent of pupils' school experience; that such achievement rested more on family background than on anything the school did. A year later the Plowden report drew a similar conclusion in Britain. Jencks and his colleagues in the early 1970s found much the same when they analyzed data from a number of investigations and concluded that equalizing the quality of the high schools would make little difference to student test-scores. These empirical studies, along with other assessments that showed that the innovations coming out of the period of curriculum reform had not had much success, raised serious doubt about the ability of the school to make a difference in student learning.

After a decade of such doubts the well-publicized British study *Fifteen thousand hours* (Rutter, Maughan, Mortimore, Ouston and Smith, 1979) produced results which showed that school climate did make a difference in what and how students learned. This study, carried out in 12 secondary schools in Britain, asked questions such as: Does a child's experience in school make a difference? What are the features of schools that matter? and, Does it really make a difference which school a child attends? They concluded that the 15,000 hours a student spends in school do indeed make a difference to the cognitive development of that student; such differences vary from school to school. 'Effective schools', those in which students achieve higher test scores, are characterized by certain factors. In the words of Rutter and his colleagues (1979) these include, among others, '. . . the degree of academic emphasis, teacher actions in lessons, the availability of incentive and rewards, good conditions for pupils, and the extent to which children were able to take responsibility' (p. 178). These factors, which were all associated with outcome differences between schools, can be altered by teachers.

At the same time work was moving ahead in other countries to identify the characteristics of schools that were found to be making a difference. The work of Edmonds (1979), who focused on making schools more effective for the urban poor, and Brookover and Lezotte (1977) who examined changes in school characteristics as linked to changes in student outcomes, along with a number of other researchers in different parts of the world, produced a set of factors that were to come to be associated with the effective school. A review of the American literature by Purkey and Smith (1983) identified eight such factors linked to student achievement. Others such as Fullan (1985) and Hargreaves and Hopkins (1991) would extend and modify that list. The characteristics that follow in the box below (from Hargreaves and Hopkins, 1991) summarize a decade of research in this area.

Effective schools: organization and process factors

(reprinted with permission of the authors)

The following eight factors are representative of the so-called 'organization factors' that are characteristic of effective schools (see Purkey and Smith, 1983)

1 Curriculum-focused school leadership.
2 Supportive climate within the school.
3 Emphasis on curriculum and teaching (for example, maximizing academic learning.
4 Clear goals and high expectations for students.
5 A system for monitoring performance and achievement.
6 Ongoing staff development and in-service training.
7 Parental involvement and support.
8 (District LEA) and external support.

These factors do not, however, address the dynamics of schools as organizations. There appear to be four additional factors which infuse some meaning and life into the process of improvement within the school. These 'process factors' provide the means of achieving the organizational factors; they lubricate the system and 'fuel the dynamics of interaction.' They have been described by Fullan (1985, p. 400) as follows:

1 A feel for the process of leadership; this is difficult to characterize because the complexity of factors involved tends to deny rational planning — a useful analogy would be that organizations are to be sailed rather than driven.
2 A guiding value system; this refers to a concensus on high expectations, explicit goals, clear rules, a genuine caring about individuals, etc.
3 Intense interaction and communication; this refers to simultaneous support and pressure at both horizontal and vertical levels within the school.
4 Collaborative planning and implementation; this needs to occur both within the school and externally, particularly in the District (LEA).

The result of this work — which was international in scope — produced broad agreement that the factors shown in Figure 1 constituted an effective school in terms of student achievement. Hargreaves and Hopkins (1991) note further that the effective schools' literature shows agreement on at least two other issues. The first being that as these characteristics vary from school to school so does student achievement. Second, schools have the capability of making changes that can lead to a school becoming effective. These findings from a decade and more of research, provide optimism about schools making a difference in the lives of children and give promise that those in schools can work toward developing a better vision of schooling.

The effective schools' movement is not without its problems, however. The first comes from the research itself and involves notions of cause and effect. The links between the characteristics of an effective school and student achievement can only be described in terms of relationships rather than causal links. The effective schools' research tells us that teachers should hold high academic expectations for students because in those schools where teachers do, students achieve higher test-scores. The clear implication here is that the high expectations of teachers cause students to achieve better. The question remains though, which came first, the high expectations on the part of teachers, or the high achievement on the part of students? Perhaps it is easier for teachers in schools with a history of high student test-scores to have higher expectations for their students. So, one must be cautious about attributing all the success of student achievement in the so called 'effective' schools to the factors identified for effective schools, however appealing that notion might be. Yet that is exactly what many policymakers have tried to do through contrived programs that attempt to plaster over a weak school with some semblance of the effective schools' characteristics.

Identifying the characteristics of an effective school is one thing, putting them into practice quite another. Even when we can state with some assurance what an effective school looks like, we are still faced with the problem of how a school becomes effective. Those who work in the effective schools' movement often appear quite oblivious to what the characteristics they have identified mean to schools or to how schools might work towards achieving them. Not surprisingly, the implementation of the findings from the effective schools' research, apart from selected demonstration projects, has been disappointing.

Another, related, difficulty with the effective schools' movement rests on its tendency to focus too narrowly on the academic not social outcomes of schooling. This emphasis has led to a failure to think deeply about the educative nature of schooling and to move beyond the simple achievement indicators of the effective school. It failed to address the question of whether test-scores represent the sum total of education. In short, rather than take a more educative view, the effective schools movement narrows the purposes of schooling and trivializes its mission.

The lack of connectedness to school improvement provides the second example of the isolated nature of the school effectiveness group. Reynolds (1991), in commenting about the field of school effectiveness, observes that if a Martian were to visit our planet to look at educational research, he would be astounded by the lack of connection between school effectiveness and school improvement.

He attributed this lack of connection to the very distinct intellectual traditions and histories of the two fields. He points out that only in selected locations such as the project conducted by the Halton Board of Education in Toronto (Stoll and Fink, 1992) do we find attempts to bring together the research base from these two areas.

Despite these weaknesses, in showing that good schools do indeed make a difference in the academic achievement of students, the school effectiveness research has given us reason to be optimistic. Moreover, that research identified the characteristics that make schools effective and also provided a strong research base.

Teacher research

For many people, staff development and certain kinds of in-service training conjure up the notion of teachers having something imparted to them because they suffer a deficiency or lack. They sit, they listen, they learn what others apparently know about how they should do their job better. The 'teacher as researcher' concept produces another image which is that of a practising professional who identifies her or his own problems and seeks ways of solving them. Such a model takes a very different approach development.

The concept of 'teacher as researcher' (or in some quarters, 'action research') has been around for a long time. In this paradigm, research in classrooms and schools becomes a powerful means through which teachers can both improve their work and grow professionally in the process. Corey (1953), building on the work of Lewin, first discussed the concept in a paper presented to a conference in 1953. He argued that the focus of research in education ought to be on the solving of classroom problems by teachers. He used the term 'action research' to describe such activity. The last few years have seen an increasing interest in a variety of teacher and school-based activities which roughly fall under the notion of teacher as researcher. These are not esoteric projects that teachers take on in addition to their work, nor are they research in the traditional university sense. Rather, they involve activity closely tied to the work teachers do, much as Corey described. Hopkins (1985) in *A teacher's guide to action research*, refers to it as 'an act undertaken by teachers either to improve their own or a colleague's teaching or to test the assumptions of educational theory or practice (p. 3).'

The thread of the teacher research movement has continued to find its way into selected parts of the educational fabric over the years since Corey's (1953) work. Today, however, we see an increased emphasis on teacher research. It has become a partner within a larger movement connected to teachers changing their view of themselves and their roles. Other areas such as constructivist learning theory and reflective practice have become conceptual allies, producing yet another movement under the social reconstructivist banner which places reform within the realm of schools and teachers.

The interest in teacher as researcher comes in part from a simple desire to improve schools and teaching. However, the roots run deeper than that. Authors such as Kincheloe (1991) see the teacher as researcher notion as a way of teacher emancipation. Citing Habermas, he contends that 'the emancipatory interest connects the act of knowing with the immediate use of knowledge' (p. 70). But the knowledge in question is to be produced by teachers themselves. Such knowledge leads to freedom from the dominance typical of knowledge produced by outsiders.

My own contact with the notion of teacher as researcher comes both from my work with teachers who attempt to apply what they have learned from university coursework and also from my observation of teachers who have simply undertaken on their own to change their practice to achieve some type of improvement. Let me illustrate the notion of 'teacher as researcher' by describing an experience unrelated to the present study, but one in which I spent several days observing and talking to teachers and where I learned how one teacher saw herself as action researcher (Wideen, 1987).

A case in point

The classroom. The students are told that this is language arts period and that they have three choices. They may write, read, or illustrate their stories. Following some housekeeping chores, the third graders begin different activities. Some remain in their seats and begin printing on what appear to be rough notebooks, others are drawing. Several others proceed to corners created by carefully arranged and colourfully decorated bookcases to sit on cushions and share in reading books.

Two queues have also formed. One leads to a student teacher who types student stories, the other to a volunteer who assists the students in editing their materials. Cheryl, the teacher, moves about the room helping different individuals. Sometimes students talk to one another in a friendly, joking manner, but most seem to be on task. As a visitor, I am presented with a ten-page story book and experience surprise that a third grader had produced it.

My first impression of this classroom was how different and how changed it was from the language arts teaching typical in most classrooms. I saw no evidence of prescribed textbooks or basal readers. In questioning Cheryl on why she taught this way, I learned that she had developed the approach herself with the help of another teacher in the school and that all teachers in the primary section of the school now use a similar approach to language arts. What was the background for this innovation?

Background. Woodfort, the school in which Cheryl teaches, is located in an older school district in a still rapidly-growing suburban community. Its residents are upper middle class and are relatively ambitious people. It was in this community that Cheryl took her first teaching position seven years ago after graduating from a local teacher-training institution. She had not found her teacher preparation particularly useful in preparing her for her first job, nor had it offered her any fresh perspectives on how to improve classroom instruction for children. In fact, it appeared to be a re-run of her own experience as a student, an experience she had not particularly enjoyed. She reports having disliked her first year of teaching simply because she knew it was not the best learning experience for children. In language arts (the subject area that I concentrated on during my observation) she found herself teaching from a basal reader, using workbooks and worksheets.

During a year's leave of absence from teaching she substituted in a third grade classroom in nearby Cameron Heights. Here she encountered a very different approach to language arts teaching. The classroom teacher was Pat who had initiated the approach four years earlier amid storms of protest. Cheryl requested a transfer to Cameron Heights primarily to learn from Pat and others in the school. Cheryl attributes much of her success to the earlier efforts of Pat who had introduced an alternative to language arts into her classroom. However, her first realization in coming to the school was that she could not adapt what Pat was doing in her classroom. She had to develop her own approach. The association with Pat and other teachers in the school was critical, however, in providing people with similar experiences with whom to discuss her difficulties. Cheryl talked about the long process of trial and error that she found necessary, both to clarify what it was she wanted to do in language arts, and how she was going to implement the new program.

Can this be called research? Normally when we think of research, we think of it as solving problems, testing ideas and accumulating knowledge by building on our work and the work of others. Can we see these practices at work in this example?

One way of viewing a problem is to see it as a discrepancy between an ideal condition and one that currently exists. Sometimes discrepancies arise out of something we do not know, such as when we see an event that we cannot explain according to our expectations of reality — certain magic acts come to mind. Other times we may wish to do something that we feel we cannot do. Our struggle as people to understand our universe and to make it better is essentially one of solving these sorts of problems.

In the case of both Cheryl and Pat, their teaching of language arts concerned them. Each had a vision of how it could become better, however fuzzy that vision may have been in the early stages. The discrepancy between current practice and idealized practice became the problem for both of them. Clarifying that vision and putting it into practice became their way of solving the problem. In many ways the problems faced by Cheryl and Pat are no different from those with which scientists and social scientists grapple. To be sure, there are differences in scale, and perhaps generalizability, but the essentials are the same.

Once a problem is identified, its solution comes about through a process of testing and refining hypotheses or ideas that will solve the problem. The garage mechanic will successively test such things as spark plugs and the battery using the hypotheses that a faulty electrical system is the problem. Scientists in the 1930s systematically tested different strains of wheat to find one which best resisted wheat rust. In the same way, Cheryl, in her attempt to find a better way of teaching language arts, tested different approaches until she found one that worked in her situation.

In terms of building on past experience, we are well aware of the tremendous background of skill and knowledge that a scientist brings to a problem. What is often overlooked is the background of experience and knowledge the teachers also draw upon in solving problems. Cheryl drew on the work of Pat and others in the school in developing the program that was eventually to solve her problem. Both she and Pat also drew on a background of information gained through in-service education, university coursework and a variety of other sources.

The cases of Cheryl and Pat are similar to more accepted notions of research in two other ways, reflection and support. Research activities are often distinguished from non-research activities by what someone once termed the constant application of intelligence. People who engage in research think, ponder and struggle with ideas and alternatives. They take time to reflect in rigorous and deliberate ways. In the case of teachers, the mindless application of programs passed on from high places does not constitute research. What is impressive in the case of Cheryl and Pat was how they both struggled with their problems. Cheryl took a year away from teaching simply to explore alternatives and think about teaching. Pat took on a school board. Both actions required thought and reflection.

People who are engaged in problem-solving rarely work alone. They normally benefit from a support group of peers: scientists consult other scientists, read journals, and attend conferences. It is interesting to observe how Cheryl joined a school where a certain type of language arts program was occurring in order to benefit from it. The entire primary section of the school became her support group.

While we do not normally think of teachers as potential researchers, this brief analysis was intended to illustrate that when teachers attempt to solve the problems they face they are undertaking a form of research. It is this recognition that has prompted numerous projects throughout Europe, Australia and North America aimed at promoting the concept of teacher as researcher.

Why classroom research?

Those who have studied and written about the concept of classroom research point to a number of advantages. They describe it as a powerful means for staff development, as an effective method of school improvement, and as a means for teachers to control their own professional activities. These reasons are imbedded within certain social and political perspectives.

As Elliot Eisner points out in *The educational imagination* (1979), people take different perspectives on curriculum. The commonly-held view that underpinned much of the activity during the curriculum reform movement and one that has persisted in developments since, sees curriculum as a top-down process. Once developed by experts, curriculum becomes a blueprint to be implemented and followed by teachers who are agents responsible for carrying out policies set by policymakers often well removed from the classroom. This perspective views research, designed to determine principles of learning and practice on which such curriculum is to be based, as an activity also undertaken by experts. In short, theory developed by experts drives practice. Supervision then becomes a process of judging the extent to which such a curriculum or teaching practice is implemented or put in place. This perspective also favours standardization of curriculum and teaching and favours the use of final examinations as one way of achieving that standardization.

Those who argue for the concept of teacher as researcher take a very different perspective. For them curriculum becomes what teachers organize and plan for their own classrooms. They talk of the teacher as an autonomous professional who designs curriculum. Within this context the teacher is a potential researcher testing out ideas. Research findings and the curriculum guide are not facts and directives to be applied, but hypotheses to be tested. Thus, the theory/practice relationship is more of a dialectic. Supervision takes on much more of a helping and developmental role and exists to improve the teacher's performance against a standard set by the teacher. This scenario runs counter to the more frequent notion of supervision existing to assess whether curriculum has been implemented. Consistency of practice across teachers becomes relatively unimportant in this perspective and progress is seen as taking on a broken front approach.

One of the most compelling reasons for encouraging classroom research is to engage teachers in staff development. By now it has been established that staff development is a learning process, but as educators we all know too well that learning does not occur without participation, involvement and practice. Classroom research means that teachers do something about their performance by becoming active participants in their own improvement. In all the project reports that I have read, the opportunity for learning on the part of the participants is the fact most frequently emphasized as the most important by-product of such projects.

Classroom research on the part of teachers offers much hope in terms of achieving the goal of improved education. Wherever exemplary schools have been singled out the message is always the same. They have become effective because teachers and principals have worked to make them that way. How that process actually begins and works remains a moot point so far, but it usually starts with teachers beginning to work on improving some part of their practice. The larger the number of people working toward this goal in any one school the better.

Classroom research also allows the teacher to take control. One of the most impressive aspects of my talks with Cheryl and Pat was the acknowledgment that they were in control of what they were doing. They were not engaged in social revolution in the sense that they were trying to subvert the system wherever possible. Rather, they were exercising the freedom they had as teachers.

In terms of school improvement, the advantages of teacher research can also be its disadvantages. Because teacher research is an individual or small-group activity, progress often appears patchy. This unpredictability in where improvements are likely to occur and what they might look like, is not always cherished by policymakers. Teacher research also has a potential for insularity. If no knowledge or information comes from the outside and forms part of the process, teacher research can become a lot of activity around nothing.

Teacher development

Another recent line of research — teacher development — grew out of many of the developments I have just reviewed. Its roots probably extend back to the 1970s and 1980s when developmental stage theorists sought to identify concerns, problems, or tasks common to most teachers at various times in their professional lives (Burden, 1990). Teacher development was seen as a series of stages through which people progressed during the course of their career.

The notion of teacher development has now moved beyond stage theory to include a more situational and personal frame. Fullan and Hargreaves (1992) have grouped developments into two broad phases, the 'innovative-focused' phase and the 'total teacher and the total school' phase. During the 'innovative-focused' phase teacher development is linked to successful innovation. They argue that because specific innovations require alterations to teaching materials and changes in beliefs and understandings on the part of teachers, implementation is essentially a learning process. Hence, they contend that teacher development and implementation go hand in hand.[8] This connection has long been recognized by those at the district level who would involve teachers in the preparation of curriculum materials on the assumption that the experience would provide a rich source of professional development and, thus, would improve the chances of implementation. But, as different authors have recently pointed out and as we see in the case of Lakeview, school change involves much more than the implementation of single innovations.

The second phase of teacher development posited by Fullan and Hargreaves involves the 'total teacher and the total school.' This frame takes into account the teacher's purpose, the teacher as a person, the context of the teacher's work, and the culture of teaching. The position stems from the view that teaching is a moral craft having purpose to those who engage in it. When school change was seen as a function of implementing innovations, the voice of the teacher was undervalued and underdeveloped as a source of school change.

Teacher development as it is currently being thought of, focuses upon the teacher as a learner and an active person in the process of school change. This understanding has led people such as Lieberman (1984) to focus on the dilemmas and meanings surrounding innovations and what teachers find important about them. This perspective takes a more teacher-centred approach, recognizing the limitations of outsiders who mandate programs such as clinical supervision or staff development designed to promote change (Grimmett and MacKinnon, 1991). This shift in thinking has led authors such as these to promote and advocate the notion of teacher development as a way to place the teacher more centrally within school reform rather than simply as a means to implement innovations better.

Teacher development has only recently begun to attract attention. As Fullan and Hargreaves (1992) point out, if it is to survive as a field it requires a much more thorough conceptualization than it has had to this point. At issue, among other things, are questions concerning those teachers who show no motivation to develop and become part of the reform process. Nor has most of the literature on teacher development up to this time progressed beyond mere description of situations and contexts that have reportedly led to teacher development. While equating teacher development to learning has an appealing ring few authors have yet moved beyond that notion in their reported work.

The broad picture

These developments describe the broad, historic picture of attempts to improve schools and set a general framework for the present case study and its analysis. Before turning to the local picture that provides the more immediate context for the school we are about to look at, let me make three comments about these general developments.

First, the different pressures for reform and the problems on which they were based remain today; the political pressures, for example, are just as evident now as they were following the Second World War when we saw the beginnings of the curriculum reform movement. While we may not have to contend with communist hordes trying to storm the walls, we do have to face the issue of global competition and all that it implies. And, in searching for a solution, many, if not most of us, will still look to the schools to provide the engine for economic growth. The charge that schools do not appear to be keeping up with changes in society, made with such fervour by insiders and outsiders alike in the 1960s, only intensify as the years roll by.

Second, although the four areas — curriculum reform, school improvement, the effective schools' movement and teacher research — set themselves up for strong criticism, and although they appear to have gone on independently, one does find a residue of educational improvement and an evolutionary character in them. Each of the three grew out of existing conditions and in one sense or another represent a reaction to the perceived failure of previous developments. The concept of school improvement, for example, was a reaction to the perceived failure of curriculum reform which in turn found its origins rooted in the perception that the existing education system would not serve post-war needs. School improvement has also evolved through stages, from the documenting of the failure of school innovations to the more current focus of attempting to understand success. The two fields — school improvement and school effectiveness — once seen to be only distant conceptual relatives, are now being brought together in significant ways. Because each development leaves behind a wealth of knowledge and a record of thinking about how schools improve, we now have a rich context in which to set this present study.

While we do see some evidence of change and progress, we also see the persistence of practices that continue to hinder attempts at reform. These practices can best be illustrated by the persistence in which those in policymaking positions continue to take the view that to mandate a change or to develop and impose a new curriculum is to change the system. Where that approach has been documented, the evidence suggests that nothing much happened. As has often been pointed out, you can't mandate what matters. Yet strategies for bringing about school system change still typically include top-down approaches where the teacher is viewed as an instrument for carrying out policy.

A third theme to persist through every development that has occurred since the Second World War — and probably earlier — involves the tension between those who want to view the schools in relatively simplistic terms and those who stress their complexity and ambiguity. For the first group, school change can be achieved through manipulating the proper variables to accomplish certain outcomes. The school effectiveness movement, with its roots in quantitative analysis, typifies this approach — best illustrated in the testing movement which seeks to establish change through test-driven instruction (Popham, 1987). On the other side of this tension lie those who take a cultural orientation which stresses the complexity of schools and the ambiguity associated with school goals. For them, the school is seen as an ecological unit with a life of its own. The school improvement area typifies this view, and those who advocate teacher research bring this understanding to the classroom level. This tension has been well-established since the beginning period of school reform and continues today, as we will see in the section that follows.

The local context

While the developments on the international scene just described provide the general context for this study, the developments played out at the local level provide a more focused look at the context. These developments create pressures for change on the one hand, yet often stand in the way of bringing about change on the other.

School improvement in a country as large and diverse as Canada is understandably complex. The various groups of players complicate the activity, especially when each claims to be on the inside track in making schools better places. Some promote new practices, others study them; some develop new policy, others implement it. School improvement has become a growth industry with new players regularly appearing on the scene. Frequently, it becomes hard to distinguish between sincere attempts to improve the schools and mere self-interested promotion.

The new understanding and awareness surrounding the field of implementation has brought new complexities to the social system in which school change occurs. Typically, many new initiatives not only involve changes to teaching, but also require sophistication in planning implementation strategies. At one time, particularly during the curriculum reform movement, a transmissive model of curriculum change saw teachers as conduits through which other people's ideas were to be implemented. Here, people worried largely about changes in curriculum content and how best to learn what the new curriculum was about. Things have changed. With what we have now learned about implementation, we must consider plans and skills in order to bring about desired change. Moreover, as Miles and Huberman (1984; 1986) have pointed out, what some people see as an improvement in the schools — an elusive and slippery concept itself — often depends through which lens the beholder is focusing.

All levels of government undertake initiatives that potentially impact on schools. Although the Federal government has no legal jurisdiction on education, it still attempts to influence the direction schools take by funding certain initiatives that match its priorities, typically linked to economic needs.[9] Because education is a provincial matter, Ministries of Education carry considerable weight in setting curriculum guidelines and often supporting policy initiatives aimed at implementing changes in those guidelines. Schools in the province where this study took place find themselves subject to varying degrees of Provincial Ministry control. The Ministry of Education produces curriculum guides in most subjects and, when this study began, was responsible for authorizing textbooks that could be used. The Ministry also sets provincial examinations in grade 12 for the main subjects taught. Local school districts have varying degrees of control within these guidelines. By the end of this study more flexibility in textbook selection became available to districts. Further, in 1986, the provincial government allowed municipalities to set their own tax rates, thereby allowing school districts to raise monies outside Ministry grants if they so wished.

These governmental and district initiatives result in a constant barrage of initiatives, policy statements and mandates that carry implications for what is to be taught in the school. Some are fairly straightforward while others require substantial changes. Further, the policy initiatives frequently conflict. The sheer number of changes proposed disconcerts most teachers. In a recent study, Fullan, Anderson and Newton (1986) show that typically schools and districts deal with multiple innovations, a finding that underscores the complexity of the social systems in which change comes about. In a recent study in British Columbia, the investigator found that 26 separate changes had been proposed by the district and the Ministry of Education in a single year.

Universities also undertake initiatives to keep the school improvement industry alive and well, generally through in-service courses and workshops for teachers. Workshops of this sort encouraged some of the changes that occurred in Lakeview. The Achilles' heel in these efforts involves their notorious lack of value in helping teachers deal with improving practice. With some notable exceptions, such courses comprise nothing more than warmed-over undergraduate coursework presented in a theoretical way that fails to relate to classroom practice.

Still other players are involved. Many, such as the educational entrepreneur, often high on charisma and low on substance, sell simple solutions to complex problems. The distance travelled by such hired help appears to be in direct proportion to the expected impact that he or she will have. As we shall see later, these efforts often have highly questionable outcomes. Many of these groups (and here one could add an array of teacher organizations) do not work from any particular power base; they sponsor their own projects. The result is a huge array of sometimes unconnected options available to schools and teachers for staff development and school improvement.

The interaction of these many and varied players establishes a context of conflicting traditions about the way school improvement should come about as well as the purpose of the changes themselves. They go beyond the simple dichotomy of a bottom-up versus top-down approach to improving schools. Rather, we see a complex cluster of initiatives, proposals and writings that reflect different perspectives about how schools should change and what should be the nature of that change.

One illustration arises out of the role of the teacher in school change. The work of the late Lawrence Stenhouse (1984) typifies a group of people working both at the school and university level who strongly argue that teachers must be central to any change in the schools. He made his point this way:

> The improvement of schooling hinges on increasing the numbers of outstanding teachers, on serving their needs, and on trying to ensure that their virtues are not frustrated by the system (p. 69).

Barrow (1984) makes a similar claim from a philosophical perspective arguing that schools should be given back to teachers. Much support now exists to encourage action research on the part of teachers. In a recent initiative the Ministry of Education in British Columbia funded 21 sites in the province to carry out action research projects.

Although the research rhetoric generally supports teacher involvement in school change, many initiatives taken by Ministries and school boards, suggest that the traditional use of power in directing what schools do continues to prosper. These power-coercive initiatives come both in the form of mandates and a highly centralized system of education. In 1984, for example, the Ministry of Education in the province in which this study took place reinstituted school-leaving examinations in grade 12. That policy move has not only had a strong impact on the instructional activity of secondary teachers, but it has also effectively frozen innovation at the secondary school level.[10] And, as we shall see in the section that follows, in taking prescription as a way of life, the centralized system of education confirms teachers' views that their professional lives are tightly governed.

The picture of school improvement drawn in the sociopolitical arena outside the school delivers mixed and changing messages to teachers. It produces what appears to be an unending array of policy initiatives. Teachers, if they take such mandates seriously, are constantly kept off balance trying to adjust to changes required for one mandate before another one comes along, while all around them policymakers wax eloquently about the need for teacher ownership.

Nowhere do these conflicts become more evident than in the area of staff development. In a recent document prepared for the Ministry of Education in British Columbia we find this stated assumption about how teachers ought to approach the planning of a curriculum project:

> To learn from our experience we must think of ourselves as inquirers rather than experts about curriculum. Many effective professionals improve their practices through an ongoing cycle of planning, acting, observing and reflecting. When this cycle is framed by a focusing question we can consciously gather valuable information for our own learning.
>
> We can all become action researchers on curriculum change. The action research process involves gathering of information about events as they occur, reflecting on problematic aspects of the situation, developing theories about how to improve the situation and testing these theories in action. Through interaction with others we can compare observations and test our own interpretations and theories against the experience of others (Dockendorf and Holborn, 1992, p. 44).

The point of view expressed in this statement comes from a person who has been heavily involved with the Ministry in staff development in the province for several years. But others have approached staff development with a 'quick fix' mentality. Teachers are taken as objects to be 'in-serviced'. The empty vessel notion or deficit model clearly pervaded the thinking of many staff development people working in the schools. The account of one teacher who writes about her experience, sums it all up:

> In 1984 I worked with a staff who decided to implement a new program through the traditional staff development model. The new program on 'effective' teaching strategies was being promoted by the district administration. After receiving information from a Californian expert, we willingly agreed to buy the product being sold at the time. Our chances of success appeared high because we had a supportive administrator, extra time set aside to implement the program, and positive and friendly relations amongst the staff members. We also acknowledged the importance of continued growth.
>
> Unfortunately, after three years of in-service little real change occurred in our classrooms. What was missing from our plans? Why weren't we more successful? Of major importance was the fact that we had not

examined the existing culture of our school or considered our present classroom practices. As a staff we never asked ourselves what, why and how are we improving our teaching practices. Instead, the staff agreed to implement 'direct' teaching strategies in their daily teaching practices because existing research told them it enhanced learning. The expert from California sold us the product based on research we never questioned. We paid her to fill us with knowledge five days each year for a three year period. We became consumers of knowledge and practice. Over time the teachers became frustrated with the direct teaching approach. Little of the theory became practice. Ultimately the program failed.

Using the staff development in this way did not work for us. Thousands of dollars and hundreds of hours of our time had been spent with minimal results. Many of us could not articulate why we were attempting to incorporate 'direct teaching' into our daily lesson plans. In retrospect, our initial decision had been made without thinking about our present practice and without questioning the research supporting the product. Would critical reflection have encouraged more questions about practice and the 'new product'? Might a process such as action research have encouraged us to question the 'packaged deal'? (Wideen, Carlman and Strachan, 1986, pp. 2 and 3).

The comments of this teacher typify the reactions of many who faithfully attended staff development workshops on the elements of instruction only to find that a limited residue of classroom improvement was left behind. The problem addressed, the ways and means of solving that problem, and the results that were to emerge when the elements of instruction were put into place were all set by the charismatic workshop leader. Teachers only had to attend. It comes as no surprise, then, that where a follow-up analysis has occurred, the impact of workshops such as the one described above are typically disappointing (Wideen, Carlman and Strachan 1986).[11] Such workshops were very typical of the scene in the province where this study occurred.

The contrast shown here regarding staff development also points to a theme threading through the literature concerning how teachers use knowledge. One view contends that research findings provide propositional knowledge that teachers can apply. Such knowledge is a given; it is non-problematic. An alternative argument suggests that decisions about teaching cannot be made out of the context of a classroom; that teachers need to think about their practice and question outside theories and packages. In short teachers should become critics. Shulman, speaking to the 1991 annual meeting of the American Association of Curriculum Development, addressed this habit of viewing teachers as consumers rather than as critics of knowledge. He argues:

In general, research answers the questions you ask and that we as a community of educational practitioners have gotten into a very bad habit

> of — we have become consumers not critics. My late, great teacher, Joseph Schwab . . . asked us to keep in mind the distinction between narrative of inquiry and a rhetoric of conclusions. . . . We in the educational practice community have accepted the results of research on teaching as a rhetoric of conclusions. We have to become a much more critical and aggressive group of consumers. . . .

This contrast bears close relation to the previous discussion on the role of the teacher in school change. The concept of research findings presented as a rhetoric of conclusions has typified much of in-service education and professional development for the last several decades. Knowledge is something developed by experts and put into practice by teachers. The 'narrative of inquiry', however, finds information and knowledge more problematic and open to criticism. Research findings become items of discussion which are to be examined within a context. When used in this way research findings become a means to think about and to extend one's own understanding of practice.

The curriculum context

One further piece of the context comes out of the curriculum focus in language arts that had begun to occur just before the staff at Lakeview were to embark on the change in their school. The National Writing Project in the United States, which involved teachers and students focusing on writing across all subjects, has, according to popular reports, produced dramatic results in terms of teachers improving their practice (Goldberg, 1984). Hechinger (1983) writing in the *New York Times* reported that teachers not only swear by the program, but argue that it has changed their entire attitude toward teaching. A similar project bearing the title, The Young Writers Project, had begun in the province at about the same time. It too involved the use of writing as a means for children to learn a wide range of skills and topics. It began small in the province but spread quickly. Those who promoted the innovation were under no illusion about limiting their activity to language arts; they saw it as a way of restructuring the schools.

In this chapter I have described the developments, and the ideas coming out of those developments, that, one way or another, have come to bear on what we do in education. So, what does it all mean? Here, let me borrow an analogy from Dewey (1975), who, in discussing the role of the curriculum in schools, used the metaphor of a traveller following a map to represent how a student relates to a curriculum. Similarly, as teachers thinking of making changes to practice, we too have a map which can guide our journey. That map is made up of the external ideas such as those I have just described. Such ideas may come from other teachers, university people, policymakers and outside change agents. That such maps exist is not the question, one only has to look at the infinite variety of prescriptions for improving schools that flood the market place of school reform. But, the way in which teachers should be expected to negotiate the map becomes a moot point. The tension that has been mentioned throughout this chapter about outsiders imposing change or insiders bringing about change is essentially a difference in how one negotiates the map.

One can be given the map and told to follow it, or be led down some path by someone else with map in hand. Both represent types of imposed change. On the other hand, the map can be seen as incomplete, as a bare outline that one travels alone, often creating and filling in as the journey progresses.

Summary

This study rests on the notion that an understanding of school improvement comes through the interaction between local school conditions and the broader context of social change (Corbett and Rossman, 1989, p. 67). This section has reviewed selected areas of study that have provided knowledge about changes needed in schools and how that knowledge and information have been acted on in the national context.

This brief review shows that although much has been learned from several decades of curriculum reform about the directions that schools might take to improve their work, those ideas have done little to improve schools because the models for implementation failed to address the teacher's role in the process. Since those early days of curriculum reform much has come to be known about schools, their effectiveness, and how change comes about in them. The effective schools' literature has made a signal contribution in identifying the characteristics of the 'effective' school. Those characteristics help us to cut through conflicting views and the complexity of schooling to point to factors that constitute a 'good' school. While that literature looks most promising from a distance, problems lie in its narrowness in defining schooling and the fact that it provides little help in knowing *how* schools become effective. Here, the school improvement literature provides much more. With their passion for process, these educators point out that school improvement is a journey, not a definition. The school improvement advocates focus upon the school as the unit of change and take a far more holistic view of the process. However, apart from general affirmative statements, that literature too gives us little help in knowing how the process of school improvement actually occurs.

Both the advocates of school improvement and school effectiveness often neglect what is of most importance to the teacher — the subjects they teach and what change means there. Seldom do those who write on school effectiveness and school improvement deal with questions of subject matter and substance, and ask the question, improvement for what? The school effectiveness people appear to accept standardized tests — whatever their limitation — as a given, non-problematic, indicator of school success, while those in school improvement appear oblivious to the outcome of schooling. Thus, neither group of advocates appear to have examined the ideas coming out of the curriculum reform movement or examined what their own prescriptive statements have to say about the implementation of those ideas.

Most studies of school improvement examine how teachers implement other people's innovations. In short, they were studies of top-down attempts at change. While much has been learned from these, we find another type of reform effort now occurring in many parts of Canada. This effort involves schools taking on the task of reform on their own, seeking to both develop and implement change. The school discussed in this book was one of those. I should further point out that many schools routinely undertake this type of task but do not carry it anywhere. The study which I report here was different: here, a change occurred in the school that proved to be significant.

This study follows the pattern taken by other researchers who have turned their attention to what change means to those who work in schools by asking: What knowledge do teachers generate about changing their practice? How do they deal with the constant barrage of information and mandates that rain on their heads from those outside the classroom? Does a school focus make any sense in a school that contains people from very different perspectives? But two other notions, the role of subject matter and the role of the group, neglected in the general literature became of interest to me as I followed the efforts of the teachers described in this study. I discuss these questions in the pages that follow.

Notes

1 In selecting these particular areas, I have made a deliberate choice to not select others. The recent work on parental involvement in schools (see Coleman and Lakoque, (1990) might have been added. The progressive schools movement (Dewey, 1900) which some consider a precursor to developments now occurring could also have been discussed.

2 In 1961 Hurd described this type of science education as being harder to change than a cemetery (see Shulman and Tamir, 1973). Yet only ten years later, in the *Second handbook on research on teaching* (1973), they used the word 'revolutionary' to describe the developments occurring at that time. They gave Bruner's (1960), *The process of education*, credit for providing 'an unmistakable sign to the rest of the educational community that radical changes in the teaching of science were imminent' (p. 1098).

3 In a paper presented to the Faculty of Education, Simon Fraser University, summer, 1992.

4 Several authors have dealt with the notion of the isolationism of teaching. Lortie (1975) was among the first. But the recent work of people such as Hargreaves (1980) shows that the isolationist nature of teaching offers protection for teachers. They can use it to resist even legally imposed changes if they wish.

5 Although I make this argument partly tongue in cheek, it also has serious overtones. Many of the ideas that have emerged that were to improve the schools have been untested, resting on little more than the enthusiasm of the developers. Moreover, it

has been my observation that policymakers, particularly when they first take office, have a need to reform something. So they try.

6 One can cite numerous examples of ideas which are around today that came out of that rich period of curriculum reform. Many contend that the basis for constructivism came out of the work of Khun (1962). The notion of cooperative learning which has much currency today resulted from work carried out during the 1960s. Curriculum projects such as the Elementary Science Study are still used in some classrooms to this day.

7 Both authors brought to that national project several years of work both at the theoretical and practical levels. See for example Hopkins (1987) and Hargreaves (1982).

8 Fullan and Hargreaves (1992) support their case by citing the work of Huberman and Miles (1984), who drew on twelve case studies of innovative sites, Stalling's work (1989), which linked staff development to school change, and Joyce, Murphy, Showers, and Murphy's (1989) well-known theory-demonstration-practice-feedback-coaching model which showed conclusively the link between staff development and school change.

9 For example, *Prosperity through competitiveness* (1991) Ottawa: Ministry of Supply and Services. This document was prepared by the Prosperity Secretariat which was established by Michael Wilson, Minister of Industry, Science, Technology and International Trade and Bernard Valcourt, Minister of Employment and Immigration. This secretariat has prepared three other documents: *Shaping Canada's future together: Proposals; Canadian federalism and economic union: Partnership for prosperity; and Learning well. . . . Living well.* See also, *Learning goals for K-12 education: Learning to be out best* (1992) Montreal: Corporate Higher Education Forum.

10 I make this claim based on a study of the impact of high-stakes testing in B.C. on secondary school science (Wideen, O'Shea, Pye, Sherwood, and Ivany, 1991). While this study examined science teaching only, from discussions with teachers in other testable subjects, the effect appears to have been generally felt.

11 In this study (Wideen, Strachan and Carlman, 1986) we observed teachers systematically on several occasions before and after a series of workshops on the elements of instruction. We were unable to find anything that teachers did differently after the workshops that they did not do before. Interviews with those teachers confirmed our observations.

Elephants love the water. They like to play. They like to splash. They like to cover their bodies with mud from head to toe. They like to squirt water with their trunks. They are also very good swimmers.

John

Chapter 3

The story of one school

The story of Lakeview grows out of my several visits to that site over a period of five years.[1] What you are about to read is true to the extent that I observed accurately and with a minimum of bias. Although acted out by the people in the district, the story which follows represents my interpretation entirely. The essential details are based on fact; the place, the players and the situation all existed. The only tampering with the truth occurs in the names and situations of the different players and the obscuring of the location so that the school cannot be identified. The sequence of the story has also been altered so that it flows in a way that is perhaps more understandable than if it had been related in the order in which I learned of it. For example, the description of the school before the arrival of the new staff was not revealed to me until near the end of my visits, partly because I did not probe for it and partly because, in the early stages, not enough trust had been established to allow for revelations of this nature.

Before beginning my account of Lakeview, I should like to describe why the change that occurred there represented something sufficiently significant to warrant my attention for a period of five years. I agree with those who contend that one learns little about change from schools that retain the status quo. We learn from the deviant rather than from the norm. We learn from those who push against the system rather than from those who live within it. Or, to paraphrase Bronfenbrenner (1976), if you want to learn something about a system, just try to change it.

This school was significant in two ways. First, it strived considerably to improve its instruction. The principal and a significant number of staff took improvement as something of a moral responsibility. They devoted a great deal of their lives to it. Second, they were successful, at least within the confines of their own school. If someone from outer space — that beloved and overused creature from the social sciences — had visited this school on two occasions, one in the spring of 1984 and again in the spring of 1988, the school may not have been recognizable on the return trip. Not only had the instructional pattern changed in most significant ways, but the tone, and indeed the very ethos, of the school had altered unmistakably. It had moved from what might have been described as a little house of horrors to being a very effective school, which, by the time this study ended, had become a lighthouse school for the district.

Changes could also be seen in student results on standardized tests. The province in which this school was located, carries out province-wide assessment of core subjects on a rotational basis. Although student outcomes as measured by achievement tests were never an important part of how the school staff at Lakeview thought about their success, these scores are given a fair amount of weight in some circles. Of the students examined during the period of this study, achievement either steadily improved or remained constant throughout. We will now examine in more detail the significant change that had taken hold at this school.

Before beginning our story, however, the issue of generalizability must be addressed. The reader would be well advised to ask: How representative is this school's experience? Can it be generalized to other schools? I have two comments here, the first being a caution. How does one generalize from one situation to another? The answer to that question can be summed up in two words — very carefully. The situation described here was unique in many respects. In the first place, the school had something of a renegade staff, several of whom were new to the school. It was also located in a small, easily-managed district populated by a supportive parent group. Thus, the reader should not apply these findings to other settings without looking carefully at the context of those settings.

Yet, in another sense this school was a very ordinary school — one that you might find anywhere. And, because of this ordinariness, the tendency to generalize will prove very seductive. But here the responsibility rests with the reader. Stake and Easley (1978) once argued that the case study is a valuable research approach because it presents results in a way that relate to the epistemological understanding of the reader. This study uses that case-study approach to which Stake and Easley referred. As a reader, relate this story to your own experience, your own situation. Keep in mind that what follows is my description of the experience of the staff at Lakeview and my interpretation of what those experiences mean *vis-à-vis* the literature on school improvement. If they provide a means by which you can reflect upon your work and improve it, or improve the ethos in your own school, then my efforts and those of the staff at Lakeview to document this project and to analyze it will have served its purpose.

My first visit to the farming and fishing community of Grand Park came on a rainy, windswept day. I had arrived the night before and the principal had met me at the airport. He described the town as having a population of over 16,000 people with a generous mix, among others, of Anglos, Natives, East Indians and Chinese. He made a point of telling me that 'this town is populated by folk who maintain a keen interest in the community, particularly in their schools.' He added that many of the teachers here involve themselves in local political issues, and those who choose to stay quickly become part of the fabric of the community. I wondered if he was speaking mostly about himself or if his comments did reflect the community. I was later to see evidence for both.

This man's name was Charles Semenuk, or Charlie as he preferred to be called, and he had become principal of Lakeview only eight months earlier. He described to me the various people involved should I decide to take on the task of studying the school and the innovation undertaken there. He and the teachers would make up the central group of players. Although the innovation revolved around them, others, both within and outside the school, played important roles. Within the school, Charlie mentioned the importance of the teacher aides, the secretary, librarians and learning assistant teachers, all of whom he saw as part of the team, and as an example related how one of the teacher aids became a member of a school committee to select a new teacher. But the players also extended beyond the school to include those who conducted workshops in the school and district, parents, and other people in schools and universities who became part of an informal network for various members of the staff. The district staff including the superintendent, the director of instruction, and helping teachers also played a significant though more distant role in the innovation. A committee of parents also met occasionally with the principal and selected members of the staff to provide support for the innovation. The importance of these other players was underscored constantly in my interviews with the participants in the study. As we will see later, Charlie's initial impressions of the larger team being critical in the change were borne out.

The school, located on the outskirts of the town, was built in the early 1960s and houses 230 students and 13 teachers. The parents of the children here make their livings as millworkers, farmers, lawyers, teachers, as well as in various other aspects of the service industry. Most of them have at least a grade 12 education and own their own homes. Most of them represent the traditional nuclear family unit of mother, father and children, all living under the same roof, with roughly 85–90 per cent of the mothers working outside the home. Although the neighbourhood has remained fairly static over the years, some residents feel that the recent addition of low-income rental units has altered the ambiance of the neighbourhood somewhat.

That wet and windy night before I was to make my first visit to the school I took a walk about the town to try to get a sense of the place. This late evening ramble took me past the old City Hall with its striking totem poles, past the heavy timbers of the community college, the new mall and waterfront shops that cater to the boating and farming trade. In spite of the weather, I sensed a solid community, with roots in the past, but looking decidedly toward the future. Later I was told by Charlie that although a strong allegiance to the town and community was generally the case here, it was seen by the teachers in the district to be an isolated area with teacher turnover in the district running as high as 25 per cent. Many teachers now teaching in Grand Park had started their careers teaching in one of the surrounding small towns in the district. Several of the teachers I would meet tomorrow, including Charlie, had come to the school from 'out in the boonies', as they liked to tell me, as if this relatively small community was somehow the hub of big city sophistication.

Most people who try to put together the story of a school improvement project describe their first feeling as 'overload' — so much for the mind and senses to absorb — not just in the situation that presented itself to me that morning and as the months unfolded, but all the prehistory that sets the scene and plays such a pervasive part in all that follows. My situation as I set out to look at and document an innovation that was to have such a profound effect on so many was no different. I had come into this situation after part of the story was over, therefore, let me step out of this first visit for a moment to describe the situation at Lakeview the year before I arrived.

My key informant for this vital prehistory was Bill, who had been on the staff since 1980. Through a series of interviews that took place over my several visits he gradually revealed to me a picture of the school as it had existed prior to 1984. That picture (later substantiated by several others) was one that matched the dark and dreary look of the town on the night of my arrival.

Bill was part of the demoralized remnant of a staff which remained behind after the outgoing principal had left. Bill and others with whom I talked described the school as a place where everything had to be done according to some rule or other; where supplies had to be obtained through a secretary who kept all materials under lock and key; and where staff communicated with each other only when necessity demanded, and at all other times kept their distance both from one another and from the principal. Little in the way of innovation had taken place for some time. The only signs of collegiality occurred when teachers came together accidently in the bar after work to console each other on the running of the school. An interview I had with a parent later confirmed what Bill had had to say: this was a school she decidedly didn't want her children to attend. Bill's comments about wanting to start a school newspaper illustrate the style of the previous principal.

> I wanted to start a newspaper and he said that would be OK. But he wanted to have the final say about what went into it. He would say that you can put this in, but you can not put that in. Everything would have to go through him piece by piece to get it started.

Despite these concerns, certain aspects of the school were held in high regard by some people. The superintendent was reported to have liked the job the principal was doing in the school. From his perspective the forms had been completed on time and the school appeared to be run efficiently. Others at that time had strongly supported the highly systematic reading program which the principal had painstakingly put into place. It was seen by a large section of the education community in the province, including the Ministry of Education who set the curriculum, to be the proper way to teach reading.

It was into this setting that Charlie and seven other teachers new to the school arrived in the fall of 1985. Like any principal in a new school, Charlie was filled with certain apprehensions and concerns. How would the new and the old staff get along? How could he energize the sluggish, deeply-entrenched views held about teaching that he had heard so much about in the school? All of these concerns and historical baggage were part of the school ethos when attempts were begun to initiate the change practice which was to occupy the people in this school for the next several years.

Breaking old habits

When the new staff and principal arrived at Lakeview Elementary in the fall of 1985 they found a reading program in place that had been put together by the previous principal. Based on a set of basal readers and an accompanying workbook, this approach to reading had become entrenched in the school and had a long history in the province as well. Its best feature was its predictability; everyone understood how it worked. That program became the target of discussion over the next two months and formed the basis for the change that eventually developed in the school.

Along with the new staff came a new set of perceptions which did not square with the rigid atmosphere found in the school. The area of most conflict seemed to be in language arts where the basal reader program did not appear to be serving the needs of the children — at least not in the opinion of the new staff. These conflicts soon provided fertile ground for the change that was to come.

Two of the new teachers, Allison and Elsie, had taught with Charlie in the village of Elmwood, and had come with him to Lakeview. Because Elmwood had been a tiny, isolated community, they had spent many hours together talking about their common interests in teaching. They arrived with a shared desire to continue this interaction, to avoid the perpetual isolation that they had previously experienced, and to explore possible improvements in education. Only five of the previous staff now remained at Lakeview. The new mix of teachers included a significant number who were interested in discussing teaching approaches and different philosophies, in developing common units, and in comparing notes with one another. A new style began to develop which set the stage for the coming changes.

The changes which occurred that first year are summarized in Figure 2, where symbols are used to depict the events, influences, and the flow of change. The rectangles represent events taking place in the school and district. Generally these were one-time occurrences that teachers talked about. The ovals — innovations developed and undertaken by teachers — appear in the shaded area across the centre of the diagram and represent the flow of change in the school. The diamond shapes across the bottom of the figure represent various professional development activities such as workshops and attendance at conferences. It was through these professional activities that the teachers became aware of external ideas, or the metaphorical map described in the previous section. However, their negotiation of that map of external influences took a quite different form from that which we have traditionally thought of as staff development.

The classification shown in Figure 2 proved arbitrary at times; for example, influences came in many forms, not only those shown across the bottom of the diagram. The events that occurred represented by rectangles also influenced

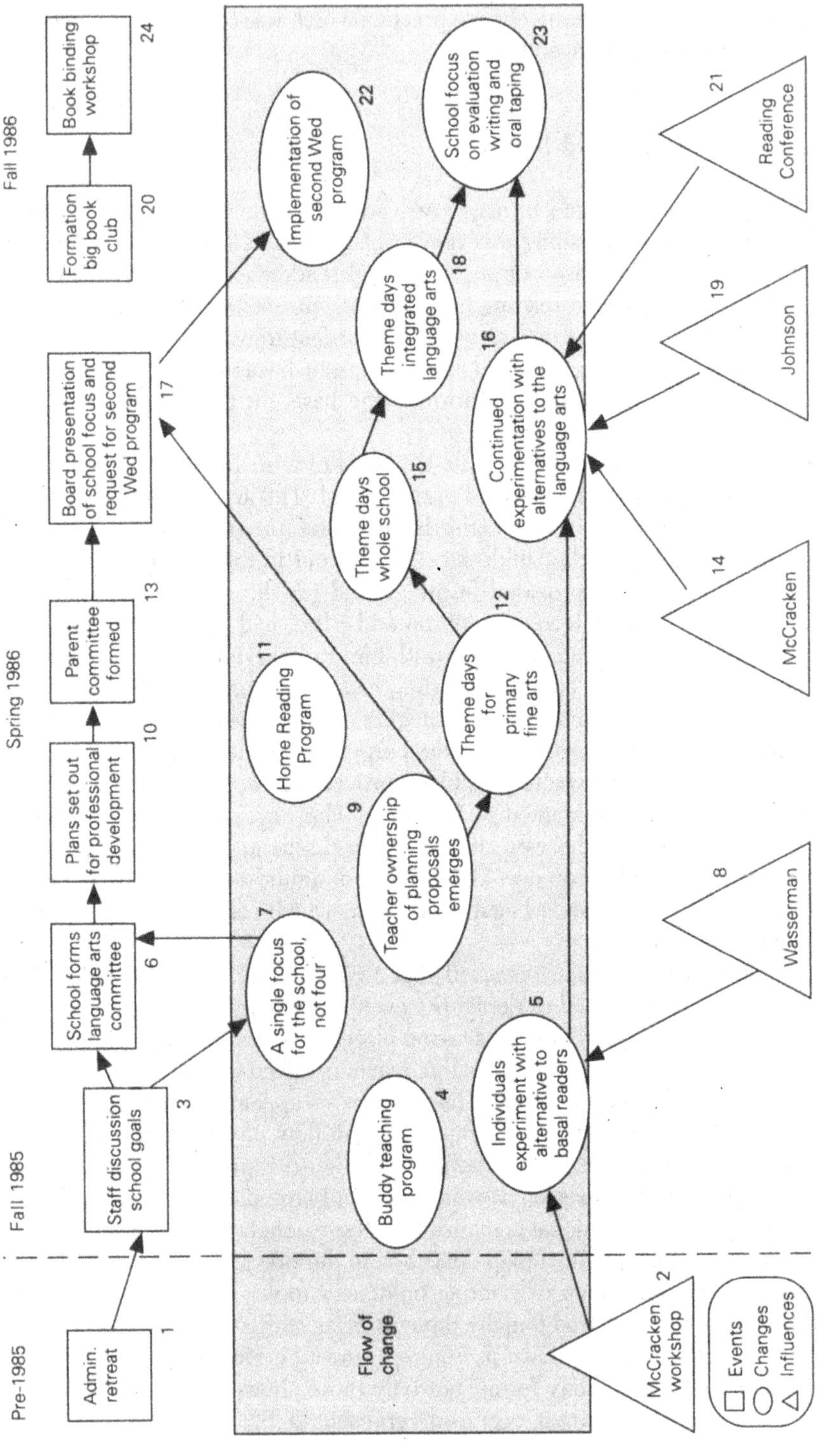

Figure 2: Year 1 at Lakeview

teachers but often in more general ways. The changes themselves often became sources of influence for further change. The lines connecting the different items show the relationships between them. The direction indicated by the arrows shows influence or what seemed to be a causal connection. More details about the items shown in Figure 2 are provided in Appendix B. For now, it is important to keep in mind that the linkages were added only where people could account for some connection.

For outsiders like me, the events, influences and innovations appearing in Figure 2 provide the substance for general statements which, as outsiders, we typically report. But, given the opportunity to express themselves, teachers often reflect feelings and beliefs that do not always conform with the generalizations about change that have been meticulously put together by so many of those same outsiders. Thus, to understand any change, one must look, not only at the events that occurred and the actions that people took, but also at the way in which people responded to those events and influences and what they meant to them on an individual level.

Thus, Figure 2, which summarizes what occurred that first year, only tells part of the story, the part that I constructed with the assistance of three members of the staff, the principal, and my field-notes. The feelings and perceptions of the players make up the other part of the picture. In describing how the change occurred in the school, I rely on both.

Two events which took place before Charlie and several new teachers came to Lakeview, the administrative retreat and the McCracken reading workshop, were talked about by the staff as having had an important bearing on subsequent innovations at Lakeview. The change which was to become the subject of the case study had roots in both these activities and reveals something about Charlie's style as a principal.

The principal traced his own thinking back to the previous year when he attended an administrative retreat which included district principals, school board members and superintendents. In addition to fairly general issues of school improvement discussed at that retreat, it was also proposed that language development be one of the main goals of the district. That aim came in conflict with Charlie's main focus for the year — improvement in mathematics. The way in which Charlie and his staff dealt with that conflict casts some light on the tension between district and school priorities. Charlie recalled a conversation he had had with two superintendents about the relationship between school and district directions. His conversation with Ben had been fairly direct. Ben had indicated that if one wanted to achieve some upward mobility in the district one should pay attention to district priorities. Here, Charlie was faced with a moral dilemma: would he follow the district direction, or would he take the path that he and his staff had decided on. Charlie held firm; mathematics would be the focus for the year. He recalls his conversation with the two district superintendents:

> I remember having discussions with Jack and Ben . . . and Ben was saying the district is moving towards language arts development. And that's

> an area that seems to be a real major concern, a major need. I said 'that is great, but we have spent some time on mathematics already' . . . and we did not feel that having done all that we could reverse it all and set off in some different direction. I checked with Jack some time later and he said 'what it comes down to is that you have to decide what your local needs are and if your school needs don't seem to fit with the district overall direction, then that is a decision you make.'

As this quotation illustrates, the district appeared to be fairly flexible provided one was prepared to take a stand. The principal and staff could go ahead and work at mathematics if they wished even though the priority was language arts. This had been the atmosphere in the district that Charlie had come to expect based on his experience, particularly this one at the administrators' retreat.

At the opening of Lakeview Elementary in September Charlie brought the staff together for a discussion of school goals, one of the expectations of the district. Charlie describes the beginnings in this way:

> When I came to Lakeview, we went through the same kind of process, a kind of needs assessment, and it was not an ultra-formal pencil and paper kind of analytical process. It was based on a lot of talk and getting to know one another in a short period of time. We did not say to ourselves, 'the district direction is in language development. We had better come up with something in that area.' We just looked at what our needs were and what our experiences had been. And it turned out that a lot of people were concerned about language development.

The 'same kind of process' he referred to was the discussion he had encountered at the district retreat with administrators. There, as in his own school 'a lot of talk' had taken place. That norm, established early in that year, was in evidence throughout the period of this study. The ensuing discussion led to certain changes in thinking among people in the school and led to the decision to take one focus instead of the four that was normally the case in schools in the district. The focus on language arts would be a single goal. This led to plans for professional development and the forming of a school-based language arts committee.

When questioned about why language arts had become the focus rather than some other subject, Charlie had this to say:

> One of the reasons for that (placing an emphasis on language arts) was that the school had previously been going very strongly in the direction of skill development, mastery and that sort of thing. They went so far as to bring mountains of booklets itemizing every skill, and sequencing all of it so it could be mastered — a tremendous amount of work. The teachers who had gone through the program did not have any faith in it

whatsoever. Not the first year teacher; not the fourth year teacher. But they had no choice. They just kept their mouths shut and went after it. So it seemed to me that we had to start at ground zero. And so we decided, based on all those discussions, that language development would be our focus.

So it appeared that the emphasis on language arts came in part as a reaction to the previous principal's carefully-structured program based around skill-based learning supported by basal readers. The rationale for focusing on language arts and for viewing it as that part of the curriculum that needed changing seemed to rest more on the aspirations of the new staff than on any evidence that the skill-based program was not producing results with children. Neither Charlie nor any other member of the staff mentioned evidence of that sort. Rather it seemed that the new staff reacted to two related aspects of the previous program. First, they had no ownership over it, and second, it did not provide the deeper structure that this particular group of teachers sought from their work.

In the case of ownership, the previous principal had developed the program and monitored its effectiveness. The teachers were merely conduits for its implementation. Nothing was problematic in this program; teachers had only to follow what was laid out. This approach did not offer much satisfaction to the new group of teachers, who, as we will see later, saw the changes in language arts as a means of examining other reforms in education. As Charlie's mixed metaphor put it some months later, 'language arts was almost used as the vehicle . . . to probe deeper issues.'

In speculating about why language arts won over other subjects such as mathematics as the school focus, one must keep in mind that language arts in the early 1980s represented a well-developed and coherent alternative to traditional teaching methods. Perhaps it was the prevailing ethos at the time that pushed the district and the school toward language arts. Would the same change have occurred if the subject area selected had been mathematics? I argue that it would not because at that time mathematics did not offer the same heuristic opportunities for reconceptualizing teaching nor would it have been supported by the same kinds of resources and learning opportunities.

The ethos in the school had now begun to encourage experimentation. Influenced by the McCracken workshop they had attended, some individuals, particularly Charlie, Allison and Barbara, had already begun to experiment with alternatives to the basal reading program. (The story which introduced the first chapter illustrates one such example.) The talk in the school about 'the writing process' gave impetus for changing the old language arts' approach. I saw students in all grades constructing their own stories which often led to what teachers called publication.[2] What became significant about these published texts was the use to which they were put. In several classes these works of the students began to replace the basal readers. The way in which such experimentation came about varied from teacher to teacher. One described the actions she took that led to a change in her work this way:

> The first year (in Lakeview) I had grade three, and I used the Ginn readers, but at the same time I was trying to do other things to supplement them that would make reading more interesting. The pressure was on writing; that was our big goal at the school, to get more writing done. So, I started incorporating a lot more writing than I ever did before. I think that was the major change. But I still used the Ginn as my backup, which was sort of my security blanket. And that's the same for all teachers that I've ever talked to. So that year I used the Ginn readers with the criterion tests and mastery tests. But I didn't have any faith in them anymore. I just did them because it was something substantial, something that was down on paper that I could show parents when they came in. Then I started using McCrackens' work that year, shortly after they gave their workshop. They came into my classroom and we taped a session in which she took my class and did an exercise with them. And then the next year I had grade three as well. And that was the year that I got rid of the Ginn altogether.

This quotation illustrates the struggle this teacher had in making a change from a structured program to the alternative approach to language arts. She was among those who began experimenting with alternatives to the basal readers early that first year. As we see in Figure 2, that experimentation continued as teachers attended workshops and conferences. The change described by this teacher (besides highlighting the not-so-subtle influence that parents have on classroom practice) shows the influence of other teachers in the school and that of the outside consultant who made a presentation at a key time in her life.

The change this teacher talked about came as a result of a process that had begun in the school that first year. Barbara, who had been at the school the previous year, recalled her experience:

> People came together to form a group those first few months and then there was a lot of talk time. There was a staff meeting. There were several staff meetings. People would go away, and think about it and talk about it. We would set a date to come back and to talk about it again. Basically what we talked about was the area we wanted to look at. Together — and the group was just forming — we began to examine some of the concerns and questions about the instructional situation. The first thing we talked about was our experience and what we knew and what areas we could agree and disagree in. One of the big things about this was getting us to share our experiences of what worked and what didn't. Coming to some sort of agreement on an area was an important step. We picked a large area, an area that we thought was broad enough that everyone could find their place in it.

What Barbara reflects in this quote is an expectation for change or at least a permission for change to occur. Her remarks also suggest the importance of teacher talk and the time to engage in that talk.

As this comment from Barbara and similar one's from other teachers indicate, the change from basal readers to what was to become known as 'the writing process' was of an experimental nature. The extent of that experimentation varied from one teacher to the next. Some appeared to be moving quickly into the new writing program, while others took a more cautious approach. A comment made by Bill in one of our interviews near the end of the second year illustrates a fairly cautious approach to change:

> I'm not one of your so-called innovators in this school. I just plug along — do the things that I want to do. And if I come up with an idea I talk to Charlie and if he says its OK I go ahead and do it. If you take a risk now you are supported in that. . . . In previous years if you wanted to take a risk you were told 'no!'

By his own admission, Bill made changes slowly, and only adopted those that suited him. He observed what others were doing and picked up ideas from them. As we see later, Bill, through his own choice, stood at the fringe of the change throughout. But when he did wish to take what he saw as a risk, he found support. When asked about a risk he had taken during that first year he made this comment:

> Instead of using the basal reader we did research reporting. For one of my language arts periods we did a research project on forensic science. I presented ten topics, from very easy to difficult, and the kids could choose two of them. They worked on the research aspect of that and it became their basic reading program. Prior to that I would have used the basal reader.

In Bill's classroom and some of the others, changes came slowly and in some respects did not always appear to be particularly innovative. But even the most minor change became symbolic of change in the school itself. The staff had begun to break down old habits. It had now become the norm to try new ideas. In short, the new language arts program signalled the beginning of a climate for change and improvement.

For everyone the gradual change from basal readers to the writing process involved breaking old habits. Experimentation with alternatives to the basal readers was helped throughout by a series of workshops that took place during this time, starting with Wassermann in the early spring of 1986, followed by McCracken, Johnson, and a conference held at a university which was attended by several members of the staff.[3] The workshops and the conferences not only encouraged teachers to continue experimenting with alternatives to the basal reading program, but served to legitimize such experimentation as well.

The second — and highly supportive — change that occurred that year involved the use of theme days.[4] This change began in the primary grades in the early fall when Barbara, Elsie and other primary teachers (some of whom had

had previous experience with theme days) decided to work together to provide special experiences for the primary students which integrated language arts with other subjects around themes. Planning was done for this activity and the proposal was taken to the school board for approval. The initial attempts grouped the primary children and combined music, drama and art in various activities organized by different teachers. Later in the spring the intermediate teachers, seeing the success of the primary theme days, suggested that the whole school might well get on board. Two groupings of children were organized — K to 3 and Grades 4 to 7. The theme, again, was the fine arts, much as before. This time, however, school board members, parents and district helping teachers became involved. The plan, as before, was to separate the children into small groups and have different individuals provide various experiences for them. Later the school was broken down into three groups, K to 1, Grades 2 to 3, and Grades 4 to 7. The third stage of this activity then began to involve other subjects in the school and occupy longer periods of time. The feeling among the teachers became, 'why not include language arts as well and combine that with the fine arts?' The program which developed, where a theme such as multiculturalism occurred every Friday for five weeks, involved the whole school, often assisted by people from outside.

The concept of theme days caught the imagination of several teachers in the school. Numerous staff meetings were held to work out details of teacher cooperation across the grades to implement the idea. One of the teachers who was instrumental in starting the project described its influence:

> One of the things that made a big change in our staff was theme day. It gave teachers a chance to do whole language for half a day. It was a time to sort of feel your way through, and no one told you what you had to do for that half a day, or full day of theme. It wasn't based on a reading series or on a reading level; there were kids of all grade levels. So you had to come up with something interesting that kids could do at their own rate, and the product wasn't the most important thing, it was the process. It led to integration. So I think that theme day was a really good way to get staff started on many things.

Two results came from the theme day experience. First, it further broke down the concept of the basal reader; teachers now saw how they could use language arts and other subjects in an integrated way and began to experiment further with alternatives. Second, the need for planning and sharing time became apparent. The school timetable was reorganized and every second Wednesday was to be set aside for planning.

While the language arts' focus and the way it was being developed were beginning to find opposition in the school, most members of the staff agreed that it did provide the focus for the innovation that first year. For a core group this program emerged as the most important need in the school. With the school focus on language arts, the principal and staff had expanded their understanding of this subject through the three workshops shown in Figure 2, as well as through professional reading and staff discussions. At this first stage people also talked a great deal about whole language; they talked about a writing school and they talked about the writing process. This discussion led to changing their program from the use of basal readers to having children write their own stories for reading. At this point the staff made a presentation to the school board on their planned new direction for the school.

What appeared to have occurred during that first year was not the introduction of one innovation, but of several. When I asked teachers to describe the innovation, most talked about the language arts program. But when pushed further, and when observed in the classroom, it became apparent that individual interpretations of the program were being acted out in the classrooms. What may have been a daring initiative to one teacher, was being seen as last year's discard to another. Innovative practice became something defined in the mind of the teacher undertaking it, not something that could be described across the entire school. The concept of a reading school was accepted by many of the teachers, as was the notion of whole language. Theme days were a bit different because they involved several teachers working together and were public events which cut across several subjects. But generally, teachers seemed to be picking up different ideas from all those approaches and working them into their practice in very individual ways. The implementation of the so-called innovation had indeed become a journey rather than an event, a journey that followed several different pathways.

One of the characteristics of that journey appeared to be permission to try different things in the school. Under the umbrella of language arts, teachers were able to try new methods. The buddy teaching program was one of them. Initiated by one of the teachers, it saw every class in the school devoting the first 20 minutes of each day to reading. The term 'buddy' came from the fact that members of intermediate and primary classrooms teamed up, with older children assisting younger ones with their reading. The 'buddy system' appeared as one of the innovations occurring as part of the developing ethos in the school and represented one more chink in the armour of the basal reading program. As an innovation it continued to spread and grow into various forms, one of which saw parents entering the school to become part of the buddy reading program in what eventually became a community of learners.

As I sit back and analyze what appeared to be happening, I sense that what we have here is a redefinition of the meaning of innovation. Traditionally, an innovation was seen as something brought in from the outside and implemented within the school. For example, in Huberman and Miles' study, *Innovation Up Close* (1984), all the changes discussed came from the outside. At Lakeview, however, innovation took the form of processes in which teachers engaged to change their teaching without any external imposition. These various teacher innovations produced the path of change shown in Figure 2.

From the observations made during my first set of visits some obvious, and not so obvious, factors that encouraged teacher innovation became apparent in connection with the developing ethos taking place in the school. The value of almost constant teacher talk about the changes and the role of the principal were among the most obvious of them. The variations among teachers in making changes in their classroom practice, the apparent anxiety of most of the staff regarding what was occurring in the school, and the role played by students in supporting the change were among those factors that are generally less talked about in the literature. Since these themes will reappear later I will comment briefly on the anxiety felt by the staff about the innovation, the students, and the leadership style of Charlie.

During my early visits to the site and conversations with the staff over an evening meal, I became aware of a further ramification of the change that was taking place. They reported, and indeed I could see, that in those early stages they were gripped by a type of innovation anxiety. Much of that evening's conversation was given to defusing the anxiety about whether the new program in which they found themselves was 'good' language arts teaching. They very quickly realized that they were now charting new waters; that they were no longer part of the main stream. They had left behind basal readers and the standardized tests that went with them. They were no longer following a prescribed curriculum as set down by the Ministry — the normal pattern for teachers in the province. One teacher made this point regarding evaluation:

> We have said we are rejecting for the most part standardized testing as an effective evaluation tool for this program. We are saying that we need other measures that arise from the kind of teaching that is being done so that evaluation is truly matched to instruction, and we don't believe that standardized testing can do that. That's great, but, because we have taken those tests away, or we are not placing any faith in them, then we don't have that comforting yardstick anymore. We cannot say, 'here are the test results that prove that we are doing a good job.' Now we have to be guided by an act of faith more than most people are familiar with taking. An article I just read points out that teachers will actually have to have confidence in their ability as professionals to evaluate appropriately, even where standard procedures are not available.

The general concern felt by the staff surfaced in two ways. On the one hand, as this teacher's comments show, the staff had left a safety net and they now had to devise other means to assess student progress. That thought was both frightening and appealing. Being innovative and being different held certain charms, but being alone without traditional supports created anxieties. The principal had concerns as well. Charlie kept raising the question as to whether this new program represented effective teaching. When I proposed that we invite an expert in language arts to critique the program, he at first scoffed at the idea, but that notion was eventually to be acted upon.

In the end, the final criteria against which the program was judged would not be expert opinion, but rather the response of students and the sense among the teachers that the new approach taken to language arts was more effective in helping students to read and write. The following comment from Barbara reflects what I heard from several.

> I have a neat feeling that I know it (the new language arts program) works. . . . It feels right. Students improve their written work and you see that improvement . . . seeing growth in their ability to talk to me about things. I can just see that the kids are more focused, they are really enjoying it. They seem to have some ownership over what they are doing . . . they are finding out about the characters; I am not asking them questions like, 'which character was like this?' There is sort of an ownership; they are trying to show me everything that they know about the character, and they are trying to find out for themselves. And I think those sort of things have really been positive.

This comment highlights the important role played by students in the change that occurred that first year, and indeed throughout the project. Their success and enjoyment of language arts became a constant source of positive reinforcement for their teachers. The teachers, in turn, also saw students' engagement in language arts being mirrored in their own learning and understanding of the change taking place in the school — a point to which I return later. This new awareness gave rise to subsequent changes in the school.

This first year became a period for the teachers to break new ground — an uneven process. The role that Charlie played here was crucial in giving the teachers the permission to break that new ground on their own terms. Comments made on separate occasions by Charlie reveal something about his approach and style that set the tone for experimentation within the school. On one occasion he commented:

> You have really got to be prepared to learn from people — to listen carefully, and really make sense of what they are saying in between the lines — and how what they are saying reflects inner needs, inner biases, and all those kinds of things.

On another occasion, Charlie said:

> So you say, 'why don't you take on the responsibility for this particular project. You may be just as good, if not better, at doing it as anyone else.' It may have a lot to do with your own professional development and growth. Then all sorts of things begin to happen. And that gives you an opportunity for dialogue and growth. And behind all of this is the principle that you don't jump on people because they are honestly, however mistakenly, trying to accomplish something for the good of other people.

This first quote shows that Charlie, too, was a learner. As such he participated in and provided support for the type of risk-taking that was taking place in the school and, in so doing, created an atmosphere for experimentation.

Much of this picture came from my first visits to the school in the spring of 1985. What I have just described also came through a reconstruction of events from subsequent interviews where I checked and rechecked my initial findings during that first visit. However, when I began a series of regular visits to the site the year following, it became apparent that I was in for a number of interesting surprises that challenged and destroyed many of my original findings and also began to undermine some of the themes that had begun to form in my mind.

Forging new ground

My first contact with Charlie during the second year came by means of a telephone call to set up my fall visit to the site. When our dates had been confirmed, Charlie informed me that what I was about to see would be quite different from what I had seen during my previous visit to the school. My subsequent arrival at Lakeview confirmed this view and proved to be a harbinger of things to come. I had taken on this task with the notion of describing the innovation in the school and then identifying those factors that led to its development and implementation. My visits to the school that second year, however, proved to be moving targets that I could never describe in any final way. Also, it became evident that the staff's perceptions about what supported the changes had changed. In many instances they had forgotten the earlier struggles they had had with the innovation and I could also see that there were enormous differences in the way they now viewed the changes occurring.

For me the innovation became something of a descriptive nightmare because of its complexity and because of its evolving nature. This complexity soon became apparent during interviews with staff members. Highly discrepant views emerged regarding what was occurring in the school. Some of those who were centrally involved saw the innovation as a highly complex program which cut across several subject areas. They also saw it as a process which was almost organic in nature. Others involved saw the innovation as an improved language arts program only. Descriptions of what took place, therefore, depended to a large extent on which player was being interviewed.

The first year had been a year of learning to break old habits. It had been a time when the teachers saw that they could change and that the act of changing was legitimate. The second year became a time for the teachers and principal to set new directions. They began to shape the change in ways that they thought it should go. As Figure 3 shows, in 1986/87, the second year of the project, the focus changed from the reading side of language arts in the first year, to writing. Whole language, as the staff described it, moved from a strategy to a philosophy. The use of alternatives extended to others on the staff, and the teachers and principal became involved in district committees and in presenting workshops.

Figure 3: *Year 2 at Lakeview*

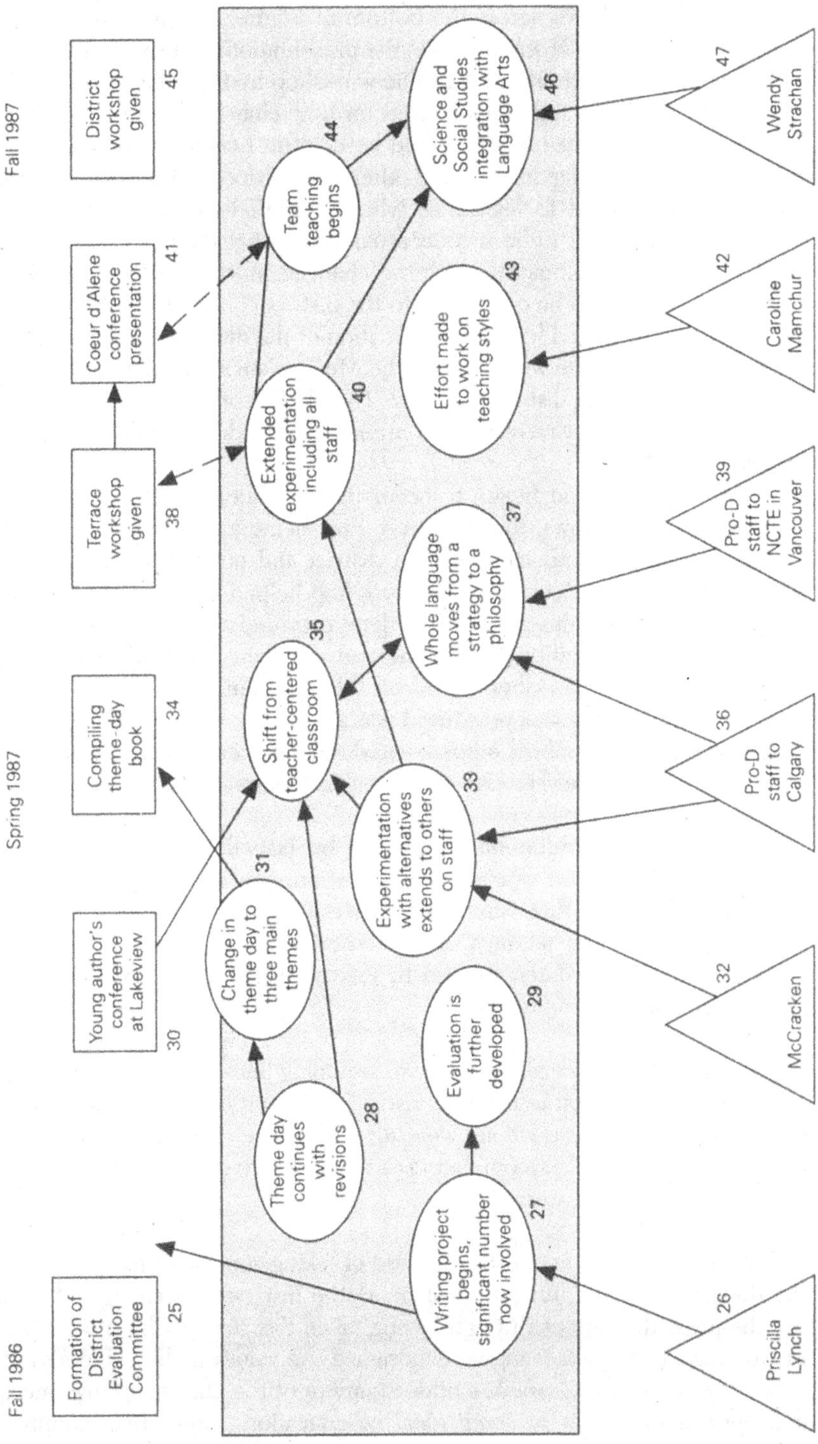

Workshops (shown across the bottom of Figure 3) again provided much of the stimulus for these changes. Here, the presentations of Priscilla Lynch and the McCrackens were both influential. The workshop by Priscilla Lynch did not deal with writing as such, rather it focused on how change occurred in the area of language arts and what supports could be helpful. Lynch also provided information on the use of taping, folders, and other ways of documenting student progress. Her workshop served to legitimize what the staff was doing in language arts because she appeared to be a conceptual ally in that the evaluation procedures she provided were compatible with the changed practice. The substance of this workshop appeared to be connected to the district concerns about student evaluation. That concern had led to the formation of the district evaluation committee shown in Figure 3. The workshop by the McCracken's provided a re-run of what had been done in the district two years earlier. But on this occasion, because all teachers in the school were able to attend, it provided a basis for further staff discussion.

Other changes had begun to occur in the school which were affecting the staff. As Figure 3 shows, the staff were now being asked to provide workshops for other teachers, both in their own district and outside. First, the staff presented a workshop in Terrace. This workshop helped build staff confidence; the conference presentations at Coeur d'Alene provided a significant number of the staff with the opportunity of resorting and clarifying their thinking. Later they presented a district workshop based on this experience.

It was also during this year that I was able to see how the changes occurring at Lakeview, and the school ethos created around them, had had a strong socializing effect on the new teachers arriving at the school, which can be seen in Isabelle's account.

The following sentiments, expressed by Isabelle, a teacher who entered Lakeview in the second year of the innovation, contain elements of several aspects of the change that was taking place and to a lesser or greater degree describe many of the feelings of the other teachers on the staff. While this experience may have been unique to this particular teacher, in many ways it represents a shared understanding.

> I feel really positive about what we are doing because I feel that through making a stamp on education, instead of letting things happen, that we are consciously as a whole, working to improve education. Not just individually in the classroom, but (as a team) we are sticking to the common goal and working towards it.

In her words we find a strong sense of taking control; of not passively allowing things to happen, but rather of being the instigator of change. We can also see the pride that comes through having taken this stance. She is conscious, too, of working as part of a team, an experience she values highly. Underlying these views one senses that Isabelle's understanding of the change springs more from a deeper commitment to some ideal of education, rather than simply to the exigencies of a particular program. She wants to make a stamp, not on her school, but on education. A sense of mission rings through loud and clear.

These words, however, uttered after a year spent working in the new program, were not always typical of this particular teacher. Isabelle came to the staff of Lakeview after having taught for many years in another school in the district. At that school Isabelle had been a devotee of the Ginn readers, which, as she put it, 'tended to use the materials that were given.' She had always been something of a cautious teacher; she felt she had always done a good job, but was reluctant to try something new until she could be sure it would work. She was a teacher who wanted guarantees.

A new experience awaited her at Lakeview. Being part of that staff gave her a sense of flexibility and greater trust in herself as a teacher; her sense of fear was slowly overcome as she watched the success of teachers who were into their second year of the innovation. The program at Lakeview worked well for her because she could adopt it incrementally; she could pick up small bits and pieces and slowly build. This aspect suited her somewhat tentative nature (which can be inferred from the following quotation). In response to the question, 'Are you convinced that what you are doing now is vastly different (from what you did in your former school?)', she replied:

> I think now I feel much more in control. Is control a good word? Control of what I am doing. I feel much more positive I am doing the right thing . . . I think because you are able to take risks so easily in this staff, and because I have learned so much from the other people on staff and we talk about education. You know, we never talked about education in the staff I was on before. It certainly was a prime concern, but we didn't really get to the meat of things, or really talk things out, or really discuss the language program. We just sort of did the language program, and we never really talked about what was going on in education. Here, we are more global; we talk about issues. . . .

In expressing these sentiments Isabelle makes four points about the innovation that I was to find characteristic of the change taking place at Lakeview. The first involves the notion of control; she senses that the teachers in the school have ownership over what was transpiring there, and this sense of 'owning' the change created the 'positive' feelings she speaks about. Second, the ethos in the school gave, and encouraged, her to be a risk-taker, a stance that was not typical of her teaching style. Third, she appears to place an enormously high value on the ability — and desirability — of the staff to talk to one another, a practice that appears to have been new to her. Aside from creating the nurturing atmosphere necessary for an innovation to take root and grow, this 'teacher-talk' also becomes an information forum where ideas can be discussed and exchanged, where 'the meat of things' can be savoured. And, finally, she sees this beginning in language arts as leading and extending to broader issues. These conditions were not unlike those outlined by Jaggar (1989) who has recently written about the conditions for teacher learning to which I return in a closing chapter.

One of Isabelle's reasons for becoming a strong advocate of the language arts program sprang from the realization that the students were reaching new understandings and that she, in turn, was learning from them.

> I was overwhelmed about how much they could speak to me about the novel. And I think that was almost what turned me on to realize that I was learning just as much. And I felt really good about that. I had been feeling that I wasn't developing, and with the personality I have, I always like to be learning. And I had been feeling that after years in this, I wasn't.

Here we can see a teacher who values learning and personal growth, who had begun to stagnate in her previous school to the point where she had taken a year off. At Lakeview she became revitalized by what was taking place in her classroom. By the time Isabelle had completed her first year in the new school, she had moved the language arts program into other areas of her teaching, into art, social studies and science, and spoke eagerly of language arts classes dealing with nuclear energy and debates between environmentalists and forestry companies. Her initial sense of fear and caution had succumbed to the nurturing atmosphere in the school and the general sense of excitement that seemed to fill the halls and classrooms. She was a teacher who needed to move slowly, who needed structure, who needed to see a program in operation before adopting it, and who needed support for each step along the way, and she found all of these needs met in her first year at Lakeview.

It was also at this time that some cracks would begin to appear in the idyllic picture that I had witnessed at Lakeview the year before. It now became apparent that the innovation carried with it not only the intent of improving instruction, but a perspective of what that improvement would look like. In short, the change to a whole language approach was not only a change in instruction, but a change in philosophy. Some staff simply did not agree with this changed view of how to teach language arts. They became marginal players in the school, outside the core group. Signs of resentment could also be seen by teachers from other schools who felt Lakeview was receiving more attention than it deserved. 'We too have a good school', a teacher from another school said to me, 'why don't you come and visit us?'

The ethos of the school that had encouraged people to break old habits during the first year continued into the second. That ethos — provided in part by the talk surrounding the workshops — was now encouraging experimentation. But another factor was at work here in which Charlie played a role. The staff were now constantly reading. Barbara describes Charlie's role in this new phenomenon:

> We talked about language arts and Charlie began getting references. He would photocopy articles from *Phi Delta Kappan* and *Educational*

Leadership that related to our topics of discussion. These would arrive in our boxes and provided the grist for further discussion.

One of the outcomes of such discussion was continued experimentation. One such experiment was the Young Authors' Conference organized by Lakeview School. This conference drew together children from other schools, as well as parents, to share their writing and attend workshops. Five children from each school in the district were invited to what essentially became a conference for the students at which one of the highlights was a workshop given by a local author. Other teachers in the district were also invited to put on workshops which were attended by some of the parents.

The year saw instructional changes taking place with every new experiment brought into the school. But, along with these obvious changes came more subtle change. The staff began to think differently about themselves and the power they had over the changes. Conflicts began to arise in the staff as it now became apparent that the changes taking place carried with them deeper philosophical currents.

The type of classroom that resulted from this process placed great emphasis on writing. In the classrooms I observed students working with students and the teacher in making two or three revisions to a written piece of work which, on occasions, would then be published. To publish a story, a student would complete it with a table of contents and a dedication and bind it in a hard cover. It was common to see students in grade 6 reading their stories to children in lower grades. Typically, students displayed their stories around the school, and many of them were taken to public forum such as the Young Writers' Conference. Even children in Grades 1 and 2 wrote their own storybooks. So at this level it was a very different language arts program than when the basal readers had provided the focus.

One event which had a substantial impact on the staff, and which would also draw them together and provide them with confidence, illustrates how the process taking place in the school was able to accommodate conflict. This event involved the visit of Wendy Strachan, an expert in the writing process who had conducted workshops in many parts of the world and was very familiar with the Bay Writing Project located in San Francisco. I set up the visit in response to what I had heard from the staff during the first year. They had repeatedly expressed concern about whether this project was 'going in the right direction'. Also, since my own area was science education, not language arts, I had similar concerns. Did the project really represent effective teaching in the area of language arts?

When I approached Charlie with the possibility of a visit from Wendy Strachan, he appeared receptive to the idea, but confessed to some apprehension about selling it to the staff. I left him with the decision and was somewhat surprised when he phoned me a week later and sounded quite enthused about the possibility. He had spoken to the staff and they had agreed. So, during my next visit to school, I was accompanied by Wendy Strachan.

Wendy was quite accustomed to visiting schools and working with teachers. For the two days of our visit she went from classroom to classroom observing and talking to both students and teachers. Each recess and noon hour saw her in the staff room discussing the teachers' work with them. A certain amount of camaraderie sprang up between Wendy and others on the staff. On the first evening of our visit we went to the home of one of the teachers for a pizza supper and a lot of talk about the teaching of language arts and the implementation of a writing program. At the end of the second day the staff, Wendy, and I gathered at a local pub for the debriefing of her visit. Somehow, there seemed to be an aura of celebration in the air; the outside expert would surely confirm our best views of the project. But in this expectation, we were only partially correct. The full text of Wendy's remarks can be found in the appendices. What follows represents some of the highlights.

> *What I saw happening.* What I would like to suggest to you is that we connect what is happening here at the school with what we know about learning. . . . When you are beginning an innovation, there is a sense in which you begin by changing your action or behaviour and your language. That is, you start doing and saying different things. . . .
>
> In regards to this process, I found teachers at Lakeview at different levels. Some of you are at the early stages; some of you have worked a good distance through the process. . . . I saw much evidence of writing. There is much evidence of writing as activity in the classroom and as display around the school. I saw much evidence of process. I saw pre-writing . . . a lot of drafting and a lot of sharing and some responding. . . . I saw some editing, some proofreading, and of course, final copy. . . . That attention to process is excellent and very encouraging . . . a very good writing climate. It is definitely there — in every classroom I went into. The children are willing to write, they take up their paper, they do it.
>
> *Where I think you are.* As a school you are moving quickly, and that has much to do with the fact that everyone on the staff is involved, that you talk a lot, that you show you are processing it all the time, and it is a serious undertaking for the whole school. It usually takes about five years for teachers to reach the stage where understanding of complex ideas and practices is fully internalized. It is then not a matter of 'we're teaching writing process' or 'we're doing writing this year, this is our language arts program', but rather that using writing is a part of the way you think and do things . . . the whole process is intrinsic to learning and teaching. If you continue as you are, I think that any of the things which I don't see now, I would expect will happen simply because you are engaging in a reflective process, you are able to identify things that you are not doing and that you want to do differently, and you are continuing to read, so you will continue to move and grow.

What we might look to see in the future. Let me say at the outset that what I have not seen in two days may of course be there and I came at the wrong time or whatever. But this is what I noticed. First, the matter of fluency. I think it is important that the first concentration at any time. . . . When we think about beginning writing in kindergarten, grade 1, grade 2, grade 3, about beginning writers, second language writers, writers in psychology, people who are trying to write physics, first they have got to get fluency — then begin to think about craft, form, and correctness. . . . Fluency first, then, for any child at any level, but particularly until the end of grade 2 where obviously, the main concentration is on quantity.

But then you begin to move into form and craft which means that you must begin to *teach* writing. At the first stage, when the children are learning what written language is for, all they need is opportunity . . . what I don't see is specific teaching of strategies to handle different kinds of writing tasks. At the moment the writing which I see mainly is story writing.

In fact, it seems in some classes everything is called story. I would suggest to you that it creates a problem if you don't distinguish writing tasks: making lists of things, writing stories, telling about, explaining something, etc. . . . Form is really important and it is important to start using the language to make distinctions. What I saw were basically generic stories which lack clear form.

The other main type of writing I saw was a sort of 'informationalizing'. It read much like the usual elementary textbook which is written in short sentences with very little subordination and with little sense of explaining much or elaborating on ideas. . . . Most of the writing seemed to be of these two types.

I think it is important to move from those types toward a variety of forms. This will mean teaching a particular form, recognizing that forms have characteristics and you teach kids how to produce them.

Lastly, I want to make a few comments about where you might think to extend further your use of the writing process. When you are teaching writing process . . . you may see it, and rightly, as a means of producing a good piece of writing, a means of improving on what comes off the top of one's head so to speak. But, another way to think about process is to recognize that all of these stages are different thinking stages.

. . . in several classrooms I saw much explicit teaching of the language of writing and teaching about the process. I think this happens and is

> necessary in part because it helps us as teachers explain it to ourselves . . . the process is not the purpose. If it becomes the purpose, then it is like teaching parts of speech. Teaching process is not teaching writing, unless the process underlies the intention, purpose, and form of the writing.
>
> . . . about the commitment you show and the involvement. I see this as closely related to your choice of project. The fact is that you chose to do language arts and you chose writing, and you chose not to buy a package designed to bring about change, a package like ITIP, for instance. . . . (T)eaching writing seems to match what we intuitively know and understand about learning. Writing has everything to do with learning and with thinking. As we teach writing, we become learners about children's learning, and that is utterly fascinating. It makes teaching so much more exciting than simply opening a book, do page 59, tick, tick, tick, you have got them right. Or even the socialization.
>
> . . . Let me repeat . . . that I feel this is a very exciting place to work and that I'm impressed and intrigued by the interesting, thoughtful things you are doing. It would be hard to leave an environment like this where so much is going on and there is such an atmosphere of professionalism about teaching. I see a strong sense of professionalism, high self-esteem, and self-respect, and the feeling of growing autonomy and control of power, the sense in you that I know what I am doing and I am learning, and that is very worthwhile to see.

In short Wendy described the writing process she had seen in the school as still being at the initial stage of story writing. She saw little evidence of work in other subjects and very little evidence at that time of students using different writing styles. She could only say that significant strides had been made in language arts at Lakeview by the teachers to change from a basal reading program to the use of a quite innovative and exciting language arts program. While major strides had been made, the staff had some distance to go to bring the writing process to other areas of the curriculum.

The teachers and principal did not agree with Wendy's assessment, and felt that their innovation was much farther along than her report indicated. They believed that coming at this time of the year gave her an incomplete picture of the project. At this particular time many of the teachers were organizing their classes for the end of the year. Had she come in early spring, they argued, story writing would not have been so evident and she would have received a different impression of the teachers' and students' work. Further, the staff noted that she did not ask for examples of technical or other styles of writing that were available. Nor did she explore with the teachers and students facets of the project that might not have been obvious on her short visit.

My own view — that the report appeared quite positive — was not shared by Charlie and the rest of the staff. Somehow the report had pricked their balloon.

Their concerns were perhaps best summarized by the conversation I had with Barbara during my subsequent visit.

M: The first thing I am curious about was your reaction to Wendy's report?
B: I had a chuckle over it.
M: OK.
B: I wish that she had been here for a longer period of time. . . .
M: Anything else?
B: I wish that we would have been very specific about what we were going to do when she was here, in terms of what kinds of things we wanted her to see in the school and what we didn't I would have liked more conversation with her. One of the things that I had a chuckle about was the whole thing about writing. Some of what she's talking about we're still working towards. But you look at things like that at one point in the year and you don't get a complete picture. I just felt like taking all the kids' writing samples through the whale unit and sending them down to her and say 'OK. Here's what you're talking about here. Here's what you're talking about there.' You know, that I just felt frustrated.
M: Do you think everybody is doing that?
B: I don't know for sure, but tend to think that many in primary work towards stories, poetry, that kind of work. The Grade 3/4 class with Isabelle probably is beyond that, because they do a lot of social studies units, and that kind of stuff, so I'm sure there are some things coming out of it.
M: So you didn't think that the report reflected what you were doing at this time.
B: No.
M: What about her notion about different stages in the process?
B: Oh, I think that's true.
M: Wendy thought that was quite interesting, by the way.
B: Did she? Why?
M: Well, I think in the schools she's worked in, she hasn't found that to be the case because people start out together. She hasn't seen a situation where you have people that are quite far advanced, and other people who are just starting, and people who are in the middle, and that sort of thing. In fact, she phoned me from Greece to insert that sentence.
B: Is that right? I quite enjoyed the conversation with her about all sorts of things. And she sent half the whale book the kids that she knew down there had read, and then, you know, that kind of stuff is fine. It's just frustrating, I think, for us, because this is a typical situation. This is Lakeview. And every year you have staff changes.
M: Oh yeah.
B: When it's two or three that change, and only four of the people who are still here, there's a lot of slow-down and a lot of trying to get very different people working together in this environment. And so you keep

going, but you know that next year the same thing will happen as at least three people maybe four will be applying out of the district. Now then you're going to have to get those four or five who replace them back in. So what you do is try and get people who have the same philosophy, the same understanding, so that you can keep going quicker. But if you can't do that, well. . . .

M: What about the good side of the report?

B: It gives us things to continue to work toward. Some things I knew, that make sense to me. So that's the kind of report it is. One minute you're laughing about what is left out, and one minute you say 'yeah, OK, this makes sense to me.'

M: By the way, I thought it was really quite positive.

B: If she had been here for a longer length of time and if we were a little bit clearer about the kinds of things she was after, we could have been much more articulate about the kind of language arts we were doing.

This conversation reveals two important issues. The first involves dealing with the problem of determining the worth of changes made in a school. Although things turned out quite well in the long-term regarding Wendy's evaluative comments, the initial reaction made me feel rather awkward. On the one hand I had followed the lead of the staff in wanting some indication as to whether they were on the right track. Yet, when that opinion was given, it created some angst. Still, I felt the report had been balanced and reasonably positive. Perhaps it suggests that at this stage of an innovation one does not want justice, only favourable reaction. Not criticism, but acknowledgment. It also gave me a sense of the power of the outsider as critic. Into the supportive and positive thinking culture of the school I had brought a person steeped in the norms of criticism typical of a university atmosphere. The clash of these two cultures produced a jolt.

The other issue which Wendy's visit seemed to highlight involved the frustration we begin to see in Barbara who expresses her concern about the turnover of staff, so prevalent in this district. It represents a source of frustration among teachers who make progress one year only to find that the next term requires a starting-over period to accommodate the many new faces on the staff.

The events around the report signalled something else about the staff and how they dealt with external input. However disconcerting their initial reaction had been toward the report, as time went on they simply talked themselves through it. The visit and the school's reaction to it illustrated that an important capacity had developed within the school. The report enjoyed a full and thorough hearing, and although it was criticized, they did attempt to act on the suggestions it made. They shaped a consensus through discussion of what they thought this expert *should* have found in their school. Their reactions to her suggestions were based on their perceptions of her criticism rather than on the criticism itself. In an effort to overcome the charge of merely 'story writing', the staff engaged in a great deal of reflection and discussion which ultimately saw further integration of science and social studies into the language arts program.

The visit of Wendy Strachan raises issues concerning the critic's role in situations of this nature. The test of the critic's appropriateness is whether or not the criticism ultimately leads to positive change, even when that change causes discomfort. The function of these interventions is to extend the vision of what is possible, but if the critic doesn't know the people, the results can be disastrous. The critic must be sensitive to the culture of the audience and aware of their prior knowledge and their conceptions of the innovation they are working with. When working with a change process, outside critics have to try to introduce this kind of dissonance only where people can handle it. In this case, what seems to have happened is that the teachers dealt with the critic's assessment as best they could given their understanding of her critique.

In some respects Wendy Strachan's visit represented a watershed for these teachers. They were now forced to decide whether they wanted to make the effort to investigate totally new concepts in language arts. Their response indicates that they probably lacked a deep understanding of the reconceptualization of writing beyond the notion of a process approach. In reflecting on what took place subsequent to Wendy Strachan's visit, it appeared to me that the staff didn't fully understand her remarks. They didn't understand what she meant by *teaching* writing because they didn't have a background of experience with the concepts to which she referred. However, perhaps this sort of dissonance — where the staff is confronted with the differences between the distance they have come and the things they have yet to explore — is not only inevitable, but necessary. If they hadn't been introduced to Wendy Strachan, they might have thought they had achieved a real writing process program instead of being made to realize that they only had some of the structures in place. Now they knew there was much more to do. In retrospect, I can now see that some intervention in the form of knowledge about language arts as a way of looking at learning in the broader sense would have made an important contribution to this school.

The central question that emerges here is when should such an intervention have taken place. How and at what point does one intervene with the difficult substantive stuff of curriculum change? Even where teachers are ready for indepth study of a change — in this case writing process — there are no easily-accessible vehicles for this intervention to occur. Perhaps because no easy access to the intervention they now needed existed, they pursued their innovation in other directions, i.e. toward subject integration. As we will see in the case of Isabelle, it was to be some time before some of these teachers became fully aware of the depth and pervasiveness of the change process in which they were engaged. The speculative question remains as to whether this depth of understanding would have occurred earlier and for greater numbers had some intervention taken place at this time.

Aside from Wendy Strachan's visit, the glow of these changes and the enhanced ethos of the school greeted me everywhere that year. But undercurrents were beginning to be felt, none the less. These came from people who did not fully support the changes in the school. The signals were exemplified in my attempts to interview Bill, a teacher who was now a learning assistance person.

Charlie had repeatedly suggested that I interview Bill, but our times never seemed to work out. When that interview was finally set up, it became obvious what the problem was — Bill was not happy with the situation, as we will see in the next section.

The other confidence-building issue that was to gain momentum in the following years involved the developments now beginning to occur in the larger community. Other schools in the province were beginning to use what came to be known as 'the writing process.' In fact, some had been experimenting with the process before it was introduced into Lakeview. But these developments had been scattered, and except for a loosely-connected organization of teachers, these efforts were mostly unknown to the teachers at Lakeview. Now, however, through attendance at conferences those projects were coming to be known to the staff. Because of conversations with two superintendents, I knew that the district too had been watching the developments at Lakeview quite closely. Yet Charlie knew little of how positively they viewed his staff's efforts. The positive signals of the staff's success came as the district began to set up committees to deal with issues such as student evaluation in new approaches to language arts. The teachers at Lakeview were much in demand for these committees. They now began to think that they were in the vanguard of something occurring in the district and indeed in the province as a whole.

The themes identified at the end of the first year could now be seen in somewhat sharper focus during the second year. The value of collegiality and teacher talk came into focus with Wendy Strachan's visit. The staff simply talked themselves through the difficulties that her visit had created for them. A capacity for dealing with change appeared to have now developed on the staff.

The general anxiety about the innovation that had been evident during the first year had now largely subsided. Besides having gained more experience with the changes, two other factors appeared to have alleviated their concerns. The first involved the visit of Wendy Strachan. They had met a critic and had survived it. That experience built confidence. The second factor involved the changes now being talked about in the district and in the province. They were both giving signals that Lakeview might be on the cutting edge of something — a bit of notoriety that the staff quite enjoyed.

What also began to emerge was the price that was being paid for the success of the innovation within the school. Although minor, some mild divisions were beginning to appear between the staff, and fatigue was beginning to set in. Both point to the tremendous effort that attends any attempt to change a social system such as a school. An active process had been put into place which brought its own problems.

Extending the change

A typical visit to the school saw me observing in classrooms during the day and interviewing teachers over lunch and after school. On this particular day I began in Isaac's room. The first period of the day involved a period of uninterrupted silent reading. For the first 30 minutes of the period, he and the students read silently. At the end of that time he gathered the group around him and, in a circle, they proceeded to discuss the writing of a story. They next began work at their desks on the redrafting of a story they had written in first draft form the day before.

The next classroom involved Barbara and Kelly team-teaching to a group of 60 students. They were brainstorming in connection with the hatching of chicken eggs, identifying things they would like to know about this process. Barb and Kelly were at the board classifying comments and then writing them on a large sheet of paper. I was quite impressed with the quality of the questions being asked by the students about the hatching of chickens. The students then moved into groups to undertake research from books and other sources about the questions they had generated. Some discussion also went on about the actual hatching of the eggs. The lesson provided a good blend of science and language arts, and was to occupy much of the school day. My next stop was a math class. There I found the students receiving instruction about the addition of fractions. After a few minutes of that introduction, they then turned to their textbooks to do several questions to apply what had just been taught.

My thoughts about the morning were somewhat mixed. The language arts lesson had reflected many parts of the whole language concept that I had seen demonstrated in the school during previous visits and which had been described to me. The science/language arts lesson had been quite interesting. It combined the two subjects in what seemed to be an effective way. The curious part involved the mathematics lesson which seemed to represent little change from the 'chalk and talk' that one typically finds in mathematics courses. I saw no use of manipulatives, or nothing out of the ordinary here. In reflecting back on my previous visits, that pattern of mathematics teaching had been quite typical throughout the school. The innovative spirit, it seemed, that had infected other subjects had not yet struck math.

Such was my introduction to the school in the third year. My interviews with the teachers that year suggested that after having experienced almost frenetic activity in the first year and a period of experimentation, reading and reflection the second year, the third year of the project — 1987/88 — had become a consolidation year. The main innovation had been implemented and the staff's attention now turned to other aspects of the curriculum and the school. When Barbara was asked to describe the third year of the project, she did so in terms of theme connections.

> Connections, we started to make connections, to understand it, to be able to express it, articulate it, and share it. We began to network with teachers in other schools and make connections in that way too.

These connections came in different forms. The workshop given by Susan Kovalik shown in the lower part of Figure 4 provided the subject theme for a unit that connected science and language arts. The workshop on learning styles that

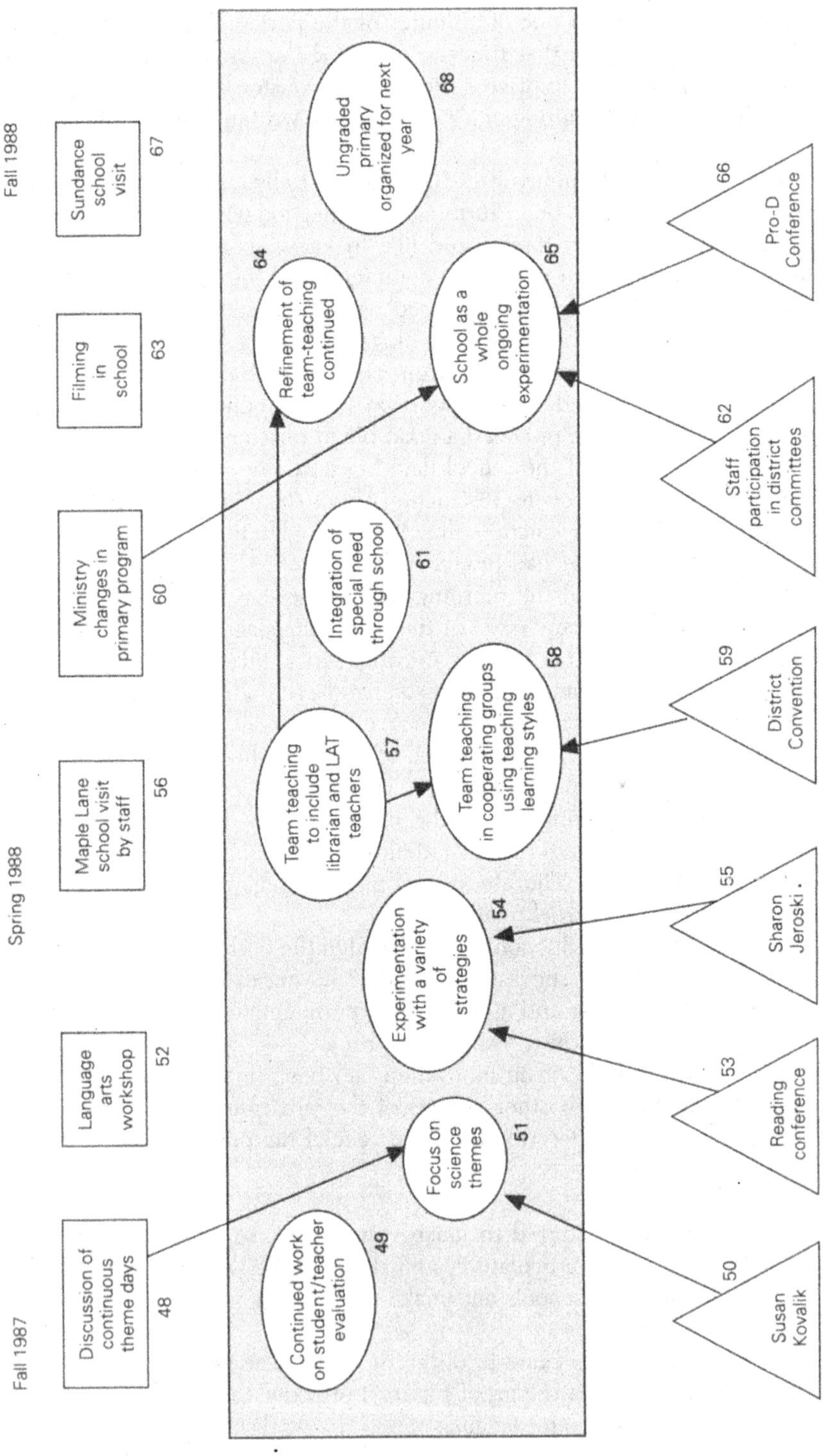

Figure 4: *Year 3 at Lakeview*

had occurred the previous year reinforced the importance of connecting teaching with learning. The Jeroski workshop served as a follow-up and led to the experimental use of different teaching strategies. Another teaching strategy, co-operative learning, came at a district convention attended by several teachers; they began to link co-operative learning to their team-teaching. The year also saw the beginning of a project aimed at integrating the 'special needs' children into regular classrooms. Students began to receive other types of attention as well. One concept — the notion of student as teacher — involved the process of having students reflect on teaching themes or learning themes that work for them and explore how they could be used to teach other students. The student as teacher concept produced a couple of interesting findings for the teachers. For example, they found that some of the students who may have experienced difficulty under other forms of teaching had developed very valuable strategies of learning which were of considerable use to other teachers.

Several of the changes that had begun earlier continued and evolved. The theme day notion continued but took an interesting shift which reflected how a change becomes part of the fabric of a school. In previous years, the theme days had been a major event both in terms of planning and execution; the entire school and community had turned out for them. But this year the lustre around the theme day had begun to tarnish; it had become an innovation that had run its course. Teachers began to discuss whether theme days were actually needed. In many respects they began now to get in the way because much of what they represented was being adopted individually by teachers in their classrooms.

The changes that had taken place in the language arts program in previous years, namely the use of whole language, had by now become part of the work of several teachers in the school. But another development occurring in the province was to give further emphasis to this change and to encourage its consolidation within the school. This development was the rather sweeping reform that came about through the implementation of the *Year 2000*.[5] The staff saw the philosophy underpinning this reform being mirrored in the changes occurring at Lakeview. That reform gave the changes that they had worked to achieve legitimacy; it also meant that several members of the staff were now asked to give workshops in the district and to serve on various district committees.

The confidence that came with this change was reflected in a comment made by Charlie during one of my visits. He had just talked about the conflicts and problems associated with making a change within the school. I had reminded him of his earlier concerns about what those in other schools thought about the innovation. He had this to say:

> It's not an issue any more. When you have covered enough ground, you wake up one day and realize that the project is successful and that you do not have to explain yourself anymore.

It was interesting to see in this third year that the teachers did not follow up on the directions for writing process suggested by Wendy Strachan. Instead they had begun to explore some other manifestations of curricular and philosophical change. The teachers seemed to be working back and forth between specific innovations on the one hand and the broader philosophical change happening in education on the other. Specific program and curricular changes became vehicles for a broader rethinking of teaching which moved from curricular thinking to philosophical and foundational thinking. Teachers were slowly weaving a tapestry by picking up on different colours at different times, playing with them and incorporating them into the larger whole.

This activity seemed erratic unless one stepped far enough back from it to view the larger picture. This activity speaks for a broader conception of the educational change process than the traditional program implementation perspective and at first blush seems to argue against my position that the subject mattered. But, on closer reflection it becomes apparent that the subject matter was the place people began their journey and it was only after comfort was established there that they could move on to more general philosophical and foundational thinking.

Isabelle, who had joined the staff a year after the project was underway, reflects these changes. Some of this introspection can be seen in the following when she speaks about plans for the coming year.

> People are talking of reorganizing for the fall. A lot of teachers were thinking, what is it going to mean for them, individually, and as a school. What changes will it mean to me, as an individual to take on those changes for next year? So I think we're reflecting and looking at ourselves, looking to the future, looking at our teaching selves and our learning selves. And getting ready to make some decisions about changing. . . .

Isabelle's growth, both professional and personal, could be detected from the way she described her previous year and from the sorts of activities she had engaged in. She had been one of the staff members who had gone to Idaho to make a conference presentation which she described as 'an incredible learning experience'. She felt that:

> . . . having that sort of goal makes you work so hard and means so much, and become so much more aware. . . . I think pushing ourselves that far we certainly learned a lot about staff development ourselves. Because we certainly broke down and had our differences and learned a lot about the whole staff process within a small group. . . .

Literature and research also started to play a larger part in Isabelle's life at this time. She talks about changing from being a 'practical' teacher to becoming a more 'theoretical' one, and gives credit to peer interaction for the change. She told me that she had become more competent in the classroom because she now had more knowledge. This knowledge came from observing teachers she wanted to emulate and then reading the literature that had influenced the classroom behaviour she had admired. I asked her what important incidents had stood out in the preceding year, she replied:

> Professional growth and professional reading. Becoming more aware of the literature and the research output. That's something I wasn't doing before and that's something that I certainly have done here. That's the major difference between before and after. Before, I didn't do it.

Isabelle's description of herself as being a more 'theoretical' teacher suggests the kind of change that happened to selected teachers in the school. She now approached her professional development from a perspective of beliefs and values rather than from external behaviours. She, and others, had developed the capacity to continue to change based on a careful examination of what was possible. This is a more important kind of change than the uncritical adoption of innovations that frequently typify school change.

Part of this capacity was a type of mental toughness that developed. Isabelle felt that the process in the school was not without its problems. For example, communication broke down and some people felt left out; the staff started asking questions — about themselves and the system. Through this process she had, in her words, become 'stronger and more assertive'. In fact the confidence Isabelle gained as a result of her experience at Lakeview, led her to apply the following year for a position at the district as an itinerant support teacher.

While the innovation at Lakeview was greeted with cheers by some, it cast a different shadow for others. Not everyone threw themselves wholeheartedly into adopting, or even considering, all the various aspects of the change. Bill, who had been at the school prior to Charlie's arrival, describes a different experience. He had been teaching at Lakeview for two years under the old principal, and five years in another district before that. Never an outward going person, Bill had got into the habit of keeping to himself, both in his classroom and as a staff member.

> In previous years I never went to the staffroom. I would spend all my time in the playground with the kids. It was more fun. Everybody came here (to the staffroom), everybody sat, nobody said a word. There were people on the staff who didn't get along with each other too, but it wasn't just the principal. Everybody sat around and really did nothing. There was no talking going on, no cooperation — maybe one or two cooperated, but that would be about it.

A tentative teacher from the beginning, Bill never liked to push himself or take any risks: 'I'm not one of your so-called innovators . . . I just plug along — do things that I want to do.' Bill appeared very content to simply move at his own pace. He never joined any of the committees during the time the change was taking place, held the idea of workshops in some suspicion, claiming that out of a whole day workshop, 'there would be only one or two things that are of any use', and felt that none of his teacher training had benefited him in his career. He saw himself as a 'lone wolf' who liked to have his own structures in place and was content with his 'own biases'. As he put it, 'I'm not one of those who put a lot of input into ideas and things like that. I'm sort of — just there.'

But if Bill was content with his own way of doing things, he was not completely immune to what was taking place in the school. He recognized that if he wanted to try something new, support would be there. And Bill did make some modest attempts at innovation — but in his own time and at his own speed.

> I see myself more of — at the beginning — an outside observer. And the problem with the project going on in the school — I guess I'm quite picky — I see a thing I like and I'll do it. I'll also backup any decision that's made in the school itself.

One of the things Bill liked was the new approach to language arts. He had never thought much of the Ginn readers although as he put it, 'they came hyped as the saviour for teachers in terms of language arts because they came with the skill-packs, study books, and teacher's guides with all the answers.' He felt that the Ginn system had never been the right approach for him because he saw himself as more 'student-oriented, than book-oriented.' So, when he was told he no longer had to use the Ginn readers, he felt that he had been set free. This new freedom led him to adopt the idea of a class newspaper, something he claimed would not have been possible — at least not in its present form — under the previous principal, or under the old system. In spite of this small innovation, Bill didn't see himself making any radical changes, rather he appears to have been caught up in events taking place in the school.

> . . . I'm basically doing the same thing I've always done but I have a better focus on things I'm doing. People have been telling me, or I've been talking with them, and finding out that we're using this whole language approach and it seems at this moment in time for me the right thing and the right direction in which to go.

Although Bill might never be the sort of teacher who experiences a profound need for change, the new ethos of the staff and the support coming from Charlie appeared to have affected him in a positive way. Over a beer one night, he told me how much he valued Charlie's approach to staff relations, that Charlie had given him a new confidence that had not been possible when he felt that 'someone was always looking over my shoulder to see if I was doing it right.' In looking at Charlie's leadership, he said:

> If I come up with an idea I talk to Charlie about it and he says, 'Fine, OK. Go ahead and do it'. . . . And if we want to take a risk we're supported in that. Charlie will say 'OK. Go ahead, try it out and see if it

> works.' So, I think that's a big innovation. In prior years, if we wanted to take a risk, we were told, 'No!'

It was no surprise to me that Bill chose 'Principal Support' and 'Peer Interaction' as the two most important aspects of the change taking place at Lakeview. He is the sort of teacher who relies heavily on colleagues. All his ideas, he told me, had come from other teachers; he was 'good at stealing or borrowing.' Although he seldom read anything in the way of research, Bill valued hearing from other people who had done the reading so that he could then either discard or accept what he had gleaned second-hand. And, while not much of a joiner or doer himself, he was not impervious to the effect the innovation was having on the rest of the staff.

> A lot of them learned a lot of things here, a lot of ideas, a new way of looking at things, and they improved themselves with all that was happening. They're just full of energy in that regard.

It would be difficult to establish, with any pretence at accuracy, the causal chain that led to the views Bill held as a teacher. Given what I know about him and about the situation at Lakeview before this study began, I might want to speculate that the oppressive regime under which he had operated prior to the change there had somehow caused him to withdraw and seek the isolation — and comfort — of his own classroom; that over time, change and innovation had become uneasy, if not forbidden, concepts for Bill. There is no way of knowing the extent to which his training and experience had shaped him into the teacher I found at Lakeview or whether he would always have been the 'outside observer'.

Another interpretation of Bill's reaction would be that it sprang primarily from his own learning style. He, like many teachers, approach change differently from the risk-takers who lead the way. Perhaps they have just as much capacity to change, but they need different conditions, different models to follow, acceptance for doing what they can do well, support for slow, minor changes, and a voice in staff discussions. They begin to explore changes when they see others having success, and they have to go step-by-step in a somewhat structured fashion. Their learning needs are seldom acknowledged in change models. This perspective on Bill is reinforced by his words which I cite later. Bill simply needed conditions where 'borrowing and stealing' are encouraged, approved and celebrated. That is why the notion of a learning community is so important in the current literature.

But, one thing does seem clear: he somehow managed to benefit from all the activity that was taking place around him. Because of the high voltage energy created by the rest of the staff, the unfailing support of the principal, and the fact that language arts became the vehicle for change, Bill found himself caught up in the net of the innovation, an innovation he could not completely ignore. In spite of himself, Bill appears to have been pulled into the change at Lakeview, dragging and yawning perhaps, but a participant none the less.

It was during this third year of consolidation of the changes within the school that some of the problems and conflicts began to appear in higher relief. For many like Isabelle, Barbara and Charlie the period could not have been better. For others, however, the changes had begun to present problems. Fatigue and burn-out began to be experienced by some. One teacher who left the school expressed the situation this way:

> When I think back on being in this school . . . I was very happy to be leaving Lakeview, just because I felt really worn out. I think the teachers here, they put so much out, and where do you get it back? Because it's really hard to get all that energy back. And I wonder where it's going to lead to. Where does it all end? Are people going to have nervous breakdowns, or are they going to find a point where they've just got to stop and take a break from all the workshops, and all the committees, and all this, and all that. I think it's great — it keeps you going in some ways. It can also wear you down pretty fast.

While the intense and ongoing activity on the part of the critical mass of teachers at Lakeview had been one of its strengths, it had also drained some energy from the staff. Charlie too spoke of the conflicts and tensions that wore on him. He described them in personal terms:

> One of the conflicts is an internal one that is always eating away at you. It was one of the things that left me not quite comfortable at Lakeview. It was part of my own personality, some insecurity on the one hand, and some bullheadedness on the other, created an imbalance most of the time. I am not sure what effect that had, but I suspect people reacted to my personality as much as the intellectual activity. My personality is not one that is as laid back as other people's. I believe that if you are going to get things done you have to call a spade a spade and lay things out on the table so people can deal with them. When you do that you lay your personality on the table along with them.

The other tensions that had been simmering throughout the project involved the split among the staff. A small group of teachers remained outside the core group and consequently were less involved. Bill was one of those. Although he witnessed many of the same things in the school that I have described about the project, he had this to say when asked about his involvement in the project and what it had meant to him:

> Others were not involved. If you did not have the same background as those in the inner circle, and if you were not directly involved in this process of change, and if you did not have that background situation, the project looked very different.

When I asked him to expand further he said:

> Maybe one day I can sit down and write it down, but I don't want to. . . . And particularly at this time — June is not a good time to be reflective because all kinds of other things are happening.

Bill left the school that year.

By the end of the third year the innovation was well established in the school. What had begun as a change in the teaching of language had led to several changes. By the end of the study period, in June 1989, both the teaching in the school and the school as an organization had changed considerably. Instruction moved from basal readers to an integrated approach to language arts, to a writing school, to team teaching, and to subject integration. The student achievement scores improved considerably during this period. The school as an organization moved from being a closed shop, where teachers used the isolated classroom as protection, to one in which doors were open, conversation centered on instruction, and an ethos for risk-taking had been created. A number of themes run through my observations; these will be picked up in the next section.

Notes

1 Although the study period reported here spanned three years, I continued to visit the school up to the completion of this manuscript.

2 The notion of publishing a particular story involved making several revisions, writing a dedication, then binding the story in a hard cover.

3 International Reading Conference held in Vancouver in 1986.

4 For a description of these and other items mentioned in this section, see Appendix B.

5 This reform was the result of a Royal Commission in Education in the Province of British Columbia. It involved a move toward non-graded primary, integration of subject areas as well as other notions such as active learning. See Ministry of Education (1990) *Year 2000: A framework for learning*, Victoria: Province of British Columbia and Ministry of Education (1989) *Primary program: Foundation document*, Victoria: Province of British Columbia, Program Development.

Fish

Fish are fast.
Sharks have very sharp teeth.
Fish are slipery.
Flying fish can fly.
Balloon fish are fat.
Fish like to play.
Fish liv in water.
Fish eat fish.
We eat fish.
Bears eat fish.
I like fish

by Emmanual
Grade one

Chapter 4

The substance of the change

In this chapter I will argue that the content of the change in the school is much more important than has previously been reported in the literature. As I stated in the introduction, the literature on school improvement seldom deals with the substance of change, of what it is we are trying to change. As a case in point, the literature on the effective principal speaks of instructional leadership in a cavalier, offhand way, assuming some unspoken or unacknowledged understanding of what is meant. Yet few programs for administrators ever deal with instruction.

This case illustrates the importance of looking very carefully at what it is that we are changing by arguing that teachers are seldom interested in generic issues of school change or climate (unless that climate becomes unbearable). What interests them most is the stuff they teach, the day-to-day contact with children over mathematics, science and language arts. But those writing in the school improvement literature have ignored this fact, preferring to concern themselves with the things that interest them, such as school climate, school organization and an array of other issues that hold little interest for school people.

The work of teachers revolves around the teaching of school subjects such as mathematics, science, and language arts. If we are to expect significant school reform to occur in ways that improve student learning, then it is only reasonable to expect changes and improvements to occur in the way these subjects are taught. Improving the school climate may make the school a better place for teachers to teach, but if the day-to-day teaching of math, science and language arts continues through a rhetoric of conclusions by means of 'chalk and talk', then it is difficult to see how the learning of children will improve. Similarly, we could train teachers to spend more time on task (an important finding from the school effectiveness research), but again, it is difficult to imagine how that rather anaemic innovation would have any lasting effect unless some change had also occurred in the way teachers thought about the subjects on which they were spending more time.

The literature on school improvement and school effectiveness has mostly been silent on this issue of such importance to teachers — the subjects they teach. The content of school subjects, the primary focus during the period of curriculum reform, has not found a high prominence in educational developments since. Those working in the area of school effectiveness have focused on general characteristics related to high scores on achievement tests. Although some of those characteristics involve an emphasis on instruction, one finds little in the literature to indicate what that means in any important way. Shulman (1986) calls the absence of subject matter in research on teaching the missing paradigm. His comments apply equally well to school effectiveness:

> Policymakers read the research on teaching literature and find it replete with references to direct instruction, time on task, wait time, ordered turns, lower-order questions, and the like. They find little or no reference to subject matter, so the resulting standards or mandates lack any reference to content dimensions of teaching. Similarly, even in the research community, the importance of content has been forgotten (p. 6).

In a strangely similar way, those in school improvement who profess to be close to the schools and the teachers in them have also ignored the content of the curriculum. Their emphasis has been on the processes by which schools come to be successful. In both areas, the generic aspects of the school overshadow the subjects that teachers teach on a daily basis. Interestingly enough, it is those subject areas which are frequently the subject of change when innovations are brought into the school. So when change agents approach schools to assist them in the process of change they keep pointing to generic concepts which involve the school as a whole, concepts over which teachers often have little control, while the teachers' need is to bring about improvement in the subjects they teach.

Not only has subject matter been ignored in the recent literature on teaching and change, but the innovations themselves — which may or may not involve subject matter — do not seem to have received much attention as factors influencing the change process. Innovations in a subject such as mathematics are treated the same as a change in language arts, reading, or the more generic changes that might be expected in a workshop designed to improve the elements of instruction.[1] The particular stuff of the innovation is rarely of much consideration among those who propose to help teachers in the change process.

This emphasis on the generic aspects of schooling can be seen in other ways. As I mentioned at the outset, we typically find the literature on the principalship pointing to instructional leadership as a necessary characteristic of the good principal, but one is hard-pressed to find any program in administrative leadership that provides courses in curriculum and instruction. It becomes a curious question as to where principals are to learn about the instruction for which they are to provide leadership. Anyone, it appears, can become an instructional leader, whether they know anything about instruction or not. This unspoken assumption perhaps underlies the almost cynical disregard those in these different fields have for the subjects that make up the bulk of a teacher's day-to-day work.

Only recently has the literature once again turned to the importance of subject matter in teaching. The work of Shulman (1986; 1987) has underlined the critical nature of content to the work of teachers. In drawing the attention of the research community to the importance of the knowledge base for teaching, he puts a new twist on the research on teaching paradigm. He argues that the basis for reform lies in a better understanding of the knowledge base of teaching. He also points out that the disregard for subject matter is a recent occurrence. More recently, Brophy (1992), one of the key figures in the research in teaching paradigm to which Shulman directed his critique, has also begun to acknowledge the role of subject matter in teaching by identifying the purposes for teaching different school subjects. But, although he uses the words, the simplicity with which he defines those purposes suggests that his analysis does not take into account the deeper structure of the disciplines and what that structure means to teaching.

Others too have drawn our attention to the importance of the subjects taught in schools. Stodolsky (1988) contends that, 'with respect to classroom activity, the subject matters' (p. 1). She carried out a detailed examination of elementary social studies and mathematics lessons and drew the conclusion that teachers arrange instruction in different ways depending on the subject they are teaching. Goodson (1983), through his analysis of changes in school subjects over time, says that historically what constitutes subject matter itself changes.

This emphasis on subject matter as the content of change does not simply involve a tinkering with the content that has made up the traditional curriculum. Little or no reform ever emerges from that process. What hopefully becomes apparent in this section is that the focus on subject matter as a means for change begins with seeing subject matter as problematic and in need of substantial reform. It also involves coming to an alternative vision regarding how that subject can be taught differently. The fundamental shifts in thinking that had occurred in language arts in the decade previous to this study provided that vision for the teachers at Lakeview.

I return to the case study at Lakeview Elementary to review the role played by language arts in the work of the teachers there as they sought to bring about change. The very nature of the subject area became a source of constant renewal for these teachers, and thus, produced a means for ongoing innovation.

The subject mattered at Lakeview

It soon became evident at Lakeview that several aspects of language arts as a subject area became of major importance in the general strategy of change that was to run throughout the school for the three-year period that I observed. Besides being a pervasive subject in the school curriculum, language arts provided both conceptual and instructional complexity. It also provided a complex source of stimulation for the staff. Not only were selected staff members able to find deep intellectual satisfaction from the innovation, others were able to join in at different points and use specific strategies to improve their teaching. One sees here, then, a general concept of an innovation in the school, but one that held different meanings for different people.

While not every teacher staked out the same claim on the innovation, they did appear to have shared values and a shared set of meanings about what actually constituted that innovation. They had a common language with which to talk about the different parts and the directions in which they wanted the innovation to go. Certainly they knew what they didn't want it to be. They did not want it to be a basal reading program, for example. Nor did they want the teaching in the school to be driven by the edicts of a principal, or anyone else for that matter. The advantage of these different perspectives on the innovation was that people seemed able to become involved in changes and developments in the school at a level at which they were comfortable. And it was here that the different stages of the innovation (Figures 5 and 6) became quite important.

Figure 5 is composed of four concentric circles. The outermost circle represents changes in the language arts program which generally involved trying new strategies in classrooms. These changes provided a starting point for many teachers. They talked about whole language, and discussed having changed their teaching from the use of basal readers to having children now write their own stories for reading. For some of them the innovation went no further than that. As Bill, who was discussed in the previous section, commented:

> I just am not a person to jump in full force and do something. I have to sit back. Over a period of time I will pick up bits and pieces of what I think will work for me. And I have over the past three years taken little bits and pieces and used them. I don't really see myself as a follower of the whole language approach. I know how to use whole language in my class, but not to the extent of other teachers. I'm not into the really deep structure of it . . . I use what is offered in the school, but I still have my own biases. . . .

But for others, considerably more was at stake than simply improving the teaching of language arts. Stage 2 in Figure 5 shows some teachers integrating subjects and becoming involved in the writing process. At this stage the larger issues of teaching and learning occupied much of their thinking and staffroom conversation. They actively contemplated changes that worked for them, and changes that they were planning to initiate. At this level, they generated changes in their own teaching rather than seeking to adopt someone else's method. The comments of two teachers are pertinent here:

> And that was the year I thought that I had finally broken totally free of Ginn and I felt very strong about whole language. And I knew what I believed in and what I didn't for the first time. And I was growing professionally as well, it was really a good year. My second and third years were excellent that way. And then doing our workshop, that just topped everything off and made me feel like a professional. So once you start to feel that you're doing something for the kids and for yourself at the same time a different view of teaching emerges. . . . A lot of teachers

Figure 5: Stages of instructional change

When this figure and the one following are read, the innermost circle is intended to convey the deeper structure.

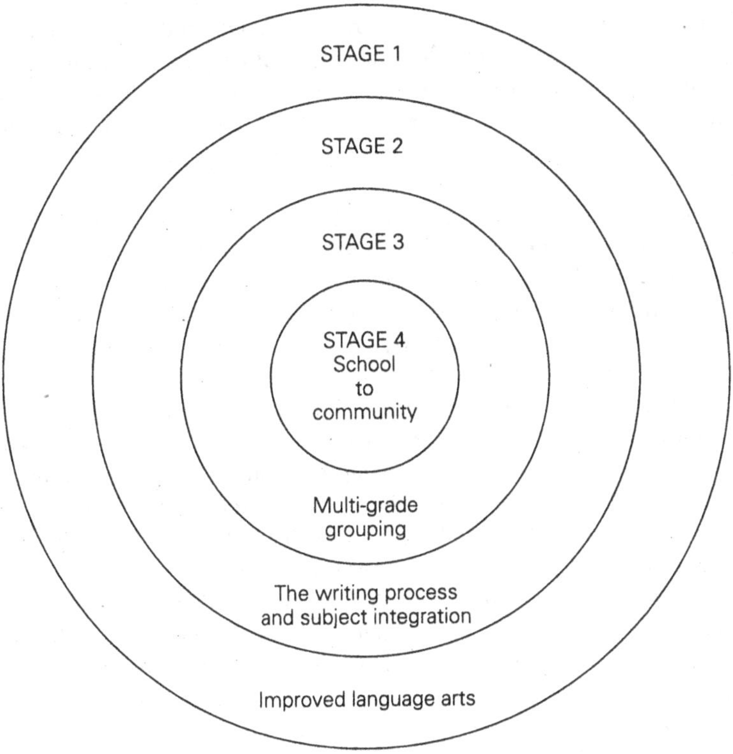

do things only for the kids; that was me for many years; just working in the classroom. And I thought that was it, that I would always be a classroom teacher, and then the next stage was principal or some other job I guess, in the district, or working for the Ministry. But I didn't think of growing as a professional myself. I didn't realize there was more to work. I went to university and teachers' college, and thought that was all I need to know. . . . But it's not. It's a continuous process.

It was so different from the basal reading approach and some of the things they read out to us; the activities that they used just seemed to be a lot more open-ended and interesting for kids to do. So I started some of that in my own classroom. And then you find that even that . . . even that's not enough, so you start looking at other things, like the writing process, just trying to use different types of books in your reading program, that kind of thing. And, I guess I'm still evolving in

> that particular point. It's only two and a half years; I am still working on that process, its still going on.

Stage 3 of the innovation involved still closer and more frequent interaction between peers. The staff struggled, experimented, and taught themselves to team-teach and try various types of multi-graded groupings. This metaphorical removal of the walls between their classrooms seems to have come about as a result of a momentum that had gathered force in the school. One of the teachers describes it like this:

> People share quite freely their ideas and people are really quite excited sometimes, and they will come into the staff room and talk about something. And you see the excitement in people and you want to be part of that excitement, so you try and learn what the process is so that you can try it in your own room.

These teachers have begun to view teaching as a changing, ongoing activity. In the first situation, for example, the teacher now sees her own professional development occurring as a result of changes she makes to her teaching.

For some of the teachers the change in the school went beyond language arts teaching, and indeed beyond the subjects being taught. They saw the change as an opportunity for growth, both for themselves and for the students. For them it was being engaged in a process of change and improvement, and enquiry into their own teaching. While this deeper structure remained something of an ephemeral notion throughout my study of the school, it nevertheless held meaning for many of the teachers participating in the project. The complexity of the innovation became one of its strengths because it provided a never-ending source of inspiration and engagement. For those engaged at the inner level it had now gone far beyond teaching strategies and procedures to a kind of inner notion about what teaching was, how one improved at it, and how one could create excitement around teaching and learning.

Stages 3 and 4 in Figure 5 reflect deeper levels of change in teaching; here teaching becomes a form of inquiry which leads teachers to contemplate the broader issues of education as a whole and its role in society. For some at Lakeview it became a personal inquiry into teaching and into themselves as teachers.

The fourth, and innermost, circle which I have termed 'from school to community', began occupying more and more of the teachers' time as the change progressed. Some staff members saw their commitment to the inquiry process as extending outside the boundaries of their school into a larger community of educators. Some of them gave workshops in their district and in other districts in Canada as well as in the United States. Others left the school to become district consultants. The staff increased their involvement in district committees and various district projects. As one moved from the outermost to the inner circles it appeared that the conceptualization of the change became more complex and required a deeper understanding, which many teachers managed to

Figure 6: Stages of reflection

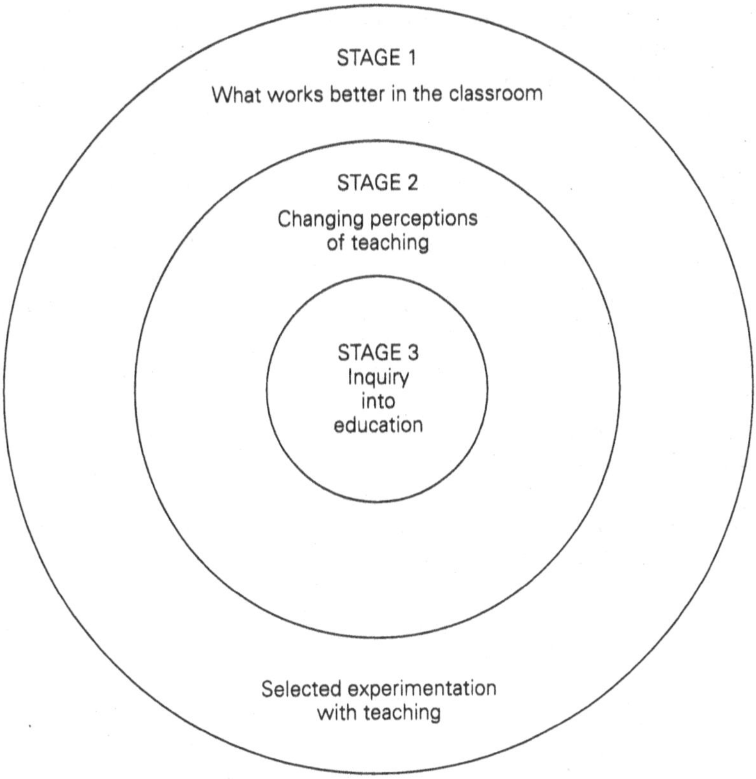

achieve. For others, however, this understanding never reached beyond improving their own language arts approach, or blending this focus into the teaching of other subjects, without being drawn into deeper interaction with their colleagues in team teaching and multi-graded group situations.

These four patterns of the change that I observed illustrate its complex nature. It reveals not one innovation, but several. I found teachers working at each of the levels illustrated here. The norms of the school were such that those differences were respected. Yet the complex nature that the change required at the innermost levels seemed to provide a challenge for those teachers who longed to be challenged. In short, the change provided something for everyone.

These patterns of change at Lakeview, which I not only observed but which teachers reported to me, corresponded to different levels of thinking on the part of teachers and principal. These are shown in Figure 6. At one stage, shown in the outermost level, teachers appeared concerned about experimenting with new teaching strategies. Their thoughts centred on how this or that practice might be put into place and how it worked in the classroom. Others had moved beyond the specific practices themselves to think about how their teaching was changing, or in some cases, how it should change. This became evident as teachers took ownership of the changes going on around them and began to take a proactive stance in creating those changes.

Beyond that, the concern focused on a deeper level of inquiry that involved the school, and in some cases education in the more general sense. I inferred from some of the comments that at times the teachers were dealing with a more fundamental concern about society itself depicted by the innermost circle. So, in short, two things were occurring. On the one hand, teachers were changing their practices; on the other, those changes were anchored within deeply-held values about the purposes and meanings associated with the changes.

In looking at the stages displayed in Figures 5 and 6, it might be tempting to argue that these layers represent stages of teacher practice and development. And, in some cases, evidence would suggest that some members of the Lakeview staff established a progression from the outermost to the innermost circles. Certainly the change itself did appear to move from level 1 to level 4. However, regarding individual teachers, and given the scope of the study, I only claim that I saw people at different levels over the three year period and that some did in fact seem to move toward the centre of both figures. It also appeared that many of the teachers had worked through earlier stages before coming to Lakeview. But it remains for further thought and inquiry to determine if, in fact, these are stages of growth, or areas where people find themselves most comfortable.

Discussion

This examination suggests that the subject area of language arts had certain characteristics that assisted the staff to make the change in the school, and, also that the nature of the innovation within that subject area became a major factor in supporting the change.

Stodolsky (1988) points out that the area of language arts carries with it certain characteristics which sets it apart from other subjects such as mathematics or science. First, it is a nonsequential subject in which teachers can choose topics of study without having to worry about any particular place in a hierarchy of learning; one story can be selected for study as opposed to another without any particular handicap. Further, the subject is not well defined or circumscribed. Both these characteristics make the subject different from mathematics where the sequence of topics is more critical to the way in which the students learn the subject. These characteristics allow teachers in the school working side-by-side to engage in a variety of different activities in language arts. Concerns over sequence of topics or consistency of teaching those topics which might arise in mathematics assume less importance in language arts. It was this characteristic of the subject which appeared to allow so much flexibility in it at the different stages shown in Figures 5 and 6.

Another characteristic of language arts that sets it apart from other areas involves its strong presence in the school curriculum. Teachers generally teach this subject every day. Talk about teaching at recess and noon is more likely to be about language arts than about any other subject. In contrast, a subject such as science is often taught infrequently, if at all, in the elementary school.[2] The teachers at Lakeview saw in the language arts curriculum an area in which they could exercise a great deal of flexibility which enabled them to experiment and make choices without worrying about upsetting the work of other teachers.

Another feature of language arts involved its encompassing nature which allowed teachers to teach other subjects within its rubric. In Bill's words:

> Everything that we are doing is refocused toward language arts. And then from there it takes off. Even in social studies and science, whatever we are doing reverts back to our basic goals of language arts.

Bill is here referring to the way in which several teachers used language arts as the subject into which they integrated other areas of the curriculum. Although from my observations such integration was not as pervasive as Bill's comment would indicate, I did see evidence of many teachers drawing other subjects into their teaching of language arts.

The unique character of the subject also allowed for the development of much deeper roots, shown in Figures 5 and 6. The content of the subject, or perhaps the way in which the staff had conceptualized it, appeared to give the teachers permission to develop their own personal and practical knowledge, not only about the content of literature and writing but also about how to teach it; that knowledge became an important wellspring of change in their teaching. They were not simply implementing some outsider's notions of how to teach language arts better, they were developing their own concepts of how the subject could be approached in a variety of ways. The content was not fixed or immutable; answers did not come from the textbook as one might expect they would in a subject such as mathematics.[3] The multiple interpretation of a story (such as Hansel and Gretel) can be carried into the arena of teaching where various different interpretations are needed in the way teaching can be carried out. At no time did the teachers say 'the subject does not allow us to teach it in that way', a comment so prevalent among teachers in mathematics and science.

The following question obviously arises here: suppose this school had decided to focus on math or science instead of language arts. Would the change process have been different? Obviously, the data from this study cannot provide a definitive answer to that question. While one can only offer a hypothesis, my best guess is that the change would have been very different. I find it hard to imagine how the kind of change that took place at Lakeview could have occurred if these teachers had been dealing with mathematics or science. For example, it is very difficult to imagine the extent to which teachers could have used either science or mathematics as a basis for integration. As Stodolsky (1988) points out, teachers approach different subjects in very different ways. In her analysis she contrasted mathematics and social studies. She acknowledges that the skills, abilities and attitudes that students are expected to develop in math and in social studies are quite distinct from each other. The same kind of differences would seem to be evident between language arts and mathematics or science.

Quite apart from the differences inherent in these two subject areas, another characteristic of language arts made it a particularly responsive vehicle for the change at Lakeview. Language arts had been the focus for change and reconceptualization over the fifteen years prior to the events at Lakeview, whereas mathematics had not undergone the same reconceptualization at that time.[4] The new vision for the teaching of language arts came to the teachers of Lakeview through workshops, conferences and the discussion that occurred between teachers on the staff.

At this point, my claim that change such as the one that occurred at Lakeview would not have taken place had mathematics or science been the medium comes in the form of a hypothesis to be tested. The point that seems much less speculative is that the subject area and the content within that subject area was an important factor in the change process there. If other subject areas had been involved, the way teachers approached their work in those areas would have been very different. In all likelihood, the change that resulted would have been different as well.

In closing this section I should like to return to a familiar theme, that the nature of the innovation itself and the content that that innovation is intended to change become important parts of the change process. But, the importance of the subject area must be kept in perspective. It is not the subject matter itself that is critical but how we conceptualize what it means to learn the subject matter. The subject matter did not sustain the change over time, but it did present teachers at Lakeview with a starting point for change. As both Figures 5 and 6 illustrate, teachers who ventured into the deeper structure of philosophical change did so through the door of language arts. Once they had entered that arena they discovered a whole range of issues to explore.

The importance of subject matter has largely been overlooked in the literature. School improvement people have focused upon the sociology of change. School effectiveness people have focused on broad characteristics of successful schools. Those in between harp on about some mystical concept of the school being the unit of change. Policymakers it seems have followed their advice and focused upon general school characteristics aimed at school change. Meanwhile, teachers on whose shoulders any real reform must rest deal with school subjects. The outsiders — who typically write for each other — have never really recognized the nature of the work that goes on in schools and tempered their theories about it. It should come as no surprise, therefore, that reforming over and over again (Cuban, 1990) brings so few results.

Notes

1 Here I refer to the series of workshops carried out by Madeline Hunter called 'The Elements of Instruction'.

2 See British Columbia Assessment of Science (1991), Technical Report IV: Context for Science Component.

3 This is not to suggest that all math educators would see mathematics in this way. What is important in this instance is how these teachers saw that mathematics. As I watched them teach the subject they appeared to be taking a view that it was an area to be covered.

4 Mathematics has since been the subject of quite far-reaching reconceptualization as seen by the documents developed by the National Council of Teachers of Mathematics (1989; 1991).

Melanie: Horses

Horses have horse shoes

Horses have babys.

Horses eat grass.

Foals drink milk from its mother.

They are prity.

Female horses are called mares.

Male horses are called stallions.

Baby horses are called colt foal (male.) and filly foal (female?.

Horses have one baby at a time

by Melanie
Grade one

Chapter 5

The people who tried to change what they taught

The teacher

Few would question the centrality of the teacher's role in bringing about changes to make schools more effective places for children to learn. Any proposed change, whether it comes from within the school or from outside, will ultimately be put into practice by classroom teachers. However obvious that statement might appear, policymakers and change agents often act as though reform mechanisms can be put into place without consulting teachers; that some sort of divine intervention on the part of change agents will suffice. The failure of such attempts does not seem to discourage these outsiders from trying again and again. A cynic might be attempted to argue that policymakers and change agents do not really want the system to change, they only want to use it to further their own careers by stirring up the schools from time to time. Then, if they can point to little or no change occurring, that must surely mean they will require larger budgets to stir even harder next time.

Lest I be accused of building a straw person here, I will comment on an example from the current literature which, although it appears to have the correct sentiments, goes about things in the wrong way. The example comes from a paper by Caldwell and Wood (1988) who begin by pointing out that

> . . . school-based improvement holds the promise of producing substantial positive change in our schools, yet it is a complex process involving new expectations and roles and a reorientation in the way we think and operate schools at the district level. It means moving many decisions about improvement out of the central office and into the school.

So far, so good. But then the authors present a flow chart showing all the arrows coming down from the district with teachers scarcely being mentioned. The board selects goals, identifies procedures for planning, etc. Teachers, when they do get mentioned, are to work collaboratively with principal and central office staff and '. . . assist in the implementation of these programs. . . .' In short, the authors describe a very top-down model of school-based improvement which misses the central need for teachers to be involved directly in initiating the process and developing the product. That model will do little for school change in the sense in which we seem to be thinking of it today. The type of school-based development that I observed in Lakeview placed the onus on the principal and teachers to initiate and sustain school improvement on an ongoing basis. This model requires a very different view of teacher change from those normally found in the literature and assumed in many jurisdictions.

But cynicism and examples aside, attempts at reform and concomitant research over the past few decades point to certain characteristics of teaching that provide a context for any discussion of the teacher's role in school change. Much of the literature also makes certain assumptions about what these characteristics of teaching mean in terms of reform. The results from this case raise questions about such assumptions.

Research about the teacher

Teaching is a complex business; changing it becomes even more complex. It is, therefore, not surprising that research on the role of the teacher in school change remains fraught with contradictions and ambiguity. The different perspectives brought to bear on teaching also bear on the change process as well. Research has shown that teachers typically work in the isolation of their own classrooms in a set of tasks that are largely unbounded and unfinished. The isolated setting of the classroom (isolated from other adults) provides a poor place for change in school practice and professional development. The isolation of teachers in their work has been amply documented in the literature. From Lortie's (1975) seminal work, *The school teacher*, to more recent works, the central message comes through — teachers work alone. Not only do they work by themselves, they are socialized to think about their work in highly individualistic terms. They emerge from a school system which teaches competition. During teacher training, success comes through individual effort, not group activity. Their first year of teaching provides a sink or swim environment in which individual effort alone decides whether one succeeds or not. In short the route to becoming a teacher has been an individual effort to this point; it should come as no surprise that teachers, once established on the job, continue to work alone.

Research also shows that teachers pay a price for that isolation when it comes to their own professional development. In a study of six teachers who had taken a particular type of coursework aimed at improving their teaching, teachers' isolation within the school was found to be highly problematic when it came to sustaining any changes that they had begun (Wideen, Carlman and Strachan, 1987). That study illustrated that when teachers returned to the isolation of their classroom the ideas that they brought with them virtually died on the vine because of a lack of support and encouragement from other adults. We hardly have to go beyond our own experience to understand the limitations of this isolated setting for learning, reflection, or bringing about change in our lives. In an isolated setting, one's practice is never examined, one receives no feedback from another adult about that practice, and one has few colleagues with whom to interact about problems. As teachers in typical schools we have all experienced going a year or more without ever having another professional comment on our work.

The central message of this research states that no matter how sincere our efforts, the isolation of the typical classroom will severely limit both professional growth and change within a school. But the work of people such as Little (1986), Lieberman (1986) and a host of others has brought hope into this somewhat dismal picture. They have pointed to collaboration, partnership, collegiality and mutual adaptation as the means by which teachers can be engaged in intellectually stimulating professional development that will counter the isolationism of the typical classroom. Collegiality has become associated with everything 'good' about successful schools. The assumption seems to be that if people collaborate things will only get better; collaboration can never make things worse. Only recently has a critical edge begun to emerge from the writing of those who deal in areas related to collaboration. Even Little (1986), who carried out the original research, has recently argued that there is an assumption that collaboration yields benefits capable of leading to rapid and favourable changes in education. She has pointed out that collaboration can be oppressive as well as being transformative, and that collaboration requires great commitment and planning to be successful, a point seldom acknowledged by policymakers.[1]

Others who discuss the teacher's role in change point out that the teaching position is one of routine, overload and limited opportunities for reform (Fullan, 1991:118). The daily maintenance and pressure to cope with teaching leaves little space for composure, constructive discussion and simple time to think. Given that situation it is not surprising that Doyle and Ponder (1977; 1978) found what they termed a 'practicality ethic' with respect to how teachers viewed innovations aimed at modifying or improving their practice. Proposed changes that did not match a teacher's practical situation had little chance of being implemented. The further such proposed changes deviated from that view of practicality, the less likely they were to be implemented. Ungerlighter (1992) expresses the point in these terms:

> . . . the more proposed changes threaten or appear to threaten the group's customs, traditions, or values, the more likely it is that the group's members will resist the change. And, if the changes are implemented, the cost of their implementation will be significant in terms of personal and social disruption.

If one extends these arguments they lead one down the decidedly paradoxical path of innovation without change. They predict that the only innovations that will be successful are those that do not vary from the values of those who are to implement them. One could then ask, how does change — if it is to be substantial change — come about?

The experience at Lakeview casts a somewhat different light on this depressing picture of innovation without change. To illustrate, I will draw on the case of one teacher whose experience typifies that of many teachers there. It shows the importance of the right kind of leadership, how collaboration played out in this particular setting, and the limits of the practicality ethic.

A case in point

Rachel, one of the teachers who joined the staff during the second year of the change occurring in the school, provides an example to illustrate a number of points about the teacher's role in change. The new teachers at Lakeview came from a wide variety of professional backgrounds and many of them, like Rachel, reported major differences between their previous experience and what they saw taking place in their new surroundings. Rachel, a third grade teacher, made this comment after three years at Lakeview:

> I see a very concerned staff (at Lakeview), more concerned than any place else I have ever been, and I have taught in Marion for a year, and in Centreville for a year and I taught in Wawanga for two years and I've never seen more dedicated people, wanting to do, not just a good job, but a better job. You know, I know lots of teachers who want to do a good job — in fact most teachers I would think want to do a good job — but I feel that the teachers here want to do a better job.

Her history will have a familiar ring for a lot of teachers. She taught for one year in a small town called Marion where life in the school pretty much followed a pattern that seemed as old as the school itself. Rachel felt that the ambience had been friendly, support reliable, and the staff more than adequate to the job. But something was missing.

> . . . just the whole phenomenon of the staff really wanting to do better all the time. In Marion they had a really good staff and we all worked together, and we shared together, but we never — we rarely ever — tried anything new, or looked at the research and said, you know, 'Are we doing that? Are we staying on top of things?'

In her next two schools life wasn't quite so tranquil, but still innovation at both places seemed a foreign concept. At the school in Centreville, one of the largest cities in the province where Rachel taught for one year, form rather than substance appeared to be the driving force. The principal there took a bottom-line approach to education with results being determined primarily by student performance on standardized tests.

> I guess the principal, at least ours, was under some pressure to make sure the school performed well. So, on the language arts test, my grade

> 3 had something like 65 per cent. And there was another grade 3/4 where the grade 3's also had about 65 per cent. We were told that we had to reteach everything that was on that test in two weeks and then the children had to take the test again and they had to get over 80 per cent average or else we would have to reteach again for another two weeks and get the test, because the principal wanted the results to be above 80 per cent so that our school, or he, looked good. . . .

At this school the principal was the undisputed leader who maintained tight control. Some of the frustration at his dictatorial tactics can be seen in her account of life in the school:

> We were dictated to. We were told quite specifically what we could and couldn't do in that school. . . . You really weren't a teacher on your own. You were basically told what to do. . . . He (the principal) would come and shake his finger, inches from your head and make you feel like a little kid. Oh, I got it three times in one week. I went home crying.

In the third district in which Rachel taught — this time in a small interior town — life was relaxed to the point that she was unaware of the curriculum as laid down by the provincial Ministry and she complained about what she perceived of as a 'lack of guidance'. Coming from the strict confines of school life in Centreville, she was unprepared for the *laissez-faire* attitudes that held sway in the school in Wawanga.

> As a teacher I was sort of left on my own, and did what I did, and I feel guilty because I sometimes think I didn't teach them all that much. Coming from Centreville where someone was on you all the time, where everybody was told what to do, I thought that was the way you had to teach. You had to use Ginn and you had to have 80 per cent. . . . So I went to Wawanga from there . . . and there wasn't very much motivation to do those things. And again I was doing Ginn.

But, although the school may have been a laid-back experience in some ways for Rachel, the leadership style of the principal was all too reminiscent of the principal's in Centreville. She spoke of walking home at night with another teacher, complaining all the way about a principal who 'made you shake in your boots'. Although she lasted two years in this school, by the end of the second, Rachel was ready once again to move on, this time to Lakeview where the whole ethos of the school was unlike anything she had thus far experienced in her professional life.

Rachel came to Lakeview a year after the innovation had begun. The contrast between Charlie's leadership style and that of the two previous principals struck her as one of the most significant aspects of life in the school.

> So when I came to Lakeview where Charlie wants people to talk to him and feels that he is the same as everyone else, it was really a nice thing

to do. Because I had always seen principals as someone who shook their finger in your face and told you that you did it wrong or when to do it and how high you should jump. So it took a while to get used to Charlie and now I can't ever imagine going back to a principal like the other two I had.

While she felt energized and excited about the change taking place there, she also at times felt some ambivalence and self-doubt. Because the entire school staff had been swept by a 'whirlwind of ideas', she at times felt left behind or caught up in events that were out of her control. This is how she described her feelings at the time:

I often feel that I am not performing as well as some others because there is such a demand . . . such a feeling that you should do better and you should be doing this and you should be doing that. And that's not putting it the right way either, but I know I feel at times that so-and-so is doing that and so-and-so is doing that, and I am doing this. And I am not sure about that and maybe I should be spending more time doing that. There is a bit of pressure that way. I know that if I was at another school. . . . I probably wouldn't feel that pressure. The question is would I be happy not feeling it?

Rachel confessed to me that at times she just wanted to 'close my door and do my own thing'. And yet, as time wore on, she became increasingly enthused about what was happening in the school, and began to gain a sense of her own budding professionalism. Because she was not a reader, not a person who would willingly seek out new information or ideas, she felt happy to be on the periphery of new concepts and new understandings that others had gleaned from research. She told me how much she enjoyed working at Lakeview and being around people who have ideas, 'who do the research for me'. As someone who finds reading research difficult, it was important for Rachel to belong to a staff where the research could be shared, where someone else took the responsibility for making it available to those staff members who would never have discovered it on their own.

For some time Rachel hadn't been happy with the way she had been teaching language arts and, coincidentally, at Lakeview she found a staff who had also felt a need to focus on that area. Ever since she had begun teaching, Rachel had been in schools where Ginn readers and the phonics book had been the alpha and omega of the reading program. And, as she put it, 'I got to be great at running off worksheets.' While her dissatisfaction with the Ginn reading program had already begun in her previous experience in other schools, her exposure to the new language arts at Lakeview provided a fresh approach and a new understanding about teaching it. She credits much of her change and growth throughout this period to the succession of speakers and workshops put on by the school; the McCrackens, Priscilla Lynch, Selma Wassermann and Terry Johnson all had an influence. Just as importantly perhaps was the sense of legitimacy that these outsiders gave to what was taking place in the school. During the course of one interview, she confided: 'It's funny and — I hate to admit it — but if someone from a university or someone with some renown comes and tells you "this is right", you sort of feel better about it than if another teacher had told you.'

One sunny afternoon I sat in her class and watched as a boy from a disadvantaged background who spent most of the class time fidgeting or fighting rose to his feet and sang out loud and clear some words on the board that until then he had been unable to read. This episode came about in response to Rachel's own twist on the language arts program that Lakeview School had undertaken. Here is how she described it:

> I wanted to teach them to read through music. . . . I wanted them to learn rhythm clapping. I wanted them to be able to identify a quarter note . . . so we would also look at serious music. So I took a poem and made up some music to it. Some of the kids I didn't seem to be reaching through stories; I tried nursery rhymes, but that didn't work. I could see that they were enjoying themselves. Some of these kids who are sort of trouble-makers in the class, who don't seem to be listening, they are the ones who are singing. . . . This was really a breakthrough for me because here was this kid who doesn't take part very much and he was so thrilled, to stand up and sing the song in front of everybody. So, music is the way I want to teach them to read.

By the end of her third year at Lakeview, Rachel had reached a plateau in her development as a teacher. She had been one of the group of six who had gone to Idaho to conduct a conference workshop. She reported having grown, personally and professionally, as a result of that experience. When I spoke to her at this time and showed her the figure (Figure 6) she placed her own progress at the figure centre, 'inquiry into education'. She saw this not only as personal growth, but growth as a staff and as a district. At this point she seemed to be seeing herself as part of a larger whole; 'it probably started out at a personal level, but I think it has grown wider than that now.'

She appears to identify closely with the group process and rated 'peer interaction' and 'principal support' as the two most important links in school change. By the end of her third year at Lakeview Rachel gave very little evidence of the young teacher who had been shaken by a principal's wagging finger. She credits Charlie not only with encouraging her to be receptive to new ideas, but with having taught her about group process in decision-making. She now feels strongly that decisions cannot 'come from the bottom up'. She can look back at the changes in the school with a clear eye, seeing both positive and negative aspects in a healthy way, as part of the natural professional development of a teacher, a development that must continue to take place if teachers are to grow.

> It's a long process. And we have all made mistakes throughout and we've all taken steps backwards. But for every step we've taken backwards,

> we've taken a couple forwards and you can't get upset with yourself because you go backwards once in awhile. I think that anyone who's really serious about teaching has to realize that they have to continue to grow . . . and it's something I've learned only since I've been here. I always thought teaching is teaching is teaching . . . and I know how to teach. But I realized I didn't know how to teach. There are lots of things to do and lots of thing that you can change. . . .

The year after this interview took place, Rachel moved to another town in the province some distance away. But this time her attitude had changed utterly. She was resolved to making a difference in her new school: 'I feel things here work so well (and) if we are doing the right thing, I want to continue to do that in another school.' And this time, Rachel will be interviewing her new principal, rather than vice versa. Sounding nothing like the helpless teacher who often walked home in tears in other districts, Rachel told me that now,

> If a principal in another school (says to me) 'I am not interested in you because this is what you believe in', then I am not interested in him (sic). It is more me seeking him. . . . I don't have as much power to say yes or no, I'll take the job, but I know that I am going to be looking at the principal and how he relates to his staff.

Once again the first clear implication from this case study is that the teacher's role is central to school change. However, my observations put a bit of a twist on this general principle. Those teachers who were central to the change at Lakeview developed the innovation and owned it. As such they were not gatekeepers or adopters or implementers in the traditional sense — they were doers of change. This notion places a different perspective on change theory that I will refer to in the sections that follow.

A second point that follows closely from the first, arises out of our previous discussion of the practicality ethic where it was predicted that the only innovations that will be successful are those which do not vary from the values of those who are to implement them. We were then left with the question, how does change — if it is to be substantial change — come about? While it is difficult to imagine a scenario in which the teacher's practice varies considerably from the teacher's values, if we assume that in any attempt at change we must always pander to those values, then we must ask ourselves the further question, how do we attempt to change the underlying values or assumptions the teacher brings into the classroom? Real change becomes a chimera. It seems reasonable to assume that most teachers engage in practice that fits their world view. Does this then argue that the world view can never change?

The data from this case study show that the practicality ethic did not predict the actions for teachers at Lakeview, particularly of those in the core group. In fact, the opposite was true. The more complex and the more difficult the change became, the harder the teachers and principal worked to understand and achieve it. Impediments became a source of inspiration; lack of goal clarity became a challenge. The prospects of change that were to emerge from the innovation would be very different from what these teachers had done over the last few years. Why does one find this occurring when the predominant view in the literature reports something quite different? The answer appears in the way the practicality ethic was conceptualized by Doyle and Ponder (1977/78) and supported by Fullan (1991) and Ungerlighter (1992). They seem to conceptualize their notions of change within the context of changes that are mandated from the outside. Perhaps they are correct in their assertions that if policymakers wish to change teachers, then teachers will not want to deviate too much from the values they hold. But the change that occurred at Lakeview did not involve a top-down mandate, it involved a change that teachers themselves wanted. The traditional notions of change suggested by the literature apparently do not apply in such cases.

Real change seems to occur when teachers choose to wrestle with fundamental issues that challenge their values. The teachers who change are those who ask questions about what is commonly accepted as truth. For example, the commonly-accepted 'truth' that Ginn readers were the best way to teach reading was questioned by the teachers at Lakeview, partly because there was an ethos of change in the subject area that was being felt throughout the province. Most of them had not even considered specific alternatives until they began to investigate. Once they began this process, the power that comes from inquiry — pursuing one's own important questions — drove the process of change. This process is very different from the idea of implementing a pre-set program that someone else has developed.

At Lakeview the innovation became less of a threat because the teachers were in control; they owned the innovation. With the ownership of the process a reality, the innovation itself began to generate information which acted in turn to alter their prior values about teaching. The initial hurdle — their prior beliefs — once overcome allowed a new path to emerge and it was along this new path that the innovation developed.

When teachers have control they generate a sense of power over the situation and their beliefs then become just other items open to scrutiny. However, without power, the values brought into a situation become lines of defense behind which one naturally retreats in order to survive. The teachers in this school owned their own process and therefore they felt comfortable and unthreatened in examining their values and their teaching.

The data from this case point to teachers' independent and strongly held views on teaching. They brought their own meaning to the change that occurred in that teaching. This observation has been made before in other jurisdictions. Clandinin (1986), for example, argues that teachers' practical knowledge provides the basis for their work; any changes to their teaching must begin there. Similarly, Gran (1990) cites research in Sweden to show that while the wishes of the central authorities could be rather easily transferred to district officials and school leaders (principals) they did not transfer well to teachers. This observation relates very closely to the notion of constructivism, a topic to which I now turn.

Constructivism and learning to change teaching

One development currently receiving considerable attention in the literature involves notions of constructivism and conceptual change. With roots in philosophy, constructivism asserts that people must be understood as knowing beings who actively build knowledge, beliefs and understandings based on previous conceptions. The locus of control for behaviour is within the person (Von Glaserfeld, 1987) who is 'self-constructing' (MacKinnon, 1989) and continually striving to make sense of his or her own experience. Such a view of learning holds that learners (whoever they are) come to any situation with their own conceptual understanding which may be the understanding of a science concept by a third grader, or the notion of how teaching should occur held by a teacher. In any new learning situation learners undergo a process of conceptual change in which the construction first held becomes changed and developed. Learning then becomes a process of accommodating new information into the prestructured world that people bring to events. Conflict and confrontation may well occur as new understandings appear discrepant with that prestructured world. The extent to which such new information and new concepts conflict with one's prestructured world is the degree to which we can expect discomfort, or even alienation, from what has now become a potential change. If what is to be learned does not conflict with previously held understandings and values, then the degree of conceptual change might be expected to be small. However, when new ideas challenge existing beliefs, then conflict becomes greater and hence, conceptual change harder to achieve. The implications for such a perspective were stated by Olson (1982): '. . . we must consult the views of teachers if we want to understand why they make the choices they do' (p. 71).

In extending this view we can see that any change within a school must first begin with an understanding of the constructions teachers hold about teaching and learning and proceed from there. When we apply this theory to teacher change, we find a situation similar to one in which a learner comes into contact with something unfamiliar. When teachers are presented with new or different approaches to learning, according to constructivist theory, they enter that situation having an understanding of teaching and more or less strongly held values about it. The introduction of a new teaching model will be similar to the introduction of new information to students; it will run into the brick wall of the teacher's prior understanding or knowledge. The teacher, with values and understanding of teaching gained from years of experience and a host of previous coursework and in-service training, may not be particularly receptive to the new ideas being presented. He or she will more likely be comfortable with the ideas that fit prior perspectives. The more dissonant the ideas are from those perspectives, the more conflict will be created.

Approaches to change

But what is the import of constructivism with regard to change among teachers and within schools? It seems almost fundamental to suggest that change in the school involves change in the way teachers think about their teaching. As such, change in one's teaching involves a process of learning. Yet, far too many approaches to change ignore this basic understanding. One can point to many approaches to curriculum change to discuss this phenomenon but three will suffice: technical tinkering, mandated reform, and personal inquiry. In the first of these, proposed changes often come in the form of new textbooks or revamped curriculum. Such changes typically do little to change the work of teachers because teachers look for the familiar in the new material and find ways to organize it to fit their prior beliefs.[2] Prior beliefs about teaching and the values held by teachers quite predictably 'wash out' any potential change the new curriculum materials may have wrought.

Another approach that has often been attempted to change schools involves mandated reform. Here policymakers propose what often amounts to rather substantial and even radical changes to teachers' work. The *Year 2000* currently being mandated at the intermediate and secondary levels in British Columbia represents such a change. Successful implementation of its proposals would dramatically shift the way teaching occurs in BC schools. Yet the failure of this mandated approach appears to me to be quite predictable. The prior beliefs that teachers hold about teaching, the values that support those beliefs, along with the context in which teachers work, will prove a formidable barrier to such change — one which will not likely be overcome.[3]

A third approach and the one that appeared to work at Lakeview was that which could be termed a 'personal inquiry' approach. The change that occurred at Lakeview did involve certain technical elements, but primarily it required a conceptual shift in the way teachers thought about their work. They shifted from seeing the teaching of language arts as structured skill development to viewing it in a more holistic way where the skills grow out of the nature of the subject itself. To make this shift requires more than learning a new technique, it means nothing less than a major conceptual reformation on the part of the teacher that comes from engagement in inquiry into teaching.

In Lakeview we saw evidence of both sides of this conceptual change notion. Those teachers in the core group constantly talked about their values regarding teaching; they talked about new ideas within the context of those values. When challenging views confronted them, such as Wendy Strachan's critique of their writing program, rather than discount her comments out-of-hand or rushing out in a full-scale attempt to implement her suggestions, they discussed them in the light of their own understanding and accommodated those that they felt to be appropriate — but only after considerable deliberation.

Certain other teachers, who were not in the core group and who regularly left the school at 3.30p.m., did not seize the opportunity to discuss such ideas. In the case of at least one of them there may have been a good reason. Sigrund, the teacher in question, did not share the core group's values about teaching. She did not value whole language. In her mind other aspects of teaching were more important. She admitted to feeling uncomfortable on the staff and was extremely reluctant to being interviewed by me. Although Lakeview school appeared to be the epitome of a collaborative culture, from Sigrund's point of view it more nearly represented Hargreaves' and Dawe's (1990) notion of 'contrived collegiality' (p. 19). And, although she, like others in the outside group, went along with the innovation — at least up to a point — she never shared the same understanding, and hence the same enthusiasm for it. The innovation failed to resonate with the deeper values and assumptions she held about teaching. We can only speculate about whether more talk with others in the school or more ongoing contact would have changed this teacher's feelings. We do know that what was taking place in the school caused her to feel alienated and something of an outsider and that no number of staff meetings or pep talks remedied the situation.

When we look at the case of Sigrund, we perhaps see an example of what Fullan (1991) describes as a change that is 'externally experienced' (p. 127). Simply because an innovation springs from someone or some group inside a school, is not to say that other individuals within that school will not take the position that it was being externally imposed or mandated. Whether from across town or across the hall, if an idea runs counter to some basic and firmly held tenet in an individual's mind, that idea will be rejected. When suggested change fails to find resonance in the individual's ordered understanding of the world, it may seem just as alien or as onerous as if it had come from outer space or from the Ministry. In fact, Sigrund may have found it more intriguing had it come from outer space and less threatening if it had come from the Ministry.

Until we learn more about the deeper mysteries of life, perhaps we will never be able to turn teachers like Sigrund into glowing champions of any suggested change. And perhaps we never should want to. In any case, teachers such as Sigrund proved to be the exception at Lakeview. Peer interaction, which I discuss later, was seen — even by the disaffected — as a major factor in promoting the change there. The talk among teachers provided a forum to test ideas and to receive feedback, and much collaborative work grew out of this interaction. All of the teachers I interviewed rated their talk with peers as either first or second in choosing factors that influenced their lives in the school. And, as can be seen from the many quotations sprinkled throughout this study, many spoke with a great deal of intensity about how much interaction with colleagues had meant to them, both personally and professionally.

The role of the principal

The literature on the principalship, which occupies a great deal of space on library shelves, describes a position that appears to encourage stability in schools rather than change. The optimism in that literature comes from those case studies of principals who have been instrumental in working with teachers to transform the cultures of their schools in ways that support improved teaching and learning. Such principals share some common characteristics. But as Fullan (1991) points out, the processes involved are not straightforward, nor are they particularly well understood. The issues surrounding the role of the principal in school reform remain complex and context specific.

My intent here, apart from some general framing, is not to review this literature. Rather I will provide a capsule of it so that the work of the principal in the school can be put into context. The role played by Charlie in the change that developed provides an illustration of how a principal can exercise moral and instructional leadership and provide the empathy and support that must accompany that leadership if teachers are to take the risks in their classrooms that lead to change. Using the notion of big change and little change that I introduced earlier, what I describe here is a little picture of the principal's role in school change.

This case focuses on the small picture of leadership within a school and contrasts with the bigger picture in the literature which seeks to establish generalizations about principals' behaviour. Lortie's study, to which I referred earlier, along with the school effectiveness literature on leadership, tends to lead to general statements such as 'the principal needs to be an instructional leader.' Such statements often fall into the category of being too general to be wrong and too vague to be useful. As Sergiovanni (1992) points out, the yield of research on school leadership has been dismal. By over-emphasizing concerns about bureaucratic, psychological and technical/rational aspects of leadership, researchers have neglected the professional and moral aspects. As Sergiovanni puts it, 'we have separated the hand of leadership from its head and heart . . . we have separated the process of leadership from its substance' (p. 3). Following Charlie over a period of several years allowed me to look closely at his educational and academic outlook and to watch how it underpinned the instructional leadership he provided. It appeared that his success rested much more on the substance and the emotional aspects of his leadership than on the technical side of being a principal.

In *The new meaning of educational change,* Fullan (1991) begins the chapter on the principalship with a section, 'Where principals are.' He shows that the principal's role in the school has been shaped historically in ways that do not support change and reform; rather, most pressures — which principals seem only too happy to accept — work to maintain stability. He cites the work of Lortie (1988) and Sarason (1982) who claim that the conservative tendencies of the principalship have historic roots. Lortie identifies four tendencies that appear to be built into the principal's role that appear to foster stabilization. First, the group from which principals are recruited tends to have narrow experience and limited exposure to ideas. The role constraints imposed by close association with teachers and the psychic rewards of the principalship provide a second tendency toward stabilization. The third item Lortie talks about is the system itself which tends to inhibit innovative ideas. Lortie's fourth factor supporting conservatism among principals involves the fact that the people closest to principals, and those from whom they receive most feedback, are for the most part parents and teachers.

This rather sombre view of the principal's role in school change emerges from the 'big picture' in the literature. In making such generalizations it paints the principal as some kind of stone-age obstructionist who, because of his background, will tend to resist change. Given these tendencies toward stabilization, principals who do push for change find themselves swimming upstream. Yet, clearly, some do. The characteristics that set this group apart are as wide-ranging as the people who fill the position; a fact that reflects the complexity of the role and the importance of personal characteristics in carrying it out. As the data will show, the principal who was the subject of this case did not fit these conservative parameters put forward by Lortie.

In looking at the role of principal we must also look at the context of the principalship. Often the literature portrays the principal as some sort of guiding light who in some mysterious way manages to lead the flocks to the waters of enlightenment. Papers with titles such as 'The principal as white knight' perhaps help create this glowing image. Rarely does the literature point to the importance of the school and district context. As the quotations I have cited suggest, the staff at Lakeview provided a conducive atmosphere for the principal. So did the district. Charlie made mistakes over the three years of this study, both at the school and district level. But at both levels people recognized his strengths and forgave him. In short, they too provided support on what has to be a two-way street.

Charlie had a somewhat unusual background. He had gained a teaching certificate through a non-traditional route. He was part of a group of students who worked with three instructors from both the university and the field. He speaks fondly about that program, particularly about the way it made him think about education. He describes it in this way:

> Although the faculty of education I went to had a terrible reputation, my experience was absolutely outstanding. I had three faculty advisors who represented a spectrum from the far left to the conservative right. Stan would be on the left. Mrs Adelade was a bit more conservative, but highly on task. And on the right there was Dr George who was not a popular lecturer by any means but certainly well respected. It was very stimulating. In those points in your practicum where you needed stability from the person in the middle you got it. When you needed the father figure you had it from Dr George. And there was Stan who was a real stimulant. I remember him saying that if you are doing your job at all you should be just on the verge of getting fired. It was a very stimulating environment. The level of dialogue was way up there.

He describes the courses he took for his Master's program in somewhat different terms.

> I would look at a bunch of administrators, or would-be administrators, doing whatever we had to do, jumping through whatever hoops we had to go through to get the best grades possible. And I knew damn well that

> when we walked out of that door with our diplomas in our hands that most of us would go right back to doing things precisely the way we had done them — basically top-down.

So Charlie came to the job with an experience from his teacher preparation that probably laid the basis for questioning some of the purposes behind schooling and education. Throughout my discussions with him it became obvious that Charlie did not fit into the group Lortie described as having limited exposure to educational ideas. He read a great deal and seemed to be constantly probing and raising questions.

Conceptual support

The conceptual leadership of the principal (and selected members of the staff) became a critical factor in the change occurring at Lakeview. Throughout that change Charlie showed a type of intellectual persistence regarding the issues surrounding the innovation. His view of professionalism embraced certain values regarding education that he held to be important both for himself and for the staff. These values constantly guided his actions. He spoke about the need to ask such questions as: are we satisfied with what we are doing in the schools? and, how can we empower people to make changes that will bring about better schools for children? He often talked of equality with teachers in decision-making and a valuing of each other's opinion. To him, such an approach should be fundamental whether one runs a school, a classroom, or a district.

In speaking about the general goals of the innovation Charlie said:

> I am convinced that our goals are legitimate, completely legitimate. Our concerns have to do with the relationship between socialization and academic learning and the development of individual attitudes and social attitudes. And we are convinced that you can't necessarily categorize all of that and break it into little boxes.

Here Charlie expresses a view of learning and of schooling that illustrates a strong commitment to normative values. In classrooms one could see this position reflected as he talked both to children and staff. In a conversation with me later in the project he had this to say regarding his support of people who would take risks in their work.

> And behind all of this is the principle that you don't jump on the person because they (sic) honestly, however mistakenly, tried to accomplish something for the good of other people (however unsuccessful they might be).

The comments made by two teachers again show the sort of questioning that he encouraged of the staff.

> That's his personality; he loves to ask those questions. That's the kind of thinker that he is. And it's not so much that his doubts express a lack of belief in what he's doing, but that it's his nature to explore all the parameters of a problem, to really look at every side of it, to make sure he hasn't missed anything.

> Charlie's the type of person that will take your ideas and take them one step further, will work with you on it. . . . So if you have a principal who says, 'Yeah, that sounds great.' and goes next door and you never hear about it again, then I think you're going to have to look in another direction for help.

Along with this set of values, Charlie exhibited a strong commitment to instruction. Because he not only taught, but read a great deal, he never seemed far away from the instructional side of the teacher's work.

At times the literature appears to suggest that principals can be conceptual leaders without subscribing to any values of their own; that they are in some way conceptual neuters. It would be interesting to speculate whether Charlie's conceptual support would have been as effective if he had been in the position of having to lead his staff toward implementing basal readers. Part of his conceptual leadership probably stems from the congruence between his beliefs and the fundamental principles of the language arts changes happening in education at the time. However, another part of his conceptual leadership certainly sprang from the strong personal values he brought with him to the position.

Perhaps principals need access to the same kinds of opportunities to inquire and the same climate of support that teachers require. Principals can learn — they can change — just as teachers can. Perhaps if leadership were conceptualized as being a model of learning, as Barth (1990) suggests, we would have more effective principals.

Without question, the role of the principal played a significant part in the change that occurred at Lakeview. The remarks made by the teachers quoted typified those made by other members of the staff. To suggest, however, that he was a 'white knight' would be an overstatement. He certainly didn't try to be everything to all people. Leithwood (1989) recently identifed four foci that reflect a principal's style or pattern of practice: an administrative or plant manager focus, an interpersonal or climate focus, a program focus, or a student development focus. He suggests that the first two represent the style of most principals, and that the latter two are less common. Yet most educators would accept that the latter two are more effective in setting a climate for improving schools. Charlie was effective primarily on the basis of his program focus (around which everything in the school revolved) and his commitment to students. Managing the plant was not his primary concern.

When I confronted Charlie with what some saw as his neglect of plant management, he paused, then he began talking about the pressure on administrators to keep up with the volume of paper that flows across the administrative desk. This aspect of the job, he felt, was the main factor on which principals were judged. Moreover, his own teachers often became nervous when the paperwork was not done. With a shrug, Charlie, however, conceded that one of the costs of engaging in close staff interaction might well be at the expense of the paperwork.

Support leadership

The principal took several actions to support the teachers in the school. These actions included providing release time for teachers, finding money to support their efforts, and taking risks with them by trying out new teaching ideas. Teachers perceived a fairness about Charlie and a willingness to share decision-making. Early on he established the norms of collegiality and interaction and became part of the learning group that emerged in the school. The following four comments illustrate certain of these points:

> Well, you could go up to him and talk to him. He's accessible. . . . He treats everybody well; he treats them like human beings.

> I would say that he is a major part of it (the innovation), and the fact is that he has always supported whatever I have wanted to do in the classroom.

> You can't say that you need a really strong administrator or that you need a really strong staff. You need to look at them all. It wouldn't have happened without the principal. But to me, the more powerful way is through the teachers. He was an integral part of that, but whatever vision he had would never happen without the teachers pulling together, having ownership, and setting up what they felt would be a group, collaborative model.

> I think the vision of what he wanted to do has changed the way he behaved as principal, and probably much more than he would have ever expected. Because, although in the beginning he believed in the collegial model, he still thought that, in order for that to happen, somebody had to lead the way. And so lots of the things that he did reflected that sort of conflict. But people on Lakeview staff know him so well, and they're so used to working with him. They weren't afraid to say, 'Hey, wait a minute! That's not how people cooperate! That's not how you make group decisions!' And pulled him back. So that all the way along I think that there's been as much opportunity for him to grow and change as there has been for the staff.

The last two quotations illustrate the interesting interplay that occurred between the principal and a group of teachers in the school. Reflecting on their interaction with the principal, the teachers posited that his leadership style had changed during the first year partly as a result of that interplay.

The staff also expressed the view that the principal would 'go to bat for them' if necessary. In short, his commitment lay with them, not the school board office or someone else on the outside. The following comments were made by teachers when asked to describe what they meant when they talked about the supportive role of the principal:

> I mean support in terms of the teachers' interests and needs, not the principal's interests and needs. They have to wait. . . . If I needed a day to just sit down and prepare myself, I can have that day to sit down and prepare myself. And I'm not dealt with as if I'm somebody who can't handle my teaching. If I want to go down and buy three books that are just excellent books, that's what I do. Go buy them. Don't come beg, just go get 'em. If I'm interested in developing a workshop in the district, I don't have to go and beg permission. I'm seen as a person who has the right to do that. I'm a professional, and I'm dealt with as a professional, and not one of his students.

> I think the staff knows that (the principal) would just go to the ends of the earth and back for them. Whatever happens, they know he's on their side. And that he does take risks on their behalf. And . . . those things build a sort of rapport as a community that you can't get. . . .

The nature of the change at Lakeview meant that at all times teachers made changes only when they were ready to do so. This evolutionary aspect of the innovation also proved to be another highly significant part of the process. The principal did everything in his power to assist teachers, not only in learning different strategies in language arts and integrating them with other subjects, but also in giving them preparation time for implementation. At the same time other teachers report that they never felt pressure to make changes at a faster pace than they were comfortable with. The changes happened slowly — more slowly than some would have liked — but it seemed necessary to set a pace that would ensure the eventual participation of most teachers. The principal, with his vision of the kind of school he wanted to help create, supported his staff extensively while not asking them to change faster than they were ready to. Some of the teachers describe his support in this way:

> I mean support in terms of the teachers' interests and needs, not the principal's interests and needs. They have to wait. (The principal) has sort of seen things moving here, and if he'd pushed us here, there would have been problems. And as time went on there was lots of support. And the only reason we got here is because there wasn't a push to move up here. Don't push, you know, if someone here is just not prepared yet, they're waiting it out. And you don't go putting the fire under their rear

> to say, 'You're slowing us down. Come on, get going! I force you to do this.'. . . It just does not work.
>
> For me, I'm too hesitant to just jump in and do things. I take everything piece by piece, 'when I feel like it I'll do it', type of thing. And (the principal) has been gracious enough in telling me . . . 'Use it if you want, but you don't have to.' Which is great for me because I just am not a person to jump in full force and do something. I have to sit back.

It appeared that the principal had supported and helped create an ethos in the school for active concern regarding educational practices and meaningful interaction among the teachers. In doing so he was able to contribute to breaking down the traditional walls of professional isolation and provide a supportive atmosphere in which to take risks. It appears from the interviews that in increasing his own teaching time and at the same time personally covering classes to allow teachers preparation time to pull together a new idea, he was making a significant contribution toward the success of the innovation. By devoting much of his own time to teaching, and by talking about his experimental strategies that did not work as well as those that did, he provided a practical model of risk-taking for teachers. It was evident in everything he did that Charlie was highly committed to the teachers' efforts to improve the school.

What can one learn from examining the principal's role at Lakeview? Simply put, a good principal stands for something that goes beyond mere support. He or she must be committed to a view of education that propels him or her toward finding solutions for what ails schools and schooling and be willing to act on that understanding.

But the case also poses some questions about the rather static, and at times dismal, picture of the principal's role in school change that the literature depicts. Lortie's generalizations about the stable and conservative nature of people who fill the principal's role did not apply in this case. Perhaps Charlie was an odd person in this regard, some sort of exception to the rule. Then again, perhaps Lortie's generalizations simply represent characteristics of a particular group of principals that he studied and which ought not to be generalized to groups of principals in other countries, as those in the school improvement literature are so fond of doing. The generalizations have only modest predictive value given the importance of the context in which school change occurs. At best, they need to be taken as starting points only, and viewed as problematic items to be examined in the light of the local context rather than as ways to understand it.

Students

The literature has mapped the landscape of school change, identified the players, and made some valuable beginnings as to how their interactions play out to accomplish school reform. But as Ruddock (1984) points out, one area of that map has not been explored in any systematic way — the role of students. She says:

> The area I am talking about is the area of pupils and innovation: including the power of pupils in relation to the progress of an innovation in schools and classrooms; and the problems that pupils face as conscripts in the innovative campaigns launched by teachers and schools (54).

As she points out, because students and teachers live in an ongoing partnership in the everyday educational transactions of the classroom and the school, the development and maintenance of the classroom culture becomes a sort of partnership between the two. Changes to that culture, which are virtually always implied by the introduction of an innovation into the teaching in that classroom, affect the lives of the students as much as they do the teachers. Curiously, this rather apparent characteristic of classroom and school culture has been virtually ignored by those who write about change. Although Fullan (1991) devotes a chapter to it in, *The new meaning of educational change*, he points out '. . . we hardly know anything about what students think about educational change because no one ever asks them' (p. 182). A review of other works on school improvement reveals little systematic information about the student's role in educational change. Though we now see encouraging signs that educators are taking into account the student's role, that acknowledgment does not really go beyond a periodic discussion of the meaning of activities with students, and an attempt to provide them with a few skills to cope with changes. The student still remains '. . . at the bottom of the heap' (Fullan, 1991:189) with little power to bring about positive change. But as Rudduck, who I cited earlier, and as the situation at Lakeview indicated, students do have considerable influence in situations where changes are being attempted.

My analysis of the situation at Lakeview identified two important roles played by students in the change. The first role was similar to that described by Rudduck as a result of her work in the Humanities Curriculum Project (Stenhouse, 1970). Students develop an understanding of how things work for them in their classroom. They become more or less comfortable with the norms that develop over time. Parents sometimes reinforce those norms. Changes in classroom patterns and routines create management problems and conflict within the classroom. Any innovation that involves a change in routine has the potential for creating these management problems.

The situation at Lakeview proved to be no different from the situation that Rudduck described. The students had been used to a basal reader which involved seatwork and the learning of skills in a highly sequential way. The new approach to language development took a very different avenue to developing those skills. They now came about in a more incidental, rather than a deliberate way, and this approach sometimes proved problematic for the students.

The best illustration of this conflict comes from the teaching of science where Barbara was making an attempt to introduce inquiry teaching to her students during the third year of the project. In a reflective journal about her experience, she made this entry:

> The background of these students (in science) is that of research and textbook study. They had science delivered to them in a non-participatory manner. They were given a number of pages to read and then given a list of questions to answer. They completed a chapter from the text with a written test.
>
> In order to try to develop a sense of inquiry in the students, I presented them with a discrepant event where an ice cube floated part way down in a container of what looked like alcohol. I wanted them to try to duplicate what I had done and to try to develop explanations for what had happened. They did that for a while, but then after a bit one of the students asked me to just tell them how the liquid worked so they could just write it down. Other students agreed and it reminded me how far I have to go in order for the sense of inquiry to stick.

Here the new approach that Barb was trying to introduce came into conflict with the students' prevailing views about how science had been taught. Those views became a factor in making changes in the science teaching in the classroom. If Barb had been working alone in this situation she may well have left this particular innovation. But she was working with another teacher at the time who was doing similar things and they were able to discuss the problem.

One aspect of the innovation that did not prove to be a problem was the noise factor that such attempts at inquiry often created. Such activity had become the norm in the school. The principal, too, was involved in trying to 'do science' with his students and his classroom was as active as any of the others.

The significant issue arising here is the fact that the student becomes the final arbiter of educational change. One way or another, if students think that the teaching they receive is not meeting their needs, they will either make life miserable for the teacher, grin and bear it (and in doing so, learn little), or, as we have seen recently, simply leave school.

The other role students played in the changes occurring in the classroom came in an indirect way through the perceptions held by the teachers of what was 'good for the kids'. When I listened once again to the transcriptions of conversations I had with teachers throughout, it became quite obvious that they were not about to make any changes that they did not see improving the learning of students. The following comments made by two teachers illustrate what was a fairly general pattern throughout the project.

> . . . this year I'm finding that it would be more benefit to the child if I first sort of see what they want to do. Then I can see how they are thinking about writing and I can push that a bit further.

> At first I felt as if I were letting them go on their own, and that was kind of scary. I allowed kids to go into the halls to have conferences and could

not watch them. You are kind of letting them go. Now at the end of the year I am seeing a lot of good results from the students I feel much better about what I am doing.

As these comments illustrate, one of the main criteria for change to be called successful lies in its potential for helping students learn. One of the reasons that the innovation had so much support from the beginning was the staff's acknowledgment of how well students appeared to be learning to read and write as a result of the new strategies involved, strategies which came in sharp contrast to the basal readers which had been in use before the innovation.

Notes

1 These questions were raised in personal communication. Fullan and Hargreaves (1991) have also raised these concerns.

2 This observation comes from an unpublished study in which the author along with a team of peers observed the implementation of a 'new' math program in two districts where new textbooks were introduced. Classroom observation and teacher interviews found few changes in the work of a sample of teachers despite considerable in-service training conducted around the introduction of these new textbooks.

3 Indeed, as this manuscript goes to press the Premier of British Columbia was reported in the *Vancouver Sun*, September 16, 1993 as 'putting a stake in the heart of the Year 2000 education program.'

Whales

Blue whales are
the bigest. mamals
in the see. This
Whale has a big
mouth. Blue whales
eat Small animals
Whales need to
keep warm This
Whale is a kiler
whale. It eats
and seals.

by Keswick
Grade one

Chapter 6

The unit of change

Policymakers and researchers have now convinced themselves that the school is the unit of change. We see an accumulation of works and developments based on that assumption ranging from school-based management to the development planning for school change. School-based management refers to a form of educational administration where the school becomes the unit for decision-making as opposed to a central district administration (Caldwell and Wood, 1988). Developmental planning seeks to empower the school to deal more effectively with the task of improving teaching and learning (Hargreaves and Hopkins, 1991).

Goodlad (1983) has probably argued the most forcefully in this regard. He contends that 'the individual school is the key unit on which to focus for effecting improvement within the formal educational system' (p. 36). That argument, however, rests on the notion that the school can function as an appropriate unit for educational reform. That notion arises more as an item of faith rather than one based on research. Goodlad, himself, makes this qualification.

> The research necessary to a strong affirmation of the school-based postulate simply does not exist. Both scholars and practitioners cite references adding up to a rather substantial list in arguing for the school as the locus for change. But, on checking these sources, one finds the best of them to be rationales for dealing with the school from the perspective of the hypothesis, not evidence regarding its validity (p. 37).

Moreover, the literature appears quite slim when it comes to dealing with what the school should look like were it to provide an appropriate setting for teacher development and/or educational change. Perhaps no better illustration of this exists than the eighty-sixth NSSE yearbook bearing the title, *The ecology of school renewal*. Here Goodlad (1987) and an impressive group of authors make a convincing case for an alternative paradigm for school improvement. They talk of replacing one-way directives with multiple interactions, rules and regulations with room for decision-making, mandated behaviour with inquiring behaviour, and so on. The alternative set out in the first chapter by Goodlad fails to lift off in subsequent chapters. The reader leaves with the sense that while it may have been a great concept, the knowledge base to affect it remains very weak indeed.

Others are not so sanguine when it comes to the notion of the school as the unit of change. A. Michael Huberman (personal communication September 1993) contends that the logic of using the school building as the unit of analysis and intervention, when we are talking about at least 25–30 teachers and support staff and 500 pupils, is a 'goofy logic'. To offer the school as a unit of change provides a convenient administrative and structural focus, but little else. To propose that those in any school can agree on any direction for school change undervalues the enormous differences that exist between individuals within a school and the complexity of the school as a community. It provides yet another example of how outsiders treat teachers as mere chess pawns in the game of school change. The analysis of the data from Lakeview calls into question the rather glib notion of pointing to the school as the unit of change.

If the school is not the most propitious unit of change, then what provides an alternative? One alternative would be to focus on the teacher. Appealing as this notion may be, especially to those who value individualism, for several reasons the concept of the individual has not had a good track record when it comes to school change. First, except in the case of leadership which I discuss later, the concept of the individual in school change breaks down because individuals leave few footprints in the landscape of schooling. When a teacher leaves a school, so does the change he or she brought about. This point has been well demonstrated in Huberman and Miles' (1986) study of innovative sites. One of the factors working against maintaining change in schools was the transfer — and often promotion — of innovative teachers to other schools or school districts. The efficacy of the concept of the individual breaks down in still other ways. The pressures of socialization within a school are such that individual change usually operates against tremendous odds. The teacher who succeeds in changing his or her work often becomes isolated within the school. To avoid this isolation these innovative teachers often retreat to the sanctity of their own classrooms. This sort of isolation affords no protection or support. The result is that individual change usually does not work in any lasting way.

The power of group process

The literature has pointed up the weaknesses of the typical isolated classroom as providing a good setting for change and professional development. And, as I have just argued, the school, for a variety of different reasons, offers little more. What then provides a better alternative? From the Lakeview experience the group emerges as a powerful vehicle for bringing about change, but with the qualification that certain characteristics must pertain for a group setting to be effective. Certain norms, beliefs, expectations and support are needed within that group for any change to occur. But, in addition, such beliefs and expectations must revolve around instructional matters that those both inside and outside the group see as important. Knowledge also plays a critical role in providing alternatives to current practice and in some cases provides the necessary suspension in time and space to allow for reflection. The arguments behind the value of the group in this case go beyond the observations made at Lakeview. Perhaps at this point it would be useful to digress and review some of those reasons.

The first and perhaps most basic reason stems from the fact that men and women are, for the most part, gregarious beings. Why do we go to conventions? Why do we have associations? How many times have you witnessed a house party ending up in one room in your house, usually the kitchen? I suspect the answer is quite simple: we learn, become inspired, and find our identity within the group. School improvement, and the type of teacher development that supports it, carries with it the same set of needs.

The need for shelter conditions under which the risks necessary for growth can occur provide another factor that underscores the importance of group process. Anyone who has tried something new, whether it is a golf swing, a new pair of skates or a new laboratory procedure, knows that at first (and sometimes for a long while), one's performance often becomes worse. For teachers attempting a new approach to teaching, this can be very unsettling. But, in a group setting the support structure provides time to hone newly forming skills and provide encouragement to help counter initial anxiety.

As I argue elsewhere, one of Lakeview's strengths was its collegial approach. That the process was characterized by constant and intense interaction among the teachers, and that the principal did not direct the project from above, but instead was part of it, was significant to its success. The ethos that emerged from this carried the staff commitment on from year to year; essentially it was a group process. The school set the tone, but the group drove the innovation.

The experience at Lakeview suggests that while the school may provide the necessary ethos to support and encourage a change, the group itself within that school offers a more viable and productive notion to account for that change. The school was not the unit of change, despite its small and closely knit staff. The unit of change became the group of teachers that formed within the school. Several difficulties emerged as I began to apply the concept of the school as a unit. I could not define its boundaries apart from the walls of the building. The more I probed the more it became apparent that one first had a full range of influences outside the school that included prior experiences, in-service workshops, parental pressures, networks, and the influences of the district and Ministry. The core group that emerged in the school which essentially drove the innovation existed within the school but did not include all its teachers despite its small size. Some teachers (as I have described elsewhere) were threatened by the process taking place in the school. They did not like the innovation; they did not like the pressures they felt to comply to it. So, where does the concept of the school which is to be the focus for change begin and end?

The point of this argument is not to suggest that efforts should not be made to improve school ethos and to move the school from being a stuck school to a moving school. However, if change is the object of the exercise, and people are being encouraged to think of productive starting points, then a far more effective unit to consider is not the school but groups within the school. However, the ethos in the school still provides the nurturing and support in which the group process can develop. Certain characteristics of the organization are critical here.

Moving the organization

To improve education is to improve the organizations in which it occurs. Although the school may not provide the most effective unit of change, none the less, it is the organizational structure where the ethos is created to support change. Some types of schools support individuals and groups to undertake changes and encourage those changes to be adopted by others in the school. Other types of schools do not.

If we think about the types of organizational and professional climates that exist in different schools, several come to mind. I am certain that each of us could produce a different set of types. In this section, I share six types of school climates based on my own observation of schools and a reading of the literature. I put these together in an attempt to explain the changes I saw, at least in part, occurring at Lakeview. The schools described below provide a continuum.

The little shop of horrors

In this school teachers report open hostility. Arguments erupt around simple things such as library schedules, where they argue long and hard about who should have the library at a specified time. Typically in such schools the principal sets down firmly what is to be taught and how. The work of individuals occurs behind closed doors. Such isolation offers protection because it avoids the criticism which may follow a visit to a classroom. At least that perception prevails. Teachers know little about each other's work; they rarely talk about it. One often finds groups of teachers banding together outside of school to provide a type of psychic support. Problem-solving does not occur in this type of school unless the principal does it. If so the decisions are normally announced, rarely discussed.

The egg carton model

This school model distinguishes itself from the little house of horrors in two ways. First, people are friendly; open hostility can rarely be observed; people stay clear of each other. When disputes occur, someone — generally the principal — typically muddles through. Secondly, teachers are recognized as competent by the principal; this lasts as long as no problems arise in the eyes of parents. Like the little house of horrors, teachers work in isolation; no one appears to have any time to worry about what anyone else does. Indifference rather than genuine respect characterizes the view of teachers toward each other. Problems at the school level are acknowledged but avoided for the most part. The principal, after all, receives extra pay to deal with such problems. The principal usually avoids issues unless they are forced upon the school.

The community model

This school provides a most friendly atmosphere. People go to great lengths to promote harmony between the staff: parties occur frequently, each Friday finds the staff at volley ball or the bar, and people show all the signs of really liking each other. The goal of the school appears to be one of creating a good atmosphere. Teachers work in isolation under the guise of professionalism. The argument seems to be that others have professional competence, so why bother them. At times, however, the friendly atmosphere brings people around to discuss their work. However, the staffroom talk centres mostly about investments, having babies, or the sport participated in at the weekend. Problems at the school level are acknowledged, but rarely solved, since isolationism tends to work against this. The staff can collectively plan a party, but rely on the principal to make a decision about the new report card.

Harmony around teaching

This school also offers a friendly atmosphere. It differs from the community model in the basis for that friendly climate. Here the discussion tends to focus around instruction. Small groups in particular, discuss their teaching, ignoring issues related to the school as an organization. Some cases show principals at odds with groups on their staff; harmony within the staff group does exist. The result produces fewer personal disputes among teachers, because of the focus on the working atmosphere. Problems that may have become big issues in the little house of horrors or the egg crate model seem easier to resolve in this setting. Problems at the school level are acknowledged and frequently discussed, but rarely solved on a school-wide basis. The principal takes action in consultation with various groups.

The good school

This model combines many features of the community model and the harmony around teaching model. It provides a friendly atmosphere and in contrast to the norms of isolation typical of other models we now find the 'norms of collegiality' that Little (1986) identified as a result of her work. As such the school takes on the trappings of a good school. This school, in a technical sense, shows all or most of the characteristics of an 'effective school' (Purkey and Smith, 1983). Problems at the school level find solution in an atmosphere of collegiality around work. Arguments and differences occur, but they are brought out into the open and discussed.

We can take on the world

This school shows all the characteristics of 'the good school', but in addition it possesses two qualities — desire and a striving for excellence. This school aims to be number one in whatever it undertakes. The staff and principal seem to be constantly striving to bring about better results, both in terms of programs and student achievement. As one superintendent put it in an interview, '. . . some schools are permeated by an attitude in which they always expect to come out on top. In basketball, for example, in a close game they always expect to win. That attitude permeates everything they do.'

The illustrations of Lakeview school and the continuum of school organizations just described illustrate several things about school change. Lakeview as an organization could only be described as a 'little shop of horrors' in the year preceding the project that I have described in this report. When teachers talk about their experience at Lakeview in the early days they speak of 'survival' and 'protecting one's flanks' rather than professional development. As one teacher remarked about the previous principal: 'You know, he treated everybody like little kindergarten students, and this type of thing. It was like a military camp.'

Military camps do not set the stage for school reform. The ethos of Lakeview changed over the four-year period so that by the end of the study the organization I observed lay somewhere between the 'good school' and 'we can take on the world' models. The organization developed an ethos in which risk taking was encouraged; trust began to develop. Within that atmosphere a capacity evolved for dealing with issues and problems related to the change occurring, as well as for monitoring and processing the information entering the school from workshops and visits to other schools. The type of school reform that I saw at Lakeview could not have occurred had that school not been functioning at these levels.

Implications for teacher development

The school improvement project at Lakeview demonstrates the close relationship between school improvement and teacher development. The teachers talked continually about their own professional growth and the changes they had made to their practice. Both occurred within the context of a school change which they also saw improving their instruction. While it may be argued that teacher development might be an end in itself, the Lakeview experience suggests that it can be enhanced if it goes on within the context of a school improvement project. Further, the change at Lakeview would hardly have occurred without ongoing teacher development. The implications here become obvious: plans for change within schools must be accompanied by plans for professional development.

One of the assumptions that appears to underpin much of the rhetoric on restructuring is that schools can be improved through some shifts in the power relationships in them. Changing a schedule or making an administrative change will supposedly change the work in the school. This study supports a different concept of that view. It suggests that for schools to become better places for children to learn, they must first become different places for teachers to teach. The extension of that argument implies that no improvement will occur in schools unless changes occur in the minds and the action of teachers. It should come as no surprise, then, that you cannot mandate the things that matter. Mandates generally do not assume any element of professional growth. They typically assume that changes external to the system can change the system. And that in turn assumes that teachers can act as conduits for other people's intentions.

Assuming the link between school improvement and teacher development, a further implication arises regarding the sort of innovations and change schools undertake. Earlier, I pointed out that the school improvement project itself, with its complexity and diversity, became a major factor supporting the change. In the literature on school improvement, it often appears that an innovation is an innovation is an innovation. This case study suggests strong links between the change being attempted and the success of that change. The implication that follows here comes more in the form of a suggestion to those who plan school improvement projects. Much more consideration needs to be given to the nature of innovations being attempted than is normally the case.

The notion of moral commitment to teaching is a matter of those values one places on the work undertaken. If one takes a technical view of teaching then it may not matter what teaching is being done. My contention is that teaching, because of its constant ongoing nature, requires an inner commitment just to keep it alive. That commitment is tantamount to a moral commitment. How is such a commitment related to change? In teaching most subjects of the curriculum, teachers must feel connected to what they do. A change in the curriculum requires a change in the deep structure of the teacher's thinking. This varies with subjects, and it varies in the way different people think about subjects. Innovations that require little in the way of deep structure for the teacher rarely produce significant changes. For example, the Hunter approach to the elements of instruction involved the technical application of ideas and approaches that were very straightforward. Their appeal rested on their simplicity. While the model may contain deeper elements, these were not examined in its presentation. Research has found few changes of any significance that have occurred as a result of teachers being exposed to that model.

Improvements in our schools rest largely on the shoulders of teachers and principals and their development as professionals. The implications here suggest that people outside the classrooms — school administrators, Ministry officials and university professors, among others — who see school improvement as something that occurs as a result of external intentions and values will find themselves frustrated and disappointed. Plans based on such intentions and values will almost surely fail. Districts can perhaps set general guidelines for reform, but the nature of that reform and the specifics of its implementation must be left to teachers.

Cats

One cat two cats three cats four cats Playing in the house. Cats are nice to every one. Cats like people. Cats like to Play with yarn My SiSter likes cats and I do to. My Brother is alergic to cats and alergic to dogs and grass too. We cant biy cats or dogs. Cats have four legs. Cats cant roar Cats can Only purr. Cats are white and black and brown

by Neeta
Grade one

Chapter 7

Factors at work

The staff at Lakeview not only achieved a significant substantive change in their approach to instruction, they also developed a significant collaborative school ethos that encouraged trust and risk-taking while allowing people to move at their own rate. They accomplished this through the efforts of a variety of players and a focus on the group as the centre for change. However, certain factors also appeared to be at work to drive that change. Those factors that stood out included peer interaction, leadership, district support, and the way they used knowledge.

Peer interaction

The literature on school improvement has identified norms of collegiality as a critical factor in the good school. Little's (1982) work in particular pointed to the importance of teachers talking to teachers about instructional matters. The situation at Lakeview supported that notion in part, but not in the way that has been assumed in the literature — an issue to which I return in the next section. Certainly, in my observations, I saw a great deal of teacher-teacher and teacher-principal talk about instructional matters. The interviews confirmed this observation. For example, when asked about factors that contributed to the change, teachers made the following comments:

> Probably talking, just very informal talking, going out for a drink. Showing the things my kids are doing in the classroom.

> And that's the peer interaction part that is so important . . . being able to hear from other people, 'Well, have you tried this, or that. And this is a good book to read', and keep up to date.

> Peer interaction to me is a key that really has to be part and parcel of whatever movement you want to make. Definitely. And with that peer interaction, I would include the workshops. . . .

While these three teachers saw the value of the peer interaction, others went on to explain just how peer interaction led to changes in their work. In the comment made near the end of the third year of the project, a teacher described how the peer interaction led to an awareness of the type of change that was needed in science:

> I think part of it has been the discussion that's been going on for the last year or so in the area of science. Knowing that science has been an area that has been very weak in the elementary system, we decided to take that (knowledge) and figure out what we can do with that, and how we could incorporate that into our language development project. Having individual teachers saying, 'Yes, that is an area that I don't feel comfortable teaching. And it's an area that I want to improve on.' It was an area that we all said, 'Hey, that's exactly what we want to do. That's what we believe in, that's where our philosophy ties in. We want hands-on, we want children to be able to manipulate their environment, and all these kinds of things. That's exactly what science is all about.'

But peer interaction, or norms of collegiality, appeared to be only part of the picture. What occurred in Lakeview went beyond talk and collaboration to include support for risk-taking, and in some cases the freedom not to collaborate. Much of the literature on collaboration (Little, 1986) fails to address the issue of trust, in people having the courage and trust to talk about difficult dilemmas and dig beneath surface congeniality to look at similarities and differences in beliefs and values. A level of trust and appreciation needs to be established that allows outsiders to feel equally respected even though they are not involved in the change to the same degree.

The group atmosphere at Lakeview produced an ethos which allowed for risk-taking and also for people to go slower at particular points. This notion can be inferred from the following two comments.

> And the fact that people on this staff are very cooperative people helped. They seem to think nothing of helping each other to develop unit plans and sharing materials back and forth, and that sort of thing, so that has helped a lot too. No one has had to work in isolation. If they run into a problem, there is always somebody else that they could go to.

> But when someone has dealt with a program for a long time and has ownership, it's really hard to change that . . . to leave the security of their programs that were running very well. And I was a real risk person for people on staff. Not everyone was at the same level in terms of how much they wanted to change in that direction. And so people were really nervous about family grouping in grades 3, 4 and 5. They were also concerned about report cards, and how would they tell parents. So it was

> quite a heated debate. . . . And we actually had to come back as a staff again to talk about that issue.

The significant point here is that while some confrontation occurred, they managed to come back to the issue in a way that allowed them to move ahead, and group support was highly instrumental in promoting that ability to deal with issues. Other things also began to work on the staff such as classroom intervisits. As one teacher noted:

> I am sure if I went to B_, or anyone else on staff who has really worked with the writing process a lot more than I have, if I said, 'B_ would you come in and do a lesson for me?', she would definitely come in and do it. People are that willing to help each other.

The group gave individual teachers a feeling of empowerment. They saw their role in the innovation as central to what was taking place and developed a strong sense of ownership over the change.

Leadership

Leadership in innovations such as Lakeview's also proved to be an essential component of the change. I found leadership at many different levels: the school superintendent was flexible and accommodating; the consultants provided support and assistance; and the principal proved to be an invaluable friend and ally. While much has been written and said about the role of the principal, we often forget or overlook the role played by teacher-leaders within the group.

At Lakeview a small cadre of teachers undertook strong leadership roles and, in their own minds at least, acted on a par and proved just as effective as the principal himself. In fact, it was he who encouraged this attitude. Their sense of ownership of the reforms taking place instilled in these people a heady sense of authority and pride. They felt they could take on the world and were quite prepared to do just that. Perhaps because they had invested so much of themselves in the innovation, their drive for success assumed many of the attributes of a steamroller on a downhill course. This is not to suggest that they crushed everything in their path, but rather that their enthusiasm gathered momentum and grew in force as the innovation unfolded. As stated by one of the teachers I interviewed, the school became 'a whirlwind of ideas'.

As can be seen in the case of Sigrund or Bill, not everyone was swept along with the reforms. However, teachers such as Sigrund were rare at Lakeview. Those involved in what I have come to call 'the core group' all went on to enhance their professional lives in a variety of ways. One became a teacher/learning assistant for the district; another, with a renewed sense of purpose, moved on to a new school; and yet another returned to university. It was their intense desire to share what they had learned that characterized them as a group.

They went to a conference at Coeur d'Alene, described by all as a marvellous learning experience, and followed that experience with a succession of speaking engagements throughout their district. As long as the candle of reform was burning, they were eager to hold it aloft for all to see. Perhaps it would not be too great an exaggeration to say that they were shot through with a rarefied sense of mission; that they burned with the zeal of the convert.

However, each of these teachers approached the innovation on his or her own terms; some were eager to try something — anything; others adopted a more tentative approach — two steps forward, one back; and still others at first eschewed any contact with what was taking place and adopted instead a 'show-me' attitude. It was only with time and some initial success that the groundswell of enthusiasm started to build. And, when it did, it proved infectious. Staff members who had been sitting on the sidelines could see the effect of the change all around them and most of them became eager to share in what was taking place. Teachers working with each other became the norm and a strong sense of collaboration was born.

Whether through good luck or good management, teacher/leaders at Lakeview managed to avoid many of the pitfalls mentioned by Fullan and Hargreaves (1991) who said that if teacher/leaders are to improve the chances for establishing a collaborative enterprise that will lead to school improvement,

> It will require confronting norms of isolation, while at the same time avoiding the imposition of solutions, premature forging of consensus, and failure to take into account the personal situations of those with whom the teacher-leaders wish to work (pp. 139–140).

Knowledge utilization

The importance of applying what we know to the resolution of social problems has long been a concern to social scientists (Love, 1975). In fact, Glasser (1975, cited in Love) once remarked that civilization was a race between catastrophe and knowledge utilization. As Love puts it,

> . . . most would agree that knowledge utilization, transferring it to a setting where it can be applied, and using that knowledge in some form is a worthwhile aim for social scientists concerned with improving education (p. 337).

Despite such interest in knowledge utilization in some areas of the social sciences, others, often those directly concerned with school improvement, apparently do not consider knowledge, and the way teachers use it to inform their work, as an important factor in change in schools. In identifying the interactive factors affecting implementation, Fullan (1991) does not mention knowledge use. Those in the effective schools' movement, who have for the last several decades been in the business of identifying the characteristics of effective schools, typically do not identify knowledge and the ways teachers use it as a factor either in creating or defining the effective school.

For the teachers and principal at Lakeview, the use of knowledge and information about teaching and related areas of education became an important factor in supporting and directing the change. Before discussing how that occurred, however, I should like to provide a context for that discussion by looking at some of the ways that knowledge utilization has been discussed in the literature over the years. Two approaches, among others, stand out which set out alternative ways of looking at what constitutes knowledge and how it should be used to improve education.[1]

Two views of knowledge and its use

The concept of knowledge utilization has traditionally been seen from a 'producer/user' perspective. 'Producers' develop knowledge and 'users' implement it. This concept has had a long-standing tradition in the social sciences beginning with studies in rural sociology of how people adopted innovations such as radio and television. A frequently cited study in the United States conducted by House (1974) looked at the pattern of adoption among educators. He found that communication links were critical to the adoption of a particular innovation. Such work took a technical view of the adoption; certain factors were associated with adoption and certain people adopted innovations sooner than others. It was that tradition which underpinned the development of curriculum materials in the 1960s. Experts — seeking to provide curriculum materials that could be readily implemented by teachers — conducted extensive research and development followed by field-testing. Implementation then became a process of putting into practice the ideas and activities in those curriculum packages that would change teaching practice and thereby improve it in desired ways. Teachers were, in effect, conduits through which ideas developed outside the classroom would be put into effect inside the classroom.

The experience of that period showed that despite the elegance of the curriculum design, and despite the enthusiasm of those who had been involved in its development, the much heralded curriculum materials that were radically to reform the schools stopped at the classroom door. What appeared to have gone wrong here was that those involved attempted to treat what was a very personal and psychological issue as a technical one. Teachers could take the ideas and activities from workshop presentations and apply them in a technical sense in their classrooms, but the way in which they were applied did not necessarily reflect what those ideas and activities meant in a deeper sense. In short, the surface structure could be implemented, but the underlying meaning could not. Moreover, the knowledge about teaching that came as part of these curriculum projects, often so painstakingly put together by outsiders, frequently bore little relevance to the day-to-day work of teachers. Despite what has now come to be seen as a major failure of the producer/user concept of knowledge use in education, it still underpins much of the reform agenda for our schools.

In the last few years we have seen the emergence of a different sense of how knowledge is used by those in schools. Knowledge has expanded from being a set of scientific facts to include the idea of knowledge as craft, based on the experience of those engaged in practice (Louis, 1981), or personal practical knowledge (Elbaz, 1983), or pedagogical knowledge (Shulman, 1991). Different shades of expression attend each of these understandings, but generally they refer to the type of knowledge that comes from experience and that which comes from having constructed one's own meaning of the events and context in which one's work is done (Grimmet and MacKinnon, 1992). This view of knowledge brings the producer and the user together. The person now producing the knowledge is also the one who puts it into practice because in effect it becomes part of one's practice as it is developed.

Taking an exclusive view of either paradigm will probably lead those in schools down separate garden paths. A total reliance on craft knowledge denies teachers the richness of research carried out by others. And it seems absurd to suggest that each teacher must rediscover the world of teaching again and again. On the other hand, we have much experience to suggest that knowledge generated by outsiders will rarely be applied by teachers in any direct way or in any situation that really matters. Yet proponents of so-called scientific knowledge about teaching frequently discount the craft knowledge of teachers. As Love puts it, 'most writers who concern themselves with the theme of knowledge transfer and utilization are not thinking of ordinary knowledge . . .' (340). By ordinary knowledge, he was referring to Lindblom and Cohen's (1979, cited in Love) notion of that type of knowledge not produced by social inquiry but which stems from common sense or thoughtful speculation and analysis. The road to better schools may well rest on our understanding of how best to combine decades of knowledge based on research with the knowledge that teachers develop about teaching.

How the teachers used knowledge at Lakeview

Knowledge utilization played a significant role, not only in shaping and defining the innovation at Lakeview, but also in driving its implementation. The manner in which the teachers and principal used knowledge does not completely support either traditional concepts of transfer and utilization of knowledge, or the more recent notions of personal practical knowledge. In some instances information was used in fairly direct ways. On other occasions, its impact was quite unpredictable. Before discussing the use made of the information at Lakeview, I describe how knowledge about teaching and education in general became part of the ongoing culture at Lakeview.

Early in the first year Charlie started a practice that was to encourage reading by the staff. Barbara describes how she saw the practice introduced within the context of discussing language arts:

> That first year, when we talked about language arts Charlie started getting references for us. He started doing things like photocopying articles that related to our topic. They would arrive in our boxes so people who were interested could read them and discuss them at our next meeting.

That practice was later adopted by the district through the distribution of the table of contents of journals from which teachers could order articles they wished to read.

Reading provided one source of information. Others came through the workshops at the district and school level which became an ongoing part of the school activity during the first three years. Figures 2, 3 and 4 identify some of the workshop activities in the school over the period of study and some of the conferences teachers attended. The staff were virtually inundated with workshop activity, some closely related to what they were doing, others of a more esoteric nature. A significant number of staff maintained contact with people outside the district through various linkages. The principal sought to maintain contact with the universities whenever he could and many teachers attended university courses as part of their degree completion. The principal and staff made visits to other schools who were working with 'The Young Writers Project'. In addition, the teachers had now begun to set up networks that provided additional sources of information. I saw much evidence during my visits to the school that the changes occurring at Lakeview were occurring in an information-rich environment. In fact, one of the factors that drove the innovation at Lakeview was the staff's commitment to knowledge and the use they made of it.

The role played by knowledge

The shape of the change at Lakeview was directed by the use of information which came in a variety of forms. Teachers talked about several benefits of such information. Regarding reading, they cited three benefits: legitimization of change (whether that change was already initiated or being thought about); stimulation to discussion and collaboration with peers; and, as a vehicle for producing new ideas.

Legitimization. One of the books frequently mentioned as important by staff was Illich's (1971) *Deschooling society*. During a meeting with teachers, I asked what a book of this nature could possibly do for teachers engaged in changing their language arts program. The answer I received suggested that Illich's book had legitimized their challenge of the system. In short, teachers who had concerns about the system now saw their concerns echoed in print, and therefore, it became legitimate to continue steps to change the system in which they were working. Barbara identified this quotation from Illich's book:

> Schools are designed on the assumption that there is a secret to everything in life; that the quality of life depends on knowing the secret; that

> secrets can be known only in orderly successions; and that only teachers can properly reveal those secrets.

In response to this quotation Barb made this comment:

> Writing allows teachers as facilitators to guide students toward finding and sharing their own secrets to allow them to become confident, autonomous learners and teachers. Teachers too need to be learners. We need to listen and observe carefully as students discover and respond to and celebrate their learning. They have lots to teach us. The teachers talk about the staffroom as being a forum where they discuss things they've read.

Schon's (1983) *Reflective Practitioner* produced a similar type of legitimization. In it they saw permission to reflect and discuss their experience.

Knowledge as support for collaboration. In a talk given to a group of primary teachers in Britain, David Hawkins used the title *I, Thou, It* to describe the essentials of a useful and productive relationship. Drawing on philosophical traditions, he argued that people do not amount to much except in terms of their involvement in what is outside and beyond them. He further contends that we cannot gain competence and knowledge except through communication with others. 'Without a Thou, there is no I evolving. Without an It there is no content for the context. . . .' (p. 47). Although Hawkins was referring to children and their relation to teachers, his notion has currency for the way knowledge became a part of the ongoing relationship and communication among teachers at Lakeview. The collaborative relationship, which I describe elsewhere, that developed on the staff produced what might be termed the 'I' and the 'Thou'. While communication and interaction were essential to the change, particularly in the early stages, it is unimaginable how they in themselves would have produced any important changes in the school without the content produced through the reading and workshop activity. These activities produced the 'It' in the three way relationship. The information produced a means by which teachers and principal could move beyond themselves to explore other areas. It produced frames within which they could think about and re-evaluate their practice. The knowledge flow provided a constant source for discussion among the staff. Each new article, book or workshop became the substance for further interaction, particularly by those teachers who had become part of the core group.

The processing of information was not necessarily smooth; teachers struggled to understand and deal with new ideas and techniques. One teacher describes her initial confusion like this:

> (A workshop leader) spoke to us, in terms of some of the concepts . . . I didn't really have a background or a real idea of where she was coming from at the time. So when she left I was sort of still in a state of confusion.

> And at that point she spoke of a one-year unit, a one-year theme, and take off from that into other (ones). And she was talking about the whole unit going from a January to June or something. I can't recall exactly when. Anyway, it was at that point that I was thinking, you know, this is just ridiculous. I mean, how can you do that with that group of kids with one general topic area.

What did appear to happen as a result of such workshops was further discussion, reflection and interaction. In such a setting, any incoming information, whether useful or not, provided a basis for discussion. A type of critical adaptation of ideas into the framework of the change that was occurring appeared to take place. That adaptation developed partly through talk and partly through trial and error.

As a source of new ideas. Elsewhere we have talked about the importance of teachers finding practices that would improve their teaching. The reading and workshops in which they were engaged served the important function of giving teachers information they could use in their classrooms. In some cases it was the much-maligned workshop that stimulated a teacher to revise her program. In another case it was a workshop leader's demonstration that a teacher applied directly. One teacher described how reading affected her work in the school in this way:

> (in response to how the particular change came about) . . . I think mostly through my own professional reading and from observing different things that are happening. I have to use Barb as my counterpart here, because I learned a lot from her. But I would say mostly, I have always been interested in actively pursuing new ideas and new strategies and continually doing a lot of professional reading. And so I would always be changing or modifying whatever I was doing, trying to find a better way. I don't think that I am ever perfect and there is certainly a lot more room for improvement.

The interaction between her reading and her contact with other teachers becomes evident in this teacher's comments. And while the interviews indicated that not all teachers read, that lack seemed unimportant because of the intense interaction that continually took place between staff; what one teacher read would generally affect the others.

The experience at Lakeview illustrated the importance of knowledge, primarily about the innovation itself, but increasingly about the change process. Knowledge performed several functions in the school, in legitimizing, in providing a type of support for collaboration, and of course in establishing signposts regarding innovative practice. Knowledge came from various sources but reading proved the central one. The use made by the teachers did not follow the traditional view of knowledge utilization, nor did it necessarily reject it in the way that many proponents of craft knowledge suggest it might.

Metaphorically, the knowledge that came into the school, in whatever form, provided an agenda for the ongoing collaborative effort that typified those first years of change at Lakeview. The chairperson for that collaboration was often the principal, but not necessarily so. That role, as we will see elsewhere, shifted from person to person.

The findings from this study are discrepant from those of many researchers who downplay the role of knowledge and information in a school, perhaps because many schools pay little heed to articles and journals that exist. Perhaps researchers overlook the importance of knowledge because of the unpredictability of whether and what teachers and principals read. Whatever the reason, where researchers fail to study and examine the knowledge teachers draw upon, they do so in peril of missing an important factor in contributing to school change.

Linkages

In an earlier section, I argued that the school did not represent an appropriate unit for understanding how change occurs. Some of the factors limiting that notion are the linkages and influences outside the school. The lives of the students and staff extend beyond the boundaries of the school to such an extent that it was frequently hard to know where the school stopped and where outside influences began. Maxine Greene (1985) uses the term 'deep structure' to refer to an entire constellation of factors outside the school, reflected in the culture of society, which essentially determines what goes on there. I saw considerable evidence of that at Lakeview.

Virtually all teachers enjoyed connections outside the school either in the form of family or professional networks. As I have described throughout this volume, parents and others played a significant role in the school. But the one area that perhaps influenced the teachers and principal most throughout the project was the district and the administrators who occupied positions there.

Note

1 The concept of knowledge utilization is far too complex to be explained in this section. What follows are some of the more salient issues surrounding the concept and how it has been used in the literature. For a more extensive treatment the reader should consult the reviews by Love (1985) and Stanfield (1985).

Book cover by grade 6 student
THE Unexpected DOORWAY
BY DONNA

Chapter 8

Reflections and implications

The case of Lakeview provides an example of change from within which saw the school move from a traditional language arts program to an approach which some call 'whole language'. However, under that umbrella, a number of other changes surfaced, including the writing process, learning skills from context, the integration of subjects around themes, and collapsing of grades. The changes were accomplished not by one innovation but by several. Somewhat paradoxically perhaps, the sheer complexity of the change appeared to act as a facilitator since it allowed teachers to enter the change process in different ways and at different stages. The way in which teachers viewed the subject encouraged learning and experimentation among the staff. The school moved from what I have described as a 'little house of horrors' to one that assumed many of the attributes of a 'good' school.

Constraints on change

Certain factors, however, did not make the development of the project at Lakeview easy. The prevailing norms of schooling within the district and the province worried Lakeview's teachers and principal alike, who expressed doubts particularly in the early stages about whether their project was educationally sound. Seeing that other schools were achieving good results through different means contributed to the intensity and frequency of their collective self-criticism and analysis of their project. While this intense and ongoing reflection on the part of the critical mass of teachers at Lakeview has been cited as one of its strengths, it also drained vital energy. One teacher describes how she was not sorry to be leaving:

> When I think back on being in this school . . . I was very happy to be leaving Lakeview, just because I felt really worn out. I think the teachers here, they put so much out, and where do you get it back? Because it's really hard to get all that energy back. And I wonder where it's going to

> lead to. Where does it all end? Are people going to have nervous breakdowns, or are they going to find a point where they've just got to stop and take a break from all the workshops, and all the committees, and all this, and all that. I think it's great — it keeps you going in some ways. It can also wear you down pretty fast.

Staff turnover presented another problem. During the three years of the study the teacher turnover at Lakeview reached 33 per cent, low for the history of that particular school. This constant turnover required time for the socialization of new teachers to the ethos of the school, and to their acquaintance with the project which led to considerable discussion at staff meetings. This turnover is an unfortunate characteristic of the profession in general; it may also be ultimately detrimental to any consistent forward movement in education.

The continual change of curriculum by the Ministry, the mandated changes as a result of another Royal Commission, the frequent introduction of new initiatives and priorities by a district, the exposure through reading, courses and workshops to new and interesting teaching strategies, while playing a part in the attempts to improve education, also contribute to its fragmentation. For example, the introduction of a system of evaluation for principals could easily detract from a 'risky' school innovation project such as the one at Lakeview. Or, had the district office personnel in Centreville seemed to be at odds with Lakeview's focus on only one school goal, we'd have seen another example of how energy is bled away from attempts at innovation. One teacher describes the effort involved in establishing the project's initial focus as follows:

> And once we came up with that everyone of us was interested in language arts. And at that time I think, the district wanted us to come up with four goals, or something. I can't remember. And we fought . . . as a group trying to come up with a way that we could convince this district to allow us to have one goal, because that was a huge, huge goal. And (the principal) was able to do that, too. I mean, he was really . . . supportive.

The importance of Lakeview's experience comes not from the particular change that occurred there, but rather from the process of that change, and this close portrait of the school can tell us more perhaps about the individual components of the change than about that larger generic entity which we have come to call 'school improvement'. Consequently, I have described portions of the story of this school and drawn out what can be learned about school change when we look at the individual building blocks which make up the larger whole. In looking back across the preceding chapters, two thoughts occur: one involves some general reflections about the literature, and the other, some specific implications for schools who wish to undertake the type of change that occurred at Lakeview.[1]

The literature on school change

The following argument may, at first blush, be of only marginal interest to many teachers since it represents my question about educational research as it is presently conducted and reported. Yet, for those growing numbers of teachers who use the research base as an avenue to reform, they would be well advised to consider, as I do in the next few pages, casting a critical eye on much that appears in the literature. Simply because some distant 'expert' has made a pronouncement about what ails the school, teachers need not accept this verdict as gospel. And, when teachers are further told how these ailments can be remedied, they need to look carefully at the prescribed medicine to see whether the 'one-size fits all' solution is appropriate in their particular case. *Caveat emptor* should be the rule where educational research in particular, and social science research in general, is considered. The same critical eye should be cast on the proposed solutions that emanate from that research.

As I argued earlier, the literature on school change can be characterized in different ways. First, it aims at robust generalizations about schools and how they change that sidestep or ignore what teachers actually teach or the work they do. Reynolds (1992) points out in her review of literature on the beginning teacher, that 'research on teacher effectiveness had largely been the province of researchers not teachers. Therefore, what is known is not always of great use to teachers' (p. 1). In this connection, those who write about school change are fond of statements such as, 'schools should stick to their knitting' without giving any acknowledgment as to just what this 'knitting' consists of or how it affects the 'knitter'. Second, the literature, once it has acknowledged the importance of culture, typically takes a technical view of school change. A simple list or set of guidelines appears to be all that is necessary for significant change to take place, according to many researchers. Third, although acknowledging the importance of the teacher in change, most who write about school improvement then take a top-down approach to implementing it. Fourth, much of the literature presents a view of school change that appears daunting and almost impossible to achieve. Rather than approaching change in a step-by-step fashion, this view prefers to dump the whole package as some sort of global whole. Fifth, too much is claimed from too little research, and the research itself is often of dubious quality. One gains the impression that publication is the aim of the researcher rather than a firm understanding of what takes place in schools and how those practices can be improved.

This case is too modest in its undertaking to challenge many of the results coming out of this literature. However, it does raise a number of questions about many previous findings as well as raising the general question about the usefulness of many of the current lines of research supposedly designed to assist school change.

Aiming at the wrong targets

When teachers undertake to change their teaching or when researchers identify an area for inquiry, they must begin somewhere. Typically people begin from the perspective of their own values, need states and conceptual trappings. The school effectiveness people, for example, view the world in quantitative terms; they value broad robust generalizations that are linked to student achievement. The school improvement people, on the other hand, view the world from a cultural and organizational perspective and seek to identify those characteristics typical of a healthy school organization. It is not difficult to understand why teachers may not be interested in either view, particularly at the early stages of undertaking change in their practice. Teachers at the beginning stages are more likely to be interested in the teaching and learning activities in subjects they teach and how they perceive changes in teaching those subjects can improve student learning.

The case described at Lakeview illustrates the concern of teachers for the centrality of subject matter as they begin to think about change in teaching. When they consulted research, they turned to that research which spoke to improvement in teaching in particular subject areas. The lack of progress in school reform may well be the result of researchers focusing on the wrong targets. In the past we have over-emphasized the generic nature of school change and de-emphasized the work in which teachers engage on a day-to-day basis.

The experience at Lakeview illustrates that most of the anxiety about changes in the school occurred around subject matter areas and how best to improve them. Only at later stages in the change did teachers' thinking begin to expand to encompass the more general aspects of the innovation. The implication for those in schools who are interested in changing their teaching is to begin with what seems problematic in their own practice, place that against a notion of improved practice, and begin wrestling with how best to bring their practice closer to the ideal.

Another example of misplaced efforts, or focusing on the wrong target, involves the obsession on the part of some researchers regarding the school as the focus of change. This tenet — unchallenged by most — appears to be accepted almost as an item of faith. The notion of the focus on the school, however, is as problematic to those interested in reform as it is unsubstantiated. Teachers wishing to make changes to their own practice, have no access to the school as a unit around which to begin their planning. Principals perhaps have some leverage, but even there it remains doubtful that much can be done in the name of real school change apart from improving the school ethos through working toward some general notion of a 'good' school. But these efforts should not be confused with improvement where it really counts — in the instructional practice in classrooms. By targeting on the school, researchers and policymakers have not only picked the wrong target, they have miscalculated the difficulties involved in bringing about change at the organizational level. The arguments about the lack of school reform, or continuous reforming which leads to nothing, could be a function of this faulty focus.

Based on the experience of this case study, groups within the school appear to be a more appropriate unit upon which to focus. But, because of its unpredictability and unmanageability by outsiders, this approach has less appeal to researchers and policymakers than it does to those in schools. Group formation cannot be predicted in advance, nor can one always be assured that groups take on changes to their practice that meet the approval of outsiders. The focus on the school will probably continue among researchers and policymakers if for no other reason than that it will almost surely retain the status quo. This rather outrageous statement rests on the perverse theory that policymakers and researchers have much to gain by having schools remain static. The cynic's view suggests that without such a constant void to be filled, these people would be out of work. If ever schools took on the job of reform (and indeed if they were ever allowed to by outsiders) then many of the policymakers and reformers might well lose their *raison d'être*. Schools have long been made the scapegoats for society's ills. Now it appears that these scapegoats must also take on the guilt associated with lack of reform in our educational system. Meanwhile, policymakers and researchers continue to focus on non-productive lines of inquiry and policy, preferring to pursue their own targets of interest whether or not these bear any relation to teachers' needs or what actually takes place in the classrooms.

The technical pitfall

The merit of technique is of long standing. Without the techniques of teaching, for example, it is hard to imagine teachers getting through a school day. The technical side of any enterprise holds certain charms for many, for instance, the technical side of most sports' activities is pursued with vigour by most successful sports teams. But, in assuming that the techniques of planning and management can, in and of themselves, adequately provide for successful change within a school, is to misunderstand the human element that ultimately drives successful schools and changes in practice.

Earlier we saw how the technical approach to school reform in the 1960s failed at the school level. At that time the notion of planning and front-end loading in the curriculum was to reform the schools. It did not. Despite that experience, policymakers and researchers have continued to craft schemes that take on a highly technical approach to school improvement. One such example is the notion of clinical supervision which has been seen as a generic means to improve the work of teachers. It involves a series of strategies aimed at helping teachers and principals to provide other teachers with feedback about their work. In the province of British Columbia many districts provided clinical supervision workshops for teachers for many years. Yet there appears to be very little to indicate that such workshops have done anything to improve the work of teachers.[2] What appears to be lacking in schemes such as these are the substantive elements about what the clinical supervision is intended to change or improve.[3]

Hargreaves and Dawe (1990) coined the phrase 'contrived collegiality' to describe a pitfall for educational change that parallels what I have described under clinical supervision. They argue that the notion of collegiality has been seized upon by policymakers in ways that turn it into a contrived mechanical process likely to have little impact on the work of teachers.

The case experience of Lakeview suggests that while the technical side may be important, the personal and moral commitment to change are far more important to teachers and principals than are the technical aspects of change. While I do not wish to underestimate the value of technique, technique alone cannot provide the route to school reform.

The persistence of the top-down approach to change

As school reformers we have come a long way since the period of curriculum reform which saw attempts to change teaching fail rather dismally. Most people in the field now acknowledge that those in schools must be central to any effort at reform. However, once those acknowledgments are made, the plans that emerge from policymakers and reformers leave one with the uneasy feeling that perhaps we have not learned as much as we think we have. It is as though we have learned to say the words but have not really internalized the concept. In the province of British Columbia, where Lakeview is located, the Ministry has now mandated a major reform based on a constructivist approach to learning. But the teachers themselves apparently are not to be allowed their own interpretation of that reform. Rather, they are to accept the mandate and proceed with its implementation without giving it the benefit of their own understanding. So, while one might agree with the general lines of reform, it is difficult to agree with the manner in which it is now being implemented. One must ask in this regard, 'can you have one type of reform and another type of implementation for that reform.' Can you ask teachers to take a constructivist view of teaching, yet implement a program based on that notion in a top-down fashion.

Change within the school

What then can we learn from the experience at Lakeview which might provide insight for other schools interested in the type of reform undertaken there? Four themes thread their way through the case that help answer that question. These involve the interconnectedness of factors working to support the change, the importance of the context of the change, the centrality of substance in the change process, and the need for school staff to construct their own meaning of the change.

The interconnectedness of change within a school

In the previous chapters I discussed a number of factors which appeared to be working at Lakeview to support the change taking place. These included such things as peer interaction, the use of knowledge, breaking down isolationism, the power of group process, moving the organization, and the roles of outside groups.

By singling out these areas for discussion, there is the danger that one begins to think of them in isolation. Nothing could be further from what actually occurred. These factors merely represent an imposed framework that I applied to better understand what went on in the school. These factors do not exist in isolation; rather, they are inter-dependent and together contribute to an overall concept of change within a school. The focus on the subject matter of teaching could only occur because other factors were in place. Among them was the supportive atmosphere of the district and the availability of ideas that came through workshop presenters.

The sum total of these factors produced something of a special circumstance, or holistic set, which supported the change. It is difficult to imagine the change occurring as it did if any of these factors had not been supportive of the change. For example, a different kind of principal may not have had the same type of success, while a district approach that attempted some type of supportive enforcement[4] would probably have destroyed the delicate ethos developing in the school.

The message to those in schools who wish to bring about reform is simple — the more the factors working to support change, the more likely the change is to occur.

The importance of context

The special set of circumstances at Lakeview, just summarized, point to the importance of the context in which changes in schools occur. The situation at Lakeview was unique, but then so is the situation in most schools. The conditions within the province at that time were of a very special nature. Since the Ministry was in the middle of a Royal Commission, a rather benign air prevailed; for a short period of time few mandates were being imposed as the Ministry struggled to decide on the direction the province would take over the next few years. That hiatus produced the opportunity to at least contemplate change, while the arrival of a new, young staff (created in part by the rapid turnover of staff in the district) who were eager for change provided an additional factor.

The elements of this context might now appear to be rather obvious factors promoting change, but even after five years of visiting the school, it none the less remains deceptive. On the surface Lakeview looks like every other school. One or two visits would not produce data to support or explain all the unique features that occurred there. It was only through repeated visits and interviews and a broader look at what was occurring outside the school that this picture could be constructed. Yet much is written and generalizations are often made based on sporadic or single school visits. My analysis of the change at Lakeview strongly questions this approach to understanding change within schools and posits that a large part of what contributes to change is determined by its own unique factors and context. This uniqueness of context places our penchant for generalization in question.

The message for those within schools is not comforting. It suggests that the experience of others cannot easily be applied to individual cases. Rather, the experience of outsiders must be shaped according to one's own circumstance and context. However, this is not to suggest that, in an effort to bring about change, school staffs cannot be encouraged to tailor this and other case studies to suit their own context. We can learn from others, but the application has to be tempered by circumstance.

The substance of change

The experience gained from this case supports the notion, all too often forgotten in most of the school improvement literature, of the importance of substance. One can be left to think that change and school reform are ends in themselves. The over-emphasis on the processes and sociology of change can lead one away from the substance which is both the subject of change and the basis within which principals and teachers shape their vision to drive reform. The substance of the change acted itself out in both ways at Lakeview. First, the subject of the change — language arts — provided most of the focus of attention for the teachers, particularly at the early stages. This issue has been dealt with in previous chapters. But the substantive side of the change could also be found through conversations with the principal and staff as they talked about their arguments behind the innovations that led to the changes in the school. Charlie often talked about a moral commitment, both in conversations with me and in his discussions with students. He clearly stood for something, and he read widely to understand the deeper structure of his beliefs. For Charlie, professionalism brought with it a commitment to reform.

Contrasting perspectives

The question of change among those in school who must bear the brunt of it — teachers, students and principals — has typically been treated from two contrasting perspectives. The political systems approach shown in the second column of Figure 7 rests on the notion of power. Such an approach to change has been around for many years. In 1972 Baldridge described a political systems approach to change; Chin and Benne (1976) described it in terms of a 'power coercive' approach.

Another perspective sees change from a human relations, or social psychology point of view which focuses on the individual and peer group relations. The two perspectives are contrasted in Figure 7. I have drawn on the work of Baldridge (1972) and Chin and Benne (1976) to contrast these two general perspectives.

These two perspectives surfaced in the earlier chapters when I set out the context for this case. They reflect the dilemma that policymakers and those within

Figure 7: Contrasting perspectives on change in social systems (schools)

Perspective	*Human Relations (Baldridge) Normative re-educative (Chinn and Benne)*	*Political systems (Baldridge) Power Coverance (Chinn and Benne)*
Basics	• Social psychological • Focus on individual and peer groups • Emphasis on normative culture	• Political systems which emphasize power • Organization oriented • Use of legislative mandates
Assumptions	• Persons are inherently active in pursuit of impulse and needs satisfaction • Individuals and groups will work to change themselves • Person and group as basic unit of change	• Power elite governs most decisions • Economic and social power are needed to achieve social change • Organization is the basic unit of change
Strategies	• Support and encourage groups to undertake change • Adapt the organization to the needs of the individual and the group • Reduce conflict through human relation training	• Identify policy initiatives • Use rewards, support and sanctions to encourage individuals and groups to change • Accept conflict as natural
Knowledge	• Knowledge is normally produced by outsiders • People in schools are rational and will adopt a proposed change once its wisdom is revealed to them	• Knowledge comes from different sources both inside and outside • People in schools construct their own meaning
Weaknesses	• Transfer from individual and groups to larger system problematic	• Lack of ownership on the part of individuals

schools have faced historically and still face today when dealing with school reform. On the one hand, we see the legitimate desire of policymakers, researchers and others outside to encourage school reform and influence its direction. Reform becomes an organizational problem awaiting the correct mix of interventions, support and strategies for motivating those within schools to bring about desired changes that outsiders most want to see. Terms such as 'supportive-enforcement' (Coleman, 1990) implies that policymakers should and can seek the correct mix of external pressure and support that will accomplish that reform. Most of the pressure coming from the press for school reform and the mandates we see increasingly fall within this category.

But this case has illustrated an approach to change that falls almost completely within the human relations perspective. Some expectation did exist at the district level, but this was not of particular consequence to the members of the staff. The driving force behind this change were the need states of the individuals and the group within the school. The unit of change became the group not the organization at either the school or district level. What those organizations did was to establish a type of ethos that supported and encouraged individuals and groups. As I discussed earlier, knowledge is a type of trade-off between what outsiders brought in and what teachers developed for themselves.

On the other hand, to suggest that Lakeview was an island unto itself which ignored the outside world could not be further from the truth. There was much more influence from the outside than may have appeared. Perhaps the key was that much of that influence was seen as both benign and supportive. The teachers and principal were allowed to develop their own strategies for changing their practice. They did not have to attend to outsiders monitoring what they did. The case illustrates what can happen when a highly motivated staff is left alone.

The daunting web of findings

One teacher, when asked to comment on Fullan's, *The New Meaning of Educational Change*, said that reading the book produced a set of conditions in her mind which were so daunting that change within a school seemed absolutely hopeless. To have all the ingredients for change in place at one time and in one location, would be, she felt, impossible to achieve.

Her comment raises the issue of what the vast literature on school change actually means in practice. In working through the literature on the effective school the reader is faced with several 'shoulds' if an effective school is to be achieved. These range from having a principal who has a feel for leadership (a rare occurrence in itself) to placing an emphasis on curriculum and instruction. The school improvement literature makes a similar set of claims about what the school ought to be about. Having watched a group of teachers move through a significant change in their school without having much knowledge of this literature, I have some concerns about this fabric of cloth that has been woven so carefully by researchers.

First, the research base does not appear to be sufficiently secure to make the many applications it does to the complicated social system of the school. For example, school effectiveness is at best a set of relationships between conditions and school outcomes. No one really knows which is causing which. Yet the interpretation is always causal in the direction that suits the researcher. For example, those who report the school effectiveness findings often report that high achievement occurs in schools where teachers have high expectations. But this begs the question of whether teachers have high expectations in schools where students perform well. I submit that we really do not know. But the literature clearly suggests that high academic expectations produce high achievement among students. Common sense may tell us that such would be the case; that the self-fulfilling prophecy — where teachers expect students to do well, they will — would indeed apply. And no doubt at times it would. My objection stems from applying this solution too simplistically. If high expectations were all that was necessary to reform schools, no one would be writing or even considering, questions such as, 'why can't Johnny read?' And, yet, increasingly we are being filled with alarm regarding just such questions — all of them based on the perceived failure of the public school system.

Yet, while the public school system supposedly falters all around us, educational researchers bubble merrily along always at the ready with one more pronouncement about what ails schooling. Many of the central tenets of their research — now dominating the literature on school reform — come in the form of slogans, rather than as statements based on solid evidence. Pronouncements such as 'ready, fire, aim' or, 'a feel for leadership,' have a *fait accompli* gloss that seems outside any research considerations, yet are often confused with having the support of research. Somehow we have come to accept these words from on high with an almost complete lack of critical analysis. For too long, too many have seen this research as being largely unproblematic when, in fact, it is fraught with problems.

The limits to generic processes

Those who write about school change usually speak in general terms about change strategies. The literature on school effectiveness has made some robust generalizations about the conditions in schools related to high achievement on standardized tests. The school improvement literature has focused on the general conditions that comprise a healthy school. The common element among these bodies of literature and other areas lies in the generic nature of their focus and discussion. Even those who speak about the teacher's personal practical knowledge tend to do so in general terms that cut across subject areas and the work people do in schools.

This tendency of thinking in generic terms about teaching and schools received a major boost in the work of Gagne (1964) who, in developing a new science program for teaching elementary science, identified what he termed 'process in science' that cut across subject matter. The appeal is obvious — and one reason such solutions find a willing audience: if we can find principles that cut across events and subject matter, then surely that is more efficient than looking at each situation individually.

The data from this study clearly demonstrated that the subject mattered in this case. What appeared as change and improvement in this school can best be understood in the context of the subject matter in which that change occurred. Moreover, when the teachers talked about change they almost never talked about change in generic terms, but rather in subject-specific terms. My observations at Lakeview coincide, at least in part, with the work of Shulman (1987) and Stodolsky (1988) who have made similar arguments. I further contend that we must recognize the importance of subject matter within the context of school change as well.

The implications for teachers and principals who are struggling to improve their schools is to assume a sceptical stance on the literature on school improvement, school effectiveness, school restructuring, and the host of other fields that spring up each year. A healthy sense of criticism would not be amiss. At the very least, treat these findings as problematic and the statements as tentative hypotheses. Recognize that such literature is the creation of outsiders who have seldom darkened a classroom door since they themselves graduated, and less often taught in the classrooms they profess to reform. This admonition does not mean that such literature cannot be useful to a group of teachers who are attempting to change practice. It can, and often does, provide a gauge against which to measure practice or the proposed approach to changing that practice. What it cannot do, however, is provide a never-fail recipe for the implementation of any particular reform.

This book opened with a description of a group of fourth grade children being led to see the story of Hansel and Gretel as a matter of interpretation. If teachers can treat the literature about schools in the same light — as questions for consideration and evaluation — then real reform in education just might come about.

Notes

1 I should also point out that while the experience of the staff at Lakeview was not common, neither was it entirely unique. Other schools in other parts of the province were undertaking similar projects. We have seen a great deal of activity in the last five years around the implementation of the *Year 2000*.

2 In a recent study of 16 high schools in a local district (Wideen, Pye, Naylor and Crofton, 1990) teachers were asked to identify activities in that district which had had some impact on their professional growth. Despite several years of clinical supervision workshops in the district, very few teachers identified that initiative as having been important to them.

3 See, for example, the work of Acheson and Gall (1987) who have laid out a series of techniques for clinical supervision. My quarrel is not with them, but rather with the mechanical and technical way in which their work is applied to teaching.

4 Coleman (1990) has used this term both in his writing and in conversation involving school reform.

Bibliography

ADELMAN, C. (1991) 'Action research: The problem of participation', unpublished manuscript.

AINSCOW, M. and HOPKINS, D. (1992) 'Aboard the moving school', *Educational Leadership*, pp. 79–81.

BALDRIDGE, J.V. (1972) 'Organizational change: The human relations perspective versus the political systems perspective', *Educational Researcher*, **1**(2).

BARTH, R. (1992) 'A personal vision of a good school', *Phi Delta Kappan*, March, pp. 512–16.

BARROW, R. (1984) *Giving teaching back to teachers: A critical introduction to curriculum theory*, Sussex: The Althouse Press.

BENNIS, W.G., BENNE, K.D., CHIN, R. and COREY, K.E. (1976) *The planning of change: Readings in the applied behavioral sciences*, (3rd ed.) New York: Holt, Rinehart and Winston.

BERMAN, P. and MCLAUGHLIN, M.W. (1978) *Federal programs supporting educational change, vol. VIII: Implementing and sustaining innovations* (Contract HEW-05–73–216), Santa Monica: The Rand Corporation.

BROFENBRENNER, U. (1976) 'The experimental ecology of education', *Teachers College Record*, **78**(2), pp. 157–78.

BROOKOVER, W.B. and LEZOTTE, L.W. (1977) *Changes in social characteristics coincident with changes in student achievement*, East Lansing: Institute for Research on Teaching, Michigan State University.

BROPHY, J. (1992) 'Probing the subtleties of subject-matter teaching', *Educational Leadership*, April.

BRUNER, J.S. (1960) *The process of education*, Cambridge: Harvard University Press.

BURDEN, P. (1990) 'Teacher development', in HOUSTON (ed.) *Handbook of research on teacher education*, New York: MacMillan.

CALDWELL, S.D. and WOOD, F.H. (1988) 'School-based improvement: Are we ready?' *Educational Leadership*, **46**, 2, pp. 50–3.

CHIN, R. and BENNE, K. (1976) 'General strategies for effecting change in human systems,' in BENNIS, W.C., BENNE, K.D., CHIN, R. and COREY, K.E. *The planning of change*, New York: Holt, Rinehard and Winston.

CLANDININ, J. (1986) *Classroom practice: Teachers' images in action*, London: Falmer Press.

CLOUGH, E., ASPINWALL, K. and GIBBS, B. (1989) *Learning to change: An LEA school-focused initiative*, Basingstoke: Falmer Press.

COLEMAN, J.S. (1966) 'Equality of educational opportunity', Washington, D.C.: US Department of Health, Education and Welfare, Office of Education.

COLEMAN, P. and LAROCQUE, L. (1990) *Struggling to be 'good enough': Administrative practices and school district ethos*, London: Falmer Press.

CONNELLY, F.M. and CLANDWIN, D.J. (1988) *Teachers as curriculum planners: Narratives of experience*, New York: Teachers College Press.

CORBETT, H.D. and ROSSMAN, G. (1989) 'Three paths to implementing change', *Curriculum Inquiry*, **19**(2), pp. 163–90.

COREY, S.M. (1953) *Action research to improve school practices*, New York: Bureau of Publications, Teachers' College, Columbia University Press.

CRANDALL, D. *et al.* (1986) 'Strategic planning issues that bear on the success of school improvement efforts', *Educational Administration Quarterly*, **22**(3), pp. 21–53.

CUBAN, L. (1990) 'Reforming again and again', *Educational Leadership*, **19**(1), pp. 3–13.

DEWEY, J. (1975) 'The child and the curriculum', in GOLBY, M., GREENWOLD, J. and WEST, R. (eds) *Curriculum design*, Beckenham, Kent: Croom Helm.

DEWEY, J. (1900) The school and society, Chicago: University of Chicago Press.

DOCKENDORF, M. and HOLBORN, P. (1992) *Developing images of educational change: Processes of implementation*, B.C.: Ministry of Education, Victoria.

DOYLE, W. (1983, Summer) Academic Work, *Review of Educational Research*, **53**(2), pp. 159–99.

DOYLE, W. and PONDER, G. (1977/78) 'The practicality ethic in teacher decision-making', *Interchange*, **8**(3), pp. 1–12.

EDMONDS, R. (1979) 'Effective school for the urban poor,' *Educational Leadership*, **37**(1), pp. 15–18 and pp. 20–24.

EDMONDS, R. (1987) 'A discussion of the literature and issues related to effective schooling', in CARLSON, R.V. and DUCHARME, E.R. (eds) *School improvement: Theory and practice*, Lanham, MD: University Press of America.

EISNER, E.W. (1979) *The educational imagination: On the design and evaluation of school programs*, New York: Macmillan.

ELBAZ, F. (1983) *Teacher thinking: A study of practical knowledge*, London: Croom Helm.

FRAZIER, C.M. (1987) 'The 1980s: States assume educational leadership', in GOODLAD, J. (ed.) *The ecology of school renewal*, Chicago: University of Chicago Press.

FULLAN, M. (1983) *The new meaning of educational change*, Toronto: OISE Press.

—— (1984) 'The principal as an agent of knowledge utilization (UK) for school improvement', in HOPKINS, D. and WIDEEN, M. (eds), *New Perspectives on School Improvement*, London: Falmer Press.

—— (1985) 'Change process and strategies at the local level', *The Elementary School Journal*, **85**(3), pp. 391–420.

FULLAN, M. (1991) *The new meaning of educational change*, Toronto: OISE Press.

FULLAN, M., ANDERSON, S. and NEWTON, E. (1986) *Support systems for implementing curriculum in school boards*, (Report to Ministry of Ontario), Toronto: Ontario Institute for Studies in Education.

FULLAN, M. and HARGREAVES, A. (1991) *What's worth fighting for? Working together for your school*, Toronto: Ontario Public School Teachers' Federation.

FULLAN, M.G. and MILES, M.B. (1992) 'Getting reform right: What works and what doesn't?' *Phi Delta Kappan*, June, pp. 745–52.

GAGNE, R. (1964) Psychological issues in 'Science — A process approach' a lecture delivered to Regional Conferences of Tryout Teachers in Washington, D.C.

—— (1965) *The conditions of learning*, New York: Holt, Rinehart and Winston.

GLASSER, B. and STRAUSS, A.L. (1967) *The discovery of grounded theory: Strategies for qualitative research*, Chicago: Aldine.

GLASSER, E.M. (1976) *Putting knowledge to use: A distillation of the literature regarding knowledge transfer and change*, Los Angeles, CA: Human Interaction Research Institute.

GLICKMAN, C. (Speaker) (1991) *Reshaping schools: No longer pretending not to know what we know*! (Cassette Recording No. C9139), San Francisco, CA: ASCD.

GLICKMAN, C.D., ALLEN, L. and LUNSFORD, B. (1992, April) *Facilitation of internal change: The league of professional schools*. Paper presented at the annual meeting of the American Educational Research Association, San Francisco, CA.

GOLDBERG, M.F. (1984) 'An update on the National Writing Project', *Phi Delta Kappan*, **65**(5), pp. 356–57.

GOODLAD, J. (1983) *A place called school*, New York: McGraw-Hill.

—— (ed.) (1987) *The ecology of school renewal. (86th NSSE Yearbook)*, Chicago: University of Chicago Press.

GOODLAD, J., VON STEOPHASIUS, R. and KLEIN, M. (1974) *Looking behind the classroom door*, Worthington, ID: Charles A. Jones Publishing Co.

GOODSON, I. (1983) *School subjects and curriculum change*, London: Croom Helm.

GRAN, B. (1990) 'Research on Swedish teacher training', in TISCHER, R. and WIDEEN, M. (eds) *Research in teacher education: International perspectives*, London: Falmer Press.

GREENE, M. (1985) 'Jeremiad and the curriculum: The haunting of the secondary school', *Curriculum Inquiry*, **15**(3).

GRIMMETT, P.P. and CREHAN, E.P. (1992) 'The nature of collegiality in teacher development: The case of clinical supervision', in FULLAN, M. and HARGREAVES, A. (eds) *Teacher development and educational change*, London: Falmer Press, pp. 56–85.

GRIMMETT, P.P. and MACKINNON, A.M. (1992) 'Craft knowledge and the education of teachers', *Review of research in education*, **18**, Washington: American Educational Research Association.

HARGREAVES, A. and DAWE, R. (1990) 'Paths of professional development: Contrived collegiality or collaborative culture and the case of peer coaching', *Teaching and Teacher Education*, **4**.

HARGREAVES, D.H. (1982) *The challenge for the comprehensive school — culture, curriculum and community*, London: Routledge and Kegan Paul.

HARGREAVES, D.H. and HOPKINS, D. (1991) *The empowered school: The management and practice of development planning*, London: Cassell.

HAVELOCK, R.G. (1969) *Planning for innovation through dissemination and utilization of Knowledge*, Ann Arbor, MI: Center for Research on Utilization of Scientific Knowledge, University of Michigan.

HECHINGER, F.M. (1983) *The New York Times*, 6 June.

HEIDEMAN, R. and CHRISTENSON, J. (1985) 'Current criticisms and efforts to improve teaching and teacher education', in BURKE, P. and HEIDEMAN, R. *Career long teacher education*, Springfield, IL: Charles C. Thomas.

HENSHAW, J., WILSON, C. and MOREFIELD, J. (1987) 'Seeing clearly: The school as the unit of change', in GOODLAD, J. (ed.) *The ecology of school renewal*, Chicago: University of Chicago Press.

HOETKER, J. and AHLBRAND, W.P., Jr. (1969) 'The persistence of recitation', *American Educational Research Journal*, **6**, pp. 145–46.

HOLLY, P., WIDEEN, M., BOLLAN, R. and MENLO, (1987) 'The cultural perspective', in MILES, M., EKHOLM, M. and VANDENBERGE, R. (eds) *Institutionalization of innovations*, Leuven, Belgium: ACCO Press.

HOPKINS, D. (1985) *A teacher's guide to classroom research*, Milton Keynes: Open University Press.

HOPKINS, D. and WIDEEN, M.F. (1984) *New perspectives on school improvement*, London: Falmer Press.

HOPKINS, D. (ed.) (1987) *Improving the Quality of Schooling*, Lewes: Falmer Press.

HOUSE, E. (1981) *The politics of educational innovation*, Berkley, CA: McCutchan.

HUBERMAN, A.M. (1990, April) *The social context of instruction in schools*, paper presented at the annual meeting of the American Educational Research Association, Boston, MA.

HUBERMAN, A.M. and MILES, M.B. (1984) *Innovation up close: How school improvement works*, New York: Plenum.

—— (1986) 'Rethinking the quest for school improvement: Some findings from the DESSI study', in LIEBERMAN, A. (ed.), *Rethinking school improvement*, New York: Teachers' College Press.

ILLICH, I.D. (1971) *Deschooling society*, New York: Harper and Row.

JACULLO-NOTO, J. (1984) 'Interactive research and development — partners in craft', in LIEBERMAN, A. (ed.) *Rethinking school improvement*, New York: Teachers College Press.

JAGGAR, A.M. (1989) 'Teacher as learner: Implications for staff development', in PINNELL, G.S. and MATLIN, M.L. (eds) *Teachers and research*, Newark, DE: International Reading Association, pp. 66–80.

JENCKS, C., SMITH, M., ACKLAND, H., BANE, M.J., COHEN, D.K., GINTIS, H., HENYNS, B. and MICHELSON, S. (1972) *Inequality: A reassessment of the effect of family and schooling in America*, N.Y.: Basic Books.

JOYCE, B., HERSH, R. and MCKIBBIN, M. (1983) *The Structure of School Improvement*, New York, Longman.

JOYCE, B., MURPHY, C., SHOWERS, B. and MURPHY, J. (1989) 'Reconstructing the workplace: School renewal as cultural change', *Educational Leadership*, **47**(3), pp. 70–7.

JOYCE, B. and WEIL, M. (1986) *Models of teaching*, Englewood Cliffs: Prentice Hall.

KEMMIS, S. (1987) 'Critical reflection', in WIDEEN, M.F. and ANDREWS, I. (eds) *Staff development for school improvement: A focus on the teacher*, London: Falmer Press, pp. 73–90.

KINCHELOE, J.L. (1991) *Teachers as researchers: Qualitative inquiry as a path to empowerment*, London: Falmer Press.

LAMBERT, L. (1989, September) 'The end of an era of staff development', *Educational Leadership*, pp. 78–81.

LEITHWOOD, K.A. (1989) *The principal's role in staff development*, a paper presented at the OISE/FEUT International Conference on Teacher Development: Policies, Practices, and Research. Toronto.

—— (1992) 'The principal's role in teacher development', in FULLAN, M. and HARGREAVES, A. (eds), *Teacher development and educational change*, London: Falmer Press, pp. 86–103.

LIEBERMAN, A. (ed.) (1984) *Rethinking school improvement*, New York: Teachers College Press.

LINDBLOM, C.E. and COHEN, D.K. (1979) *Usable Knowledge: Social science and social problem solving*, New Haven, CT: Yale University Press.

LITTLE, J.W. (1986) 'Seductive images and organizational realities in professional development', in LIEBERMAN, A. (ed.) (1984), *Rethinking school improvement*, New York: Teachers College Press.

LITTLE, J.W. (1992) 'Teacher development and educational policy', in FULLAN, M. and HARGREAVES, A. (eds), *Teacher development and educational change*, London: Falmer Press, pp. 170–93.

LORTIE, D.C. (1975) *Schoolteacher: A sociological study*. Chicago: University of Chicago Press.

—— (1988) 'Built-in tendencies toward stabilizing the principal's role', *Journal of research and development in education*, **22**(1), Fall, pp. 80–90.

LOUIS, D. (1981) 'External agents and knowledge utilization: Dimensions for analysis and action', in LEHMAN, R. and KANE, M. (eds) *Improving schools*, Beverly Hills, CA: Sage Publications.

LOUIS, K.S. and MILES, M. (1990) *Improving the urban high school*, New York: Teachers College Press.

LOVE, J.M. (1975) 'Knowledge transfer and utilization in education', in GORDON, E.W. (ed.) *Review of Research in Education*, Washington, D.C.: American Educational Research Association.

MacDonald, B. (1991) 'Introduction', in Rudduck, J. *Innovation and change: Development involvement and understanding*, Milton Keynes, UK: Open University Press.

MacKinnon, A.M. (1989) 'Conceptualizing a reflective practicuum in constructivist science teaching', unpublished doctoral thesis, U.B.C., Vancouver.

Miles, M. (1984) *The role of the change agent in the school improvement process*, paper presented at the annual meeting of the American Educational Research Association, New Orleans.

Miles, M. and Huberman, A.M. (1984) *Qualitative methods: A sourcebook of method*, Los Angeles: Sage Publications.

Mortimore, (1991) 'School effectiveness research: Which way at the crossroads?' in *School effectiveness and school improvement*, **2**(3), pp. 213–29.

Nias, J., Southworth, G. and Yeomans, R. (1989) *Staff relationships in the primary school*, London: Cassell.

Olson, J. (1982) 'Constructivism and education: A productive alliance', *Interchange*, **13**(4), Toronto: O.I.S.E., pp. 70–5.

Patton, M.Q. (1980) *Qualitative evaluation methods*, Beverly Hills: Sage Publications.

Popham, W.J. (1987) 'The merits of measurement-driven instruction', *Phi Delta Kappan*, **66**(9), pp. 679–82.

Purkey, S. and Smith, M. (1983) 'Effective schools: A review', *Elementary School Journal*, **83**(4), pp. 427–52.

Reynolds, A. (1992) 'What is competent beginning teaching? A review of the literature', *Review of Educational Research*, **62**(1), pp. 1–35.

Reynolds, D. (1991) *What Makes an Effective School? How Do We Make Schools Effective*? Plenary address to the Third Australian Guidance Association Conference, Melbourne, Australia, 1991.

Rosenholtz, S. (1989) *Teachers' workplace*, New York: Longman.

Rudduck, J. (1991) *Innovation and change: Developing involvement and understanding*, Milton Keynes, UK: Open University Press.

Rutter, M., *et al.* (1979) *Fifteen thousand hours: Secondary schools and their effects on children*, London: Open Books.

Sarason, S.B. (1982) *The culture of the school and the problem of change*, Boston: Allyn and Bacon.

—— (1990) *The predictable failure of educational reform. Can we change course before it's too late*?, San Francisco: Jossey-Bass.

Schon, D.A. (1983) *The reflective practitioner: How professionals think in action*, New York: Basis Books.

Schwab, J. (1964) 'Structure of disciplines: Meanings and significances', in Ford, G. and Pugo, L. (eds) *The structure of knowledge and the curriculum*, Chicago: Rand McNally and Company, pp. 1–20.

Sergiovanni, T.J. (1992) *Moral leadership: Getting to the heart of school improvement*, San Francisco: Jossey-Bass.

Shulman, L. (1986) 'Those who understand knowledge, growth and teaching', *The Educational Researcher*, **15**(2), pp. 4–14.

SHULMAN, L. (1987) 'Knowledge and teaching: Foundations of the new reform', *Harvard Educational Review*, **57**(1).

—— (1991) *The changing definition of 'effective' teaching: A conversation with Lee Shulman*, (Cassette Recording No. C9149), San Francisco, CA: ASCD.

SIKES, P.J. (1992) 'Imposed change and the experienced teacher', in FULLAN, M. and HARGREAVES, A. (eds) *Teacher development and educational change*, London: Falmer Press, pp. 36–55.

SPRADLEY, J. (1979) *The ethnographic interview*, New York: Holt, Rinehart and Winston.

STAKE, R. and EASLEY, J. (1978) 'Case studies in science education', (A project for the National Science Foundation), University of Illinois.

STALLINGS, J.A. (1989) 'School effects and staff development: What are the critical factors?', paper presented at the annual meeting of the American Educational Research Association San Francisco.

STANFIELD, J.H. (1985) 'The ethnocentric basis of social science knowledge production', in GORDON, E.W. (ed.) *Review of research in education*, Washington, D.C.: American Educational Research Association.

STENHOUSE, L. (1970) 'The humanities project. Heimemaan', (Revised edition — RUDDUCK, J., 1983), School of Education, University of East Anglia.

—— (1984) 'Artistry and teaching: The teacher as focus of research and development', in HOPKINS, D. and WIDEEN, M. *New perspectives on school improvement*, London: Falmer Press.

STODOLSKY, S.S. (1988) *The subject matters: Classroom activity in math and social studies*, Chicago: University of Chicago Press.

STOLL, L. (1992) 'Teacher growth in the effective school', in FULLAN, M. and HARGREAVES, A. (eds) *Teacher development and educational change*, London: Falmer Press, pp. 104–22.

STOLL, L. and FINK, D. (1992) 'Effecting school change: the Halton Approach', *School Effectiveness and School Improvement*, **3**(1), pp. 19–41.

STRACHAN, W. (1988) *Report to the principal and staff of 'Lakeview' school: Reactions to Writing program.*

UNGERLEIDER, C.S. (1992) 'Creating the conditions for collaboration and change in education', paper presented at *Collaboration in teacher education: Seeking ways of working together*, Teacher Education Forum, British Columbia College of Teachers, Vancouver, B.C., 20–21 Nov.

VAN VELZEN, W., *et al.* (1985) *Making school improvement work*, Leuven, Belgium, ACCO.

VON GLASERSFELD (1987) 'Constructivism', in *The international encyclopedia of education*, Oxford: Pergamon Press.

WALLACE, R., *et al.* (1990) 'The Pittsburgh experience: Achieving commitment to comprehensive staff development', in JOYCE, B. (ed.) *Changing school culture through staff development (1990 Yearbook)*, Alexandria, VA: ASCD.

WIDEEN, M.F. (1987) 'Teacher as researcher', *B.C. Teacher*, **67**(1), pp. 12–14.

WIDEEN, M.F. (1987) *The long-term impact of two school improvement projects: A study of institutionalization*, Proposal submitted to SSHRC.

WIDEEN, M.F., ANDREWS, I. (eds) (1987) *Staff Development for school improvement — a focus on the teacher*, London: Falmer Press.

WIDEEN, M.F. (1988) 'School improvement in Canada', in *Qualitative Studies in Education*, **1**(1), pp. 21–38.

WIDEEN, M.F. (1992) 'School-based teacher development', in FULLAN, M. and HARGREAVES, A. (eds) *Teacher development and educational change*, London: Falmer Press, pp. 123–55.

WIDEEN, M.F. and HOPKINS, D. (1984) 'Supervising student teachers: A means of professional renewal?' *Alberta Journal of Educational Research*, **30**(1), pp. 26–37.

WIDEEN, M.F., CARLMAN, N. and STRACHAN, W. (1986) *Problem focused coursework as a model for in-service education: Case studies of teacher initiated change*, (Project Report), Burnaby: Simon Fraser University.

WIDEEN, M.F., O'SHEA, T., PYE, I., SHERWOOD, A. and IVANY, G. (1991) *Impact of large-scale testing on the instructional activity of science teachers*, Burnaby: Institute for Studies in Teacher Education, Simon Fraser University.

WILLIAMS, R., MOFFETT, K.L. and NEWLIN, B. (1987) 'The district role in school renewal', in GOODLAD, J. (ed.) *The ecology of school renewal*, Chicago: University of Chicago Press.

Appendix A

One student's story

THE Unexpected DOORWAY
BY DONNA

The Unexpected Doorway
by
Donna

"Aw mom!" I said as they were about to leave to celebrate their aniversary.

"Tough luck!" said my mom sternly.

"But mom!" I'm not going to babysit them! They're little brats!" Iyelled at her.

"Don't call your brother and sisters brats! And don't yell at me!" she shouted back.

"But I was supose to go to the movies with Cheryl!" I protested.

"Your sisters and brothers are more important than movies!" she said "and that's that! We'll be back by 12:00!" she remarked just before she slammed the door. I stormed to the window, crossed my arms, and stared at her. "What a @*#?!" I murmured.

"And don't forget to do your homework!" she said for the millionth time as she and my dad sped off in our cutlass supreme.

"The nerve of her!" I mumbled again, this time trudging up the stairs. In my bedroom, I picked up my cordless phone, phoned Cheryl and told her I couldn't go to the movies with her.

"What a bummer! she said annoyingly. "We were suposed to go to that BIG party after. Oh well, I guess I'll have to go to that awesome party by myself. I mean—it's a shame that you can't go, everyone is there—that is—all the great popular. . ."

"Cut it out! I git the picture" I said interupting.

"Well sorry Ms. Krousay!" she said.

"Ha ha." I managed to say before we hung up.

I moved to my computer and stared at the monitor. My main heading was "English assignment." Underneath was the date and my story heading "My greatest adventure." My English teacher Mr Cthvolkski, by the way, nice name eh?, had expected us to write a full detailed story of our greatest adventure. What a dope! There wasn't anything to do in Gettysborgto be classified as adventurous. What were we suposed to do, write out first day in nursery school? or maybe even our first trip to the shopping mall?

"I bet I'm going to flunk!" I muttered.

"Whatch' ya doin? said a voice behind me. It was my bratty little sister, Tina. She was cradling Ralphie, our dog, in her arms. Today she pretended to play circus and Ralphie was the clown. I could tell he felt ridiculous, or at least he looked like he felt ridiculous.

"What do you think I'm doing?" I answered her dumb question.

"What?" said Tina stupidly. I rolled my eyes facing the ceiling.

"Homework!" I blurted out annoyed.

"Oh." she said as if she were "put down".

"I wanna go to the messy room," she announced (which meant the cellar.)

"Go ahead" I said rudely "do what you want, I don't care!" I looked at my computer again and wrote "one day".

"Good enough." I said.

"What's good enough?" asked my nosey little sister Mary-anne.

"It's none of your business" I answered her.

"Well anyway," she said "Oliver found a frog, says it's his good luck charm, won't let it go, and to top it all off, he kissed it—YUCKY!"

"Good for him!" I said, "He'll get tired of it sooner or later." I concentrated on my story again. Oh well I'll do it tomorrow. Besides, it's not due till Monday (which was at that time, Friday). I went to watch t.v. downstairs with a cold pizza and cake from the night before. Oliver ran in shouting "boingle." Oh gosh, boingle again. That dumb little show with the guy made of springs.

"Tough!" I said "get lost, I was here first and your're not going to watch boingle for the millionth time because they're all replays.

"I'm gonna to tell mummy on you! he threatened.

"Oohhh I'm sooo scared" I replied.

"You better be!" he screamed as he trudged out.

Well, I was watching the Cosby show, oh yeah, my name's Laurie. My real name's . . . uh. . . too embarassing so people call me by my middle name, Laurie.

"Laurie!" It was Tina again. "Laurie! Come here", she was shouting from the cellar, coming up to the rumpass room.

"What do you want now? I said when she came in.

"Ralphie tripped and found duh door wid lites!"

"What in the world are you talking about? I asked facing her.

"Come!" she said eagerly, tugging at my sleeve. Because of her excitement, Tina tripped a few times, coming down to the cellar. Mary-anne

and Oliver were already there, awed. No, Oliver came bouncing behind us saying "it's boingle! He said he'd visit!"

Sure enough, there was a small door with lights streaming from the cracks. Ralphie was scared to death and hid behind some boxes. We crept towards the door. No Tina walked up to it and opened it while I looked for a bat. We all drew back because a sudden burst of light came from the other side of the door. Now, we crept up to it. We saw some spiral stairs and followed them down. Ralphie crept behind us uneasily, it was about 10 no, 5 flights of stairs till we got to a tunnel. It was continuously turning like the one in Disneyland, or was it Universal Studios—either one of those two.

At the end of the tunnel, we saw the queerest looking amusement park. When the whole thing turned on (by themselves) I almost ran home at 50 m.p.h. while my brother and sisters ran to the gates showing free rides! I couldn't believe it

I was totally freaked, well, not freaked, but . . . yeah, freaked!, while my younger, might I say, way younger siblings were very eager to go to it. I mean, what a disgrace! Of course I followed them because I had to look after them.

We first went to the playhouse. There was this twirling thing that I didn't know what was called that got me dizzy. Next, it was this room full of smoke. I thought I saw a lady in white, but at the time, I thought it was my imagination. Suddenly, something gave way under Tina. These ugly trolls were crowding in on us. We looked down where Tina fell and saw a slide.

We all eagerly went down it, not caring where it would go, just as long as we got away from the monsters. We ended up in the maze of mirrors.

"Laurie! Help! I'm here! Aahah"!!. .

"Tina! Where are you?" we yelled looking for her. Ralphie barked tremendously. . .

"Get away! screamed Tina, backing us.

"Once I'm done with you, I'll get your picky friend, hissed the lady in white. "Thank you for opening my trap!" she said as she waved her arms in a threatening manner.

"Nooooo . . . ." gasped Tina as she colapsed.

We desperately searched for Tina in the maze of mirrors. Ralphie quieted down a little. We all stuck together so we wouldn't lose each other like we lost Tina.

In the mirrors, we saw those horrible creatures again and stopped in terror. They were closing in on us, while the same lady I saw in the smoky room blocked our path.

She hissed "you'll never see your world again! Suddenly, a roller coaster swished by, forcing us to be knocked into it. The seatbelts wrapped themselves around us just as we made a sharp turn. The roller coaster changed it's shape rapidly into an over grown lizzard. Oliver started crying and tightly clung to already too much squeezed froggy. An old man appeared beside me and said "we must stop her!"

"Wha. . ." I said being interupted.

"My wife . . . Edna . . . when I married her . . . she gained my powers — gasp — and uses it to . . . bring children from the universe . . . and changes them to —gasp — her allies . . . so she can take over the universe!

"Where's my sister!" I screamed at him, shaking him.

"Hold it! I came to help you." he said taking my hands away.

"Then where is she?" I asked impatiently.

"Look in here." he said waving his arms. Oh my, first goblins, then a ghostly lady, now a guy who does magic! What next? In his palm, lay a figure. It was an illusion. My sister lay onconcious in a manhole.

This must of been a dumb dream I was having. Like who'd use magic tricks to turn people into goblins so they could rule the world? Who'd want to rule a world of goblins? This is crazy!

The next thing I knew, we were at the old geezer's house drinking potions when evil Edna dicided to drop in. I looked at the old geezer who stupidly disappeared in a puff of smoke. Oh yeah, go ahead, leave us alone with your whaco wife. See if I care! I looked back at Edna desperatly tried to escape. Mary-anne hid behind the bed while Oliver hid under the table. Them stupid kids! Edna's aides were already approaching them.

"I;ve got you now! she shreiked. "You're mine!" she said threatiningly as she zapped me with some rays. Surprisingly, her zap bounced

off of a force feild around me and hit her. Her high pitched scream filled the whole place. Then we suddenly disappeared just as the goblins or what ever they were jumped at us. We reappeared at the manhole where Tina was trapped.

Oliver landed on his butt and started to cry. Mary-anne was still crouched in her position behind the bed. The old man was there too, holding Tina in his arms. At the sight of her, I screamed, horrified. She had a haunch back with spikes sticking out of her back. Her nose was like a pig's snout. Her rosy white complection turned to a pale green.

"What happened!" I screamed, teary.

"Edna has already cast her spell on your sister, but she's still not fully developed yet." exclaimed the old man.

"What do you mean not fully developed?" I yelled.

"It means we can still save her. I have a potion to cure her." he said calmly.

"Wrong deary! said Edna's harsh voice, "nobody can save anybody now!"

I knew it! She'd come here, knowing we'd try to save Tina.

"YOU WITCH! yelled Mary-anne who had snuck up from behind and tried to hit Evil Edna.

"You'll pay little girl! said Edna as she struck Mary-anne.

"Don't you hurt my sister! I screamed as I grabbed Oliver's frog and threw it at her. No, that wont do, I'm lying again. Actually, Edna

zaped me, then Oliver shreiked I hate you! and threw his beloved frog at her in anger. At the moment the frog touched her, she sunk to the ground screaming, then melted away.

I later realized that it was probably all the potions that it hopped into when Oliver let it loose in the old geezer's house. Maybe the chemicals reacted to supernatural beings. Who knows? Well anyway, everything that Edna had created had either went back to normal, or disapeared, including Tina. We all went back to the old geezer's hut again. Everyone of us that Edna had kidnapped. We only had one thing left to do. PARTY! After we celebrated, the old man had everyone drink a remedy that made them return to the exact place they left. We were the last, but he didn't let us drink untill he finished his speech of thanks.

THE END

I stared at my monitor again and thought "I hope Mr. Cthvolski accepts. make-believe adventures.

Appendix B

Events, changes and influences involved in the project at Lakeview School

1 *Administrative Retreat* This retreat occurs every two years. Board members, principals and district administration attend to discuss general directions for the district.

2 *McCracken Workshop (Kelly, Isabelle, Charlie)* This workshop had a strong impact for teachers; it encouraged them to visualize some alternatives to the structured, packaged, language arts programs (i.e. Ginn).

1985–86

3 *Staff Discussion of School Goals* 1) Charlie sat down with each person on staff and asked them about their personal goals. This process then led to a whole staff discussion about the school's goals.
2) Staff discussions were part of the 'change' that took place; they were considerably different from the staff meetings several teachers had experienced in previous years. This initial one about school goals was crucial. (In many cases a wide variety of school goals are planned that don't connect in any way to each other.) Through staff discussion, the area of Language Arts became a full staff interest. It was an extremely wide goal, though all in one direction, and thus all staff members found their spot. In addition, this led to discussion of supporting a choice of 'one' goal and writing up a proposal to present to the School Board.

4 *Buddy Reading* The Buddy Reading Program was initiated by a staff member. On a school-wide basis, the first 20 min. of the day was free reading time; in most cases intermediate and primary classes were teamed for budding reading. This reading time was modelled by all personnel throughout the school including the secretary and teacher aides.

5 *Individual Teacher Experimentation* Each teacher was a part of, and comfortable with, the school goal. Collectively they were all moving in the same direction; they were at different readiness levels to experiment, or continue

to experiment with different approaches to teaching language arts rather than the structured style. Some were actively involved while others observed and discussed the outcomes, the questions, and the concerns.

6 *School Forms Language Arts Committee* The staff recognized the possible value of a school-based committee to gain some information about areas of interest and question. The school-based Language Arts Committee was set up with the teachers who chose to be involved. Professional reading, discussion and sharing with the other interested staff members was the valuable purpose. An important contribution was a shared discussion on psycholinguistics.

7 *One Focus School Goal* As a staff they decided to identify and then implement an integrated instructional approach of the whole language teaching elements. The intended outcomes were:

— to increase student acquisition of communication skills, knowledge, and attitudes.
— to eventually reflect a more 'holistic' approach to teaching.
— to increase and support students' creative and critical thinking competence.

8 *Selma Wassermann* Selma Wassermann was requested to give the staff a workshop on the use, the purpose, and way to include thinking skills within the Language Development Focus. Wassermann's workshop was valuable to a variety of staff. For some it was an introduction to an area of interest, for others, it reaffirmed their beliefs and practice. Again, consultants of any sort, who work with the staff as a whole, help initiate discussion that contributes to much of the change.

9 *Teacher Ownership of Planning Proposals* Teachers recognized their ownership and personal voice in all decisions. Teachers were an equal part of all stages, from making decisions to writing up the proposal and presenting it. Each teacher had a choice of participation at each level of planning.

10 *Plans set out for Professional Development* The staff met to set out professional development goals for the coming year. High in their priorities were the alternatives to the basal reading program.

11 *Home Reading Program* The Home Reading Program was initiated by one teacher. Teacher, student and parent participation worked well. The advantages were recognized as school/community link, interested participation and relationship to their original goal.
1) 'Reading Blitz' — the student takes home a card and along with parents keeps track of daily reading (of any material, including the newspaper) over the period of a month. Daily class and school participation percentage is kept and displayed in the hallway. Each day that 80 per cent or better had participated special privileges were given. At the end of the month a school-wide gym readathon takes place.
2) Student and parent participation in the program has been successful and does encourage home reading.

12 *Theme Days — Primary Fine Arts* Theme Day was a concept initially organized by the primary teachers in the fall of 1985. Students in grades K-3 were multigrade grouped every Friday afternoon to take part in 'theme' related fine arts activities. Primary teachers team-planned each theme which usually ran for 4–5 Friday afternoons.

13 *Parent Advisory Committee Formed* A small parent consulting committee was formed to start a communication link and to build upon the school reputation. This was viewed as an important part of any 'change' process in that it helped gain community support.

14 *McCrackens — Second visit* A district-wide professional development in-service. This second visit again reinforced the teachers' questions about structured, packaged, language arts programs. Demonstration lessons were taught in two classes in the school by Marlene McCracken. This was an important step as teachers were able to observe and then model what they saw McCracken do. Again, they found more confirmation that whole language was a more sensible way to teach language arts. Movement towards theme teaching and whole language strategies became more noticeable.

15 *Theme Days — Whole School/Half Day/Fine Arts* Intermediate teachers took an interest in the Primary Theme Day program and wanted to see the program in operation school-wide. Staff reorganized and refined existing groupings to include K–1, 2–4 and 4–7 groupings. Librarian, principal, LAT, Special Needs teachers, and on occasions district staff, school trustees and parents became facilitators for the groups so that group size could be kept to a minimum. Teachers had the choice as to which age group they wished to work with. Themes continued to run 4–5 weeks in succession (Friday afternoons) and focused on fine arts activities. Some themes chosen were water, space, back to the future, science, multiculturalism. All themes were chosen using a democratic process.

16 *Continued Experimentation* Growth, change and experimentation within the 'whole' school environment continued. The thrust, support and encouragement reinforced risk-taking and teachers' individual and collective empowerment.

17 *Board Presentation* This involved the staff in the school making a presentation to the Board. This was an important step in two ways: it gave the teachers some ownership over the change in the school which would not have been the case had the principal been the sole presenter. And, substantively, it led to a single focus in the school and to the second Wednesday program. The single school focus involved language arts; the second Wednesday program gave the staff planning time in the afternoon of every second Wednesday. To compensate for this time, they taught a half-hour longer each day.

18 *Theme Day (Integrated Language Arts and Fine Arts) — Whole Day* As observers of the Primary Theme Day Program, both the intermediate teachers, and students, gained an interest in becoming participants. Through staff

discussion, a decision was made to re-organize the program, integrate language arts with the fine arts, experiment with strategies and philosophies that had been introduced up to that date (co-operative grouping, thinking skills, family grouping of students, etc.), and finally, include all of these and extend the day from only afternoons to all day, every Friday throughout each theme.

The purpose of implementing a school-wide Theme Day was to encourage the integration and extension of holistic instructional strategies. The themes would span 3 to 4 week periods. Some examples: back to the future, science challenge, multiculturalism.

19 *Johnson* Terry Johnson was chosen by staff as a possible resource person related to the school goal and teacher interest. His workshop was considered valuable to all staff members; a number of staff experimented and put into practice the language arts strategies he had modelled and were discussed. Several of the books and resources Johnson suggested, and some he had written, were then ordered and put into use. (Donald Graves/Donald Murry/T. Johnson, *Literacy Through Literature*).

20 *Big Book Club* Some of the primary teachers formed a district 'Big Book Club' to share ideas, resources, and 'make' Big Books for their classroom. This worked very well for teachers who were ready to experiment and try out something new.

21 *Reading Conference* Six members of the staff attended the International Reading Conference at the University of British Colombia which focused on various aspects of changing the language arts program. This conference also further confirmed the value of collegiality among the four who attended.

22 *Second Wednesday Implementation* The second Wednesday program is a reorganization of the school timetable so that each second Wednesday afternoon students are dismissed at 12.00. The school day then begins at 8.40 a.m. to make up the lost time. The second Wednesday afternoon provided teachers with time to work together in pairs, small groups, or as a whole staff planning, sharing ideas, etc. The use of time was valuable particularly in creating a collective, collaborative atmosphere. One of the key aspects was that how the time should be used was determined by the staff, not by the administration or the principal.

23 *School Focus on Evaluation* Evaluation became a topic of discussion and questions. Two measures were initiated to reflect student progress in the Integrated Language Arts Project.

1) A collection of tape recorded samples of students' oral reading with various types of text.
2) A school-wide collection of students' writing samples.

24 *Book Binding Workshop* The 'Book Binding' workshop included both teachers and parents. The focus of this workshop was to have parents assist in the publishing stage of student writing.

1986–87

25 *Formation of District Evaluation Committee* The formation of this committee signalled a change in the way evaluation was to be carried out in the district. The staff at Lakeview had been working to change their approach to evaluation the previous year. The fact that the school was represented on the committee made them feel confident and empowered; interests extended to becoming active participants of district change and initiative through other committee participation and presentations of workshops.

26 *Priscilla Lynch* Priscilla Lynch was a valuable resource to support and extend the interest and question about the change process in which they were actively involved and interested in language development. Lynch provided a non-primary information resource re-text methodologies to be used with intermediate and secondary. Confirmed use of taping, folders, reading tests, cloze, etc.

27 *Writing Project* Writing became the most comfortable area for teachers to experiment with the student-centered, holistic learning environment. The implementation of classroom writing folders was initiated by some teachers and was found to be a useful tool for both record keeping and ongoing assessment.

28 *Continuous Revision of Theme Day* In the fall of each new year the staff sat down and reviewed the theme day program. Decisions were made as to whether to continue the program, change it in any way, as well as selecting themes to focus on. It was decided this year to continue having Theme Day from 10.30–3.00 every Friday with a two week break between themes. Groupings of students changed from the previous year; however, the same divisions remained K–1, 2–4, 4–7.

29 *Evaluation Tools — Further Development* Discussion continued around design, practice and experimentation with a variety of evaluation tools. At this stage writing files and reading files (taped reading) were organized and implemented by most staff members. Through discussion, the staff recognized the value of a school cumulative file of student writing development samples. These files would then be available for teachers, parents and student transfers.

30 *Young Authors' Conference* To highlight all the writing that was being done by students, the staff organized and hosted a Young Authors' Conference for students in the spring of 1987. Masterminded by Kelly, an author and storyteller were invited to be guest speakers at this conference. Teachers in the district were invited to facilitate conference sessions on a subject of writing that interested them and students chose the workshops they wished to attend. As well as attending writing workshops, listening to an author or storyteller, the students also had the opportunity to watch high-school students illustrate a book they had written, and then take it to the book binding room where it was cloth bound by parent volunteers.

31 *Change in Theme Day* At the beginning of 1987–88 it was decided to change

the theme day format since teachers were constantly feeling pressured to produce new theme ideas on top of all the theme planning they were doing in their own class. There was still an interest in continuing theme day because of the many benefits it provided the students, but it was decided to try only running three themes — one in the fall, one in winter and one in spring. It was also decided to make the first theme the Christmas concert. Second and third themes this year were multiculturalism and science.

32 *Third Visit by McCrackens* This visit was a follow-up to previous workshops.

33 *Experimentation with Alternatives Extends to Others on Staff* Recognition of and commitment to the roles of research literature and subsequent discussion as they relate to institutionalizing a programme and change process, owned by teachers, continued to develop. Belief in freedom to make honest mistakes without penalty began to grow.

34 *Compiling Theme-Day Book* Throughout the year teachers kept their Friday theme activities with the intent to put together a useful resource for theme related language arts and fine arts activities. A small group of teachers then collected the materials, organized them, and compiled what was considered a useful tool for other teachers who were involved in theme planning and teaching. It was a very valuable product of all the processes that had been worked through and it reinforced their personal self-confidence in the program's success.

35 *Shift From a Teacher-Centered Classroom* The classroom atmospheres had moved from the structured setting to a child-centered environment. Students were encouraged to become much more self-reliant learners, make appropriate choices, problem solve, and gain confidence in their decision-making. Teachers became more comfortable and confident with their role as facilitator — modelling and participating as both teacher and learner. They found this shift to be valuable in focusing on the learning process rather than the products.

36 *Calgary ProD* Two teachers (Barb and Kelly) had the opportunity to visit some schools in Calgary which were targeted as being more advanced in their use of whole language strategies. After discussions with teachers and observations in classes they were confirmed in their level of understanding. Another step in the internalization process had been taken.

37 *Whole Language Moves from being a Strategy to a Philosophy* As the year went on, teachers began viewing whole language as a concept rather than as a set of strategies.

38 *Terrace Workshop Presentation* Staff preparing the Holistic/School Staff Development workshop were invited to make a presentation during a conference in Terrace. It was a great opportunity to 'iron out the bugs' before heading to Coeur d'Alene. The workshop was very well received by conference delegates and many inquiries have been made since that time, to members of the Lakeview staff.

39 *NCTE Conference in Vancouver* This conference served two purposes for

the school and staff development. First, it confirmed for the two teachers who attended that important things were happening in the school, and second, that they were very capable of presenting a workshop at the next NCTE conference being held in Cœur d'Alene, Idaho in May, 1988. A proposal was submitted to the conference committee stating that six staff members, including the principal, were interested in presenting a workshop on school staff development. The proposal was eagerly accepted and the planning begun.

40 *Extended Teacher Experimentation Includes all Staff* Through professional development, professional literature and internal and external resource people, they continually discussed and experimented with ongoing change.

41 *Cœur d'Alene Conference Presentation* After two staff members attended the NCTE conference in Vancouver, plans were made to send a group of interested teachers to Coeur d'Alene to present a workshop on the School Staff Development Project. Following a staff meeting discussion, six interested teachers (including the principal) began the planning process. Even though there was opposition from the school district and the conference planning committee to send six people to present, the group persevered and all six did eventually present their workshop entitled 'Holistic School/Staff Development'. The three components of the workshop were staff development, evaluation and theme day.

42 *Carolyn Mamchur* A staff member invited Mamchur to provide a workshop on two areas of interest — the writing process and learning styles. This evening and full day workshop was also open to other school staffs. Districtwide, Mamchur was found to be key in initiating an awareness and discussion of the idea of recognizing the different learning styles of children.

43 *Effort Made to Work on Teaching Styles* Following Mamchur's visit, greater attempts were made on adapting different teaching approaches to the learning styles of students.

44 *Team-Teaching Begins* Through continual team committee work and discussions and planning, team-teaching seemed to originate naturally. Cooperative grouping of students and Buddy reading programs had modelled the success of 'team' learning for several. They began to plan and experiment with team-teaching in short themes such as 'electricity' and 'human body'. They found the outcome to be successful and exciting; from there planning in Graves for the next year began to revolve.

45 *District Workshops Given* After presenting the Holistic School/Staff Development Workshop in Cœur d'Alene, schools in the district requested that the staff present the workshop during a Professional Development Day. The workshop was presented to the staff of one district school and then it was decided that it be presented to all interested teachers in the district in an after-school session. More than fifty people attended.

46 *Science and Social Studies Integration with Language Arts* Attempt was made to integrate the teaching of science and social studies into the language arts program.

47 *Wendy Strachan* In the Fall of 1987, two years after the project began, Marv Wideen invited Strachan to come to Lakeview to observe and analyze the development she saw in terms of the writing project. She visited the school for two days, after which she wrote a report on what she saw. That report is attached as Appendix C.

1988–89

48 *Staff Discussion of Continuous Theme Day* As happened at the beginning of every new year, theme day became the topic for discussion — how did the staff feel about theme day; should it continue? It was agreed that the original purpose of theme day was now not a necessity as most teachers in the school were using themes as a tool for integration of curriculum. However, it was agreed to continue with two or three theme day sessions as they were still enjoyed by staff and students and they provided a good vehicle for integrating special-needs students. In the second week of the school year Kelly had the opportunity to attend a week-long in-service training at another school presented by Susan Kovalik, a consultant from the United States. A major focus of the workshop was discussion and use of one year-long theme rather than several different themes in a class. Rationale given was that it is necessary to provide connections; by using a year-long theme connections could be made and students make sense out of their learning. Individual teachers on the staff decided to try the idea of a year-long theme and found it to be a valuable tool to integrate curriculum.

49 *Continued Work on Evaluation* Evaluation and the development of comprehensive evaluation strategies have become an integral part of Lakeview's school development. This year a move was made to include many more student self-evaluation tools in the programs. Students were expected to evaluate and reflect on their own learning and participate in cooperative groups. During reporting periods (November, March and June) students were involved in writing their own report card, and both their's and the teacher's report were shared during parent/teacher interviews.

50 *Susan Kovalik* Kovalik, a consultant from the USA, was invited to a neighbouring school for a week-long in-service training on brain-compatible learning, the use of year-long themes as a vehicle for integration of curriculum and the importance of science being the subject around which all subjects are integrated. The reason, Kovalik states, is that science is the one subject that all children naturally relate to, regardless of ability or background, since children are naturally curious. This workshop led to many staff members successfully working with the model of a science-based, year-long theme.

51 *Science Theme Focus* In discussions early in the year staff made the decision that science should be the school focus. The previous four years focus had been on the development of language arts and integrating language into all subject areas. Science, it was felt, had not been made a major emphasis although science played an integral part in our world. However, science

proved an excellent focus since students are naturally curious and interested in it, and it provides an excellent vehicle for teaching critical thinking skills, problem-solving, hypothesizing, etc.

52 *Language Arts Workshops Given* Through district committee membership, some staff members began to participate in planning and presenting workshops to interested schools in the district. These workshops included a variety of topics — theme planning, writing and reading strategies, and evaluation tools, etc. Planning and articulating the philosophy and practice they believed in and used, was found to be a very powerful process of internalizing and extending their depth of understanding.

53 *Reading Conference* Barb and Charlie attended an administrative conference in Richmond. Speakers included Ministry representatives, district administrators, and school administrators; the main focus was related to school change and strategies to support it. The conference was most valuable in terms of personal confirmation in the 'school change' practice and philosophy.

54 *Experimentation with a Variety of Strategies* An environment of 'trust' and 'support' seemed to be in place. Teachers felt confident in taking risks and experimenting with new ideas and/or initiatives. A school focus on 'Science' was carried through. Team teaching with multigrade groupings was carried on through a variety of themes.

55 *Sharon Jeroski, PLAP District Evaluation Team* Two members from Grand Park attended the Ministry PLAP Assessment marking process. Jeroski was the co-ordinator of the Ministry Provincial Testing. She was asked to contribute her knowledge and experience to the district — the District Evaluation Pilot Committee — and a meeting of administrators. For a period of three years this committee focused on creating and implementing evaluation tools that supported changes in teaching strategies, from sequential to holistic. At this time the committee considered the necessity of assessing the students' developmental change, and therefore Sharon Jeroski, and two others, became an integral part of the district team to design and carry through a planned process to document district growth in language arts.

56 *Maple Lane School Visit* In the spring Isabelle, Barb and Kelly had the opportunity to visit Maple Lane School in Richmond which was recommended for its school initiative of using cooperative learning and thinking skills. These three teachers were able to compare and contrast the two schools in terms of philosophy and actual teaching practices and were able to bring back and apply these new strategies in their own classrooms. Being able to participate in a team Pro-D was also a very valuable experience since they were given the opportunity to observe and collaborate with others.

57 *Team-Teaching Focus: Changed Roles of Lib/LAT* Team-teaching was being experimented with in a variety of ways. At this stage both the librarian and LAT became active participants and therefore changed their previous roles. They took part in the planning, teaching and evaluation process in a variety of ways. For example, five teachers worked together to group multigrade students including the special education pupils. The librarian team-worked

with groups of students carrying out research projects related to the theme; the LAT facilitated small groups of students writing up lesson plans and carrying them through with other small groups. This whole process was a powerful learning experience for all.

58 *Team-Teaching* Throughout one of the team-teaching units, focused on grouping students according to their personalities and learning styles. The students then worked together in small teams throughout the unit. The focus was for students to recognize, accept and experiment with a variety of activities that incorporated the various learning styles. The students found this valuable and several were able to identify their strengths.

59 *District Convention, Organizer Assistance* At this stage many teachers gained confidence and interest in assisting with the organization and focus of the District Convention.

60 *Ministry Changes: The New Primary Program* Based on recommendations made by the Royal Commission, the Ministry introduced the new Primary program. Ministry timelines state that schools have two years before formal implementation is required. Grand Park responded by establishing a District Advisory Committee which consisted of four primary teachers, a primary helping teacher, the president of the local Primary Teachers' Association, two administrators, a school trustee, two parents and the Director of Instruction. This committee's responsibility was to oversee and support implementation in the district, as well as being involved in the process of setting district policy on matters relating to the primary program.

61 *Integration of Special Needs Students throughout the School* Both the staff and students began to accept naturally the variety of personalities and learning styles of all others with whom they team-planned and learned. The use of the word 'equality' became much more internal both in the philosophy and the practice of the school activity. The special education students were accepted, both during instructional time and free outdoor play time. A full-time integration plan was being designed to put in place the coming year. Both the teachers and students were part of the planning process, and both were comfortable with the goal.

62 *Staff Participation on District and Ministry Committees* Staff participation on district and Ministry committees was considered valuable for several reasons; a notable one was internalizing and having the opportunity to articulate their philosophy confidently, as well as providing outside expertise and connections to new resource people who have since played major roles within the school and district.

63 *Filming — Skeena Journal CBC Yale Town Productions — APASE* Lakeview was fortunate to be involved in two filming sessions this year. The first, Canadian Broadcasting Corporation's Skeena Journal, held in February during Education Week, filmed innovative programs taking place in Grand Park schools. The second, Yale Town Productions in conjunction with the Association for the Promotion and Advancement of Science Education, produced a video on science teaching.

64 *Continuation and Refinement of Team-Teaching* Throughout the year a variety of team-teaching arrangements were designed and experimented with. At the completion of each unit staff discussed the successes and refinements they considered necessary at the time.

65 *School as Whole Experimentation (ongoing)* The whole school seemed to become an active learning environment. Any new ideas staff were interested in experimenting with was consistently supported by others. It became an environment where risk-taking was no longer in question.

66 *Pro-D Conference* All primary teachers, the principal, and secretary attended a Terrace weekend conference related to the Ungraded Primary program.

67 *Sundance School* The staff had decided they would pilot the Ungraded Primary program in September, 1989. One member arranged a school visit to Sundance School where the program had been in place for several years and was highly recommended. Linking with other teachers and schools involved in similar philosophy and practice assisted them with planning and practice, and in building confidence.

68 *Organization of Ungraded Classrooms for Next Year* When they decided to pilot the Primary program next year, staff agreed that a logical next step in Lakeview's school development was to incorporate the many successes that were achieved this year. Multiage/multigrade groupings worked very well and contained many underlying philosophies about learning held by the staff, specifically, peer teaching, modelling, cooperative learning, etc. In deciding the actual groups, student and teacher learning/teaching styles, as well as personality styles, behaviour, age, abilities, cooperative grouping, and role models were all important factors.

Appendix C

Report of Wendy Strachan

Report to the Principal and Staff
of Lakeview School
February/1988
From: Wendy Strachan
Re: Reactions to Writing Program

My comments fall into four categories: 1) what I see happening, 2) where I think you are, 3) what I don't see, and 4) what I think we might look to see later on.

What i saw happening

What I would like to suggest to you is that we connect what is happening here at the school with what we know about learning. We were talking last night about how doing this project was very similar to how adults learn and to the processes they go through. When you are beginning an innovation, there is a sense in which you begin by changing your action or behaviour and your language. That is, you start doing and saying different things. And gradually there is a reciprocal process going on — a dialogue. As you do and say different things and notice yourself, and notice the effects, you also change what you think and believe. The external behaviour becomes internalized as a way of thinking. At first, as in learning any new and complex idea, one begins to use the language, the vocabulary. But at first the use is quite rigid. We can't actually paraphrase much until we've developed a full concept of what the language means and of course we learn that in experiencing the meaning. A similar process occurs with behaviour or action. At first, the behaviour is imitative, conscious, and to be practised. But as we watch ourselves doing new things, as you've watched children respond to each other's writing and seen what the effects are, then the behaviour also becomes part of how we think ourselves, we become more creative and generative, it's personal, it's our own language. We explain or describe what we do in dozens of ways because we've all kinds of experience and examples to draw upon which give our own meaning to the learned language and behaviour.

In regards to this process, I found teachers at Kantana at different levels. Some of you are at the early stages; some of you have worked a good distance through the process. So, in relation to this then, what did I see happening here at the school? What I saw, of course, you know already. I saw much evidence of writing. There is much evidence of writing as activity in the classroom and as display around the school. I saw much evidence of process. I saw pre-writing in two or three particular forms, one the idea-web, and then some use of questions and listing. The idea-web seemed the most common pre-writing strategy being used. Then I saw a lot of drafting and a lot of sharing and some responding. By responding, I mean some talk about the writing, not a great deal but some, mostly sharing. I saw some editing, some proofreading, and of course, final copy. There seems to be quite a bit of emphasis on that approach, of going through the whole process with a lot of pieces of writing. That attention to process is excellent and very encouraging. I think we talked about that. You said that it has made everyone feel relaxed and that relaxed, cooperative feeling contributes very much to what is also much in evidence — a very good writing climate. It is definitely there — in every classroom I went into. The children are willing to write, they take up their paper, they do it. While some have more difficulty than others deciding on topics and so on, they are still working and learning in a very receptive, supportive climate. There is also time for writing. That is crucial, and you have given it. There is time for sharing; that's also crucial and you have given that time. There is also some student choice which is important, and you are giving that. And I see that the climate is also respectful of the students on the whole, and it is also encouraging on the whole — all of which are essential ingredients for encouraging writing and ensuring success. I think you know all of those things.

Where i think you are

In terms of where you are in relation to what I see in other schools, I think you are moving at a good pace, you are doing very well. As a school you are moving quickly, and that has much to do with the fact that everyone on the staff is involved, that you talk a lot, that you show you are processing it all the time, and it is a serious undertaking for the whole school. It usually takes about five years for teachers to reach the stage where understanding of complex ideas and practices is fully internalized. It is then not a matter of 'we're teaching writing process' or 'we're doing writing this year, this is our language arts program', but rather that using writing is a part of the way you think and do things — you don't even think about it as only teaching writing any more than you think of using talk as teaching speaking, because it is how you work. Not, of course, that you do not deliberately teach strategies for handling writing tasks but the whole process is intrinsic to learning and teaching. If you continue as you are, I think that any of the things which I don't see now, I would expect will happen simply because you are engaging in a reflective process, you are able to identify things that you are not doing and that you want to do differently, and you are continuing to read, so you will continue to move and grow. I see no reason why that should not be the case as things are at present.

What we might look to see in the future

Let me say at the outset that what I have not seen in two days may of course be there and I came at the wrong time or whatever. But this is what I noticed. First, the matter of fluency. I think it is important that the first concentration at any time, at any level, no matter what you are teaching or what subject you are writing in, the first thing you have got to have is fluency. When we think about beginning writing in kindergarten, Grade 1, Grade 2, Grade 3, about beginning writers, second language writers, writers in psychology, people who are trying to write physics, first they have got to get fluency — then begin to think about craft, form, and correctness. Now in the elementary school, it is rather difficult to decide where to go once you have that fluency. By fluency I mean the ability to write fairly confidently and legibly in a variety of forms on a variety of topics, so that you have a child who will sit down and write an explanation or do a diary entry, who will write a story, who will write a report, who will describe a process, who can write in several forms therefore and do it fairly confidently. Not necessarily with any sense of much form, but none the less will confidently do it; who will write quantity. Fluency first, then, for any child at any level, but particularly until the end of grade 2 where obviously, the main concentration is on quantity.

But then you begin to move into form and craft which means then you must begin to *teach* writing. At the first stage, when the children are learning what written language is for, all they need is opportunity. They need all the things that you have provided: time, support, encouragement, opportunity for sharing, response. But then, once they are fluent, and I know some of you have noticed this, you want form, craft, quality. The children now need to be taught writing, and that doesn't occur only by osmosis. Certainly there has to be wide reading; you can't be a good writer if you don't read or have not acquired an ear for written language, and you certainly learn that incidentally from a great deal of reading. But as we all know, many people can read huge amounts but they still can't write. There are techniques to learn, there are strategies to be taught. So what I don't see is specific teaching of strategies to handle different kinds of writing tasks. At the moment the writing which I see mainly is story writing.

In fact, it seems in some classes everything is called story. I would suggest to you that it creates a problem if you don't distinguish writing tasks: making lists of things, writing stories, telling about, explaining something, etc. It is helpful to use more differentiating language. If everything is called a 'story', then it becomes difficult to identify story structure as distinct from anything else and to work with it. You might talk about writing 'personal experience', or writing a 'personal narrative' which would be a general recollection, more a biographical kind of thing. Form is really important and it is important to start using the language to make distinctions. What I saw were basically generic stories which lack clear form.

The other main type of writing I saw was a sort of 'informationalizing'. It read much like the usual elementary textbook which is written in short sentences with very little subordination and with little sense of explaining much or elaborating on ideas. Students tend to write this way when that is what they read in the 'content' areas, and when the writing assignment is topic-based rather than purpose and audience directed. I saw quite a bit of this report kind of writing. Most of the writing seemed to be of these two types.

I think it is important to move from those types toward a variety of forms. This will mean teaching a particular form, recognizing that forms have characteristics and you teach kids how to produce them. They read and write in those forms taking account of purposes and audience and have something to focus on in revisions. So, for instance, in one of the classes, a boy was talking about his BMX. Some of the children in Grade 3, Grade 4, Grade 5 have a tremendous amount of technical knowledge of things. As the teacher, you may decide to teach students to write directions, guides, or manuals and the student chooses what to explain. So this little boy with the BMX wanted to be a good BMX rider and knew just what he needed to learn to do. He had knowledge which he could learn how to explain to someone else in a particular form.

When the assignment is simply to write about a topic what you often end up with is a list of things, mostly *IS* sentences, like a whale is, or a dog is, and it is a grocery list of characteristics. It doesn't have any form other than essentially the list. But if you shape that information into something which is really a full description for a purpose and audience, to reveal something felt about the whale, or describe a whale in an activity somewhere, or why we should take care of whales, or whatever — when you do that, you decide on the focus and the purpose and then the writing can take shape. Then you have something to respond to when thinking about revision because you know it has a form you are looking for. And it gets much more controlled and gets much stronger. And then the children learn strategies and techniques to apply to other topics. But it is important to include this sense of choosing how to deal with the topic in the whole piece, and also to work at the sentence level, seeing how rearrangements change the meaning, how adding phrases focuses and enhances meaning. You have more substance and purpose then for revision. I am sure that you will find, if you have not already, that it is not enough to write 'stories'. They get longer as kids get older and more fluent, but not necessarily better or more shaped and controlled. So they need a whole variety of other forms to use, particularly from Grade 4 upward.

As well as teaching and using a variety of forms, it is also important to teach strategies for revision. Most of the revision I saw, the changes in the writing, are fairly superficial and mostly editing really. I did not see much revision. Since that is the most difficult thing to do anyway, it is not at all surprising not to see changes in substance. As well as knowing how to do it, it also requires recognition or belief that words create reality — that the words are the facts, that they don't stand in for something else in an external, visible world. Children will add detail in response to audience questions but real revision requires awareness of textual truth. But, we can work toward that!

The correctness seems to me not to be a problem, everyone is dealing with that because basically what is happening in the later draft is editing and correcting — all of that is happening. A small suggestion to you on the editing. I think it is really a good idea for children to correct each other's work and find errors, but if you are marking spelling, I would suggest to you that you ask the *student* to circle all the words that he or she thinks are misspelled. When they must find them, they have to read much more carefully and they go through and they circle the ones they think are wrong and often they will circle ones that aren't misspelled, of course, but then you correct the ones which are and leave it at that. If they don't circle some, leave it — it doesn't matter. Make them find them and then correct them, and they will do it. Research on spelling shows us that by the fifth grade all instruction washes out — anything is okay — no teaching is equivalent to teaching everyday; no teaching is equivalent to having lists every week, or having your own lists, or having whatever. By fifth grade everybody tests out the same across tests of all kinds of programs. And also it is a strategy. The more things about their writing that children identify for themselves, the better.

Lastly, I want to make a few comments about where you might think to extend further your use of the writing process. When you are teaching the writing process and seeing it as going through this process of pre-writing, generating ideas, and then drafting, responding, revising, editing, proofreading, presenting, you may see it, and rightly, as a means of producing a good piece of writing, a means of improving on what comes out off the top of one's head so to speak. But another way to think about process is to recognize that all of these stages are different thinking stages. They require different kinds of thinking and different things go on when you are generating ideas compared to what goes on when you are drafting and when you are responding and when you are revising. There are different thought processes. The pre-writing and drafting are really thinking out, and generally when we are thinking out something, in a draft, we are not conscious of audience. We write mostly for ourselves. We get our thoughts on paper, to look at our own minds. So the pre-writing and drafting allow the thinking out and thinking through things. But when we start getting into response and revision, we are writing for an audience and that is a whole different thing. We are putting ourselves in someone else's place. We have a new orientation to what is on the paper.

The power of the idea of process is that in teaching you can use writing to assist learning because you use the pre-draft for thinking out. When you are writing about any topics you are learning about — when you were learning about whales for instance, you write a draft of what you know and understand and have learned before, and what you think about whales and things. You write a coherent statement, a passage, of text, and you explain what you know in a full, chatty way, not making a list, but talking on paper about what you know and don't know. What that provides is the basis of teaching to go on to other strategies, not necessarily writing. Using writing to learn is using first draft writing as a means of making knowledge conscious and not going any further with it as a piece of writing. It has done its job when it does that. I think understanding the meaning of the stages, the meaning of what goes on in the thinking at those various points is something to think more about. It makes the process powerful because it becomes part of how you think about teaching and learning.

Somewhat related to that, I noticed much talk about process. By this, I mean that in several classrooms I saw much explicit teaching of the language of writing and teaching about the process. I think this happens and is necessary in part because it helps us as teachers explain it to ourselves. It's part of the process of making that language our own, and the children's. But their purpose is to engage in the process rather than learn about it. Of course they are doing both. But the metacognitive levels of understanding and knowing follow from the doing and emerge from the doing reflectively, rather than from being learned and applied. I'm curious about whether or not by focusing so much on *teaching* the language of the process and the structure as opposed to simply *using* the language we are not substituting that language for the old language of grammar? If we are teaching *about* writing, as well as doing it, we may be substituting teaching about writing for what we used to do — teaching *about* language. Then we get involved in what kinds of questions we ask, what steps we are at, and we can be teaching writing the way we teach identification of parts of speech. That's clearly not what we want. But that's a question I have — I am not saying that's happening here. I think it is something to think about, and maybe it is just a stage — it may be a necessary stage to go through to keep articulating it and having the kids learn what they are supposed to say in response and what they are supposed to say here and now. Learning the vocabulary is essential for both the teachers and students, but the process should underlie the purpose and meaning of the writing. The process is not the purpose. If it becomes the purpose, then it is like teaching parts of speech. Teaching process is not teaching writing, unless the process underlies the intention, purpose and form of the writing.

That reminds me of a question raised yesterday. A question about the commitment you show and the involvement. I see this as closely related to your choice of project. The fact is that you chose to do language arts and you chose writing, and you chose not to buy a package designed to bring about change, a package like ITIP, for instance. You didn't buy a package of stuff to learn and apply but you chose to engage in a process, to set out on a journey. It is the nature of this project, the whole writing process, that it encourages the kind of dynamics and interaction, and the kind of professionalism which you are finding is happening here, which is the larger thing. The experience you are having here is identical to experiences in all the schools where I have been, all the writing projects I have been connected with, both as director and consultant. Anybody who writes about the National Writing Project writes about the enhanced professionalism of teachers, the sense of autonomy, the sense of being in power or rejuvenation, the feeling that teaching actually is an exciting thing to do. People who want to leave the field change their minds and stay. People who are out, come back, because teaching writing seems to match what we intuitively know and understand about learning. Writing has everything to do with learning and with thinking. As we teach writing, we become learners about children's learning, and that is utterly fascinating. It makes teaching so much more exciting than simply opening a book, do page 59, tick, tick, tick, you have got them right. Or even the socialization. Many teachers compensate for the boredom of teaching the subject matter by being big social whirl people. I see this all the time.

Well, that's pretty much all I can say at this point. Let me repeat, however, that I feel this is a very exciting place to work and that I'm impressed and intrigued by the interesting, thoughtful things you are doing. It will be hard to leave an environment like this where so much is going on and there is such an atmosphere of professionalism about teaching. I see a strong sense of professionalism, high self-esteem, and self-respect, and the feeling of growing autonomy and control of power, the sense in you that I know what I am doing and I am learning, and that is very worthwhile to see. It has been a pleasure being here. Thank you.

Appendix D

Notes on the methodology

During the data gathering period, which began in April of 1986 and ended in July, 1989, I made eleven visits to the site. Each site visit typically consisted of two or three days and involved classroom observation and interview. The people I interviewed and contacted in connection with this study were primarily the staff of Lakeview school. But I also interviewed teachers who had left the school, district staff, and the superintendent and the director of instruction in the school district. As well, I also had the opportunity of meeting with school board members, and interviewed one of them. The repeated site visits enabled me to interview the participants on successive occasions. Each site visit produced tapes of interviews, samples of student work, materials of various types, and pages of handwritten field notes.

The study began with an invitation from the principal of the school to visit the school because of the change that he thought had occurred there. My first visit led to the preparation of a proposal which was later approved by the board. They provided some initial funding. Financial support for the project was later granted by Simon Fraser University and the Social Science and Humanities Research Council.

The study set out to:

1 describe the school improvement plan (writing project at Lakeview) and the contexts (i.e., district initiatives and community support) within which the plan occurred;

2 document the case histories of the main players (teachers and district people);

3 identify changes in classroom practice occurring as a result of the school improvement plan; and

4 conduct an interpretive analysis of the data, to

(a) identify the factors and events occurring within the school and external to it that led to the development of the school improvement project;

(b) examine the strategies that were used by the different players to bring about changes in the school; and

(c) relate the experience at Lakeview to the selected bodies of literature concerned with school improvement.

The first three objectives provided the basis for a case study describing various aspects of the school's improvement project, the changes in classroom practice which resulted, the background of the main players, and the setting in which it occurred. Objective four involved an interpretive and analytical stage. Here, I attempted to determine what the case study said about school change and how that related to the broader literature.

Many of the qualitative procedures used in the research were drawn from the methods outlined by Miles and Huberman (1984). These were supplemented by procedures and techniques developed by others such as Glaser and Strauss (1967), Patton (1980), and Spradley (1979).

Table 1 shows the specific steps followed in connection with the research objectives. It includes the data sources and the methods of collecting that data. The references cited in the third column represent researchers who have reported specific techniques followed in the study. The discussion that follows describes the data analysis.

The analysis of the data fell roughly into two stages — the first descriptive and the second interpretive. The descriptive stage (see objectives 1–3) provided an account of the school improvement plan at Lakeview. Here I sought to document the changes that had occurred, and the meaning that people placed on those changes. I drew heavily on the players themselves to prepare this part of the report.

The interpretive stage saw that descriptive case study examined in the light of the understanding of school change reflected in the literature on school change. This occurred through my own struggles, but also through an ongoing interaction with a selected group of peers and teachers from Lakeview over the past two years. The question we always struggled with was: What does it mean, and how can we best interpret these events? In addition to the usual techniques that have become part of qualitative research, I should like to comment on three procedural aspects of my study at Lakeview.

Role of the Researcher

The role played by the researcher is crucial in this type of research. With two exceptions, my role was that of a non-involved observer. I did speak to the parents of the school, and I was involved in the filming of a science project in the school. The visit of Wendy Strachan was clearly an intervention that might not have occurred had I not been doing the study. But apart from these, I simply observed and listened.

That admission should not lead the reader to suppose that my presence had no effect on what took place in the school. During my interviews with the staff, they were asked to reflect in ways that they might not normally have done. This

Table 1: Steps in Collecting and Analyzing Data

Objective analysis	*Data sources*	*Data collection/data conceptual analysis*
1 To describe the school improvement plans and the contexts.	• documents, minutes, school and district records • field notes from staff meetings • interviews with teachers, principals, central office staff	• concept analysis of documents and materials • structured and unstructured interviews, coding and analyses of transcribed interviews, triangulation, content charts, causal flow charts (Miles and Huberman, 1984; Spradley, 1979)
2 To document the case histories of the main players involved at Lakeview.	• deep structured interview • documents	• successive interviews and progressive focusing of case histories and events (Smith, *et al.*, 1986)
3 To identify changes in classroom practice occurring as a result of the school improvement plan.	• classroom observation • teacher interviews • stimulated recall • school objective plan (Objective #1) • deep structured interview • focused group interviews	• several periods of classroom observation which is transcribed and analyzed to establish patterns. These are then discussed with teachers to identify changes from past teaching practices • content analysis of teacher daybooks (Leinhardt *et al.*, 1984; Wideen, Strachan and Carlman, 1985) • an analysis of previously conducted data designed to construct a causal flowchart • stimulated recall with participants using causal flowchart • content analysis of recorded interview and group interview
4 To conduct an interpretive analysis of the data, including the case study, to a) identify the factors and events leading to the school improvement project; b) examine change strategies; and c) determine knowledge use.	• case study • all previously recorded data • literature	• causal flow charts • critical incident charts • interpretive analysis (Miles and Huberman, 1984; Patton, 1980)

type of reflection may well have led them to make changes that they may not have undertaken. So, my presence probably did have an effect, although that was not my intent.

Participation of the Staff in the Research

As I have pointed out the principal and selected members of the staff were interviewed on different occasions. I normally reviewed earlier interviews and based my interview/conversation with them on the issues and themes that I saw emerging. For example, in the case of the factors that appeared to be supporting the change, I developed a list which became the subject of discussion in subsequent interviews.

One of the most productive occasions of staff involvement occurred during the third year when I brought a penultimate copy of my report to Lakeview, and paid for substitute time for three teachers to meet with me along with the principal. Another item on my agenda for that two day meeting was for them to identify the key events and changes that had occurred over the three-year period so I could compare that with my own construction.

It soon became apparent that neither the teachers nor the principal were much interested in the report that I had written at that time. They were much more interested in reviewing and reflecting on the events and changes that had occurred. The two days were thus taken up in essentially constructing what appeared in the text under Figures 2, 3 and 4 which in a crude form represents a causal flow chart (Miles and Huberman, 1984). An interesting sidelight to this process was how much had been forgotten by these three teachers about their earlier struggles. This process is one that I would highly recommend to others attempting a study of this kind.

A final caution. Qualitative research of this type relies heavily on the self-reported data and that which comes through interview and observation. A whole set of inferences must be made as one moves from these data to construct a picture of the events that occurred and to interpret those events. To assume that such data reflects a true picture of events and influences (supposing that there is one) assumes that people can recall significant events accurately and can account for those things that influenced them to think as they do. It also assumes that as a researcher, I have been able to interpret the text of interviews and my observations in appropriate ways. The extent to which one has difficulty with any of these assumptions, is the extent to which one may have difficulty accepting the interpretation of the events that shaped this book.

Index